Dr Mike Smith's
Guide to Over-The-Counter Medicines

DR MIKE SMITH is a specialist in preventative medicine and a general practitioner. He was the Chief Medical Officer of the Family Planning Association 1970-75 and their Honorary Medical Adviser 1975–90. He is an elected member of the FPA's National Executive Committee and a member of the Pet Health Council. For many years he has been a 'resident' expert guest on BBC2's *Jimmy Young Programme*, LBC's *Nightline* and the medical columnist/ editor for *Woman's Own*. Between 1988 and 1990 he was the expert guest on SKY TV's *Sky by Day* and continues to appear on SKY. In April 1991, he was voted the TV and Radio Doctors' 'Experts' Expert' in the *Observer* magazine's series.

His other books include *Birth Control, How to Save Your Child's Life, A New Dictionary of Symptoms, Dr Mike Smith's Guide to Prescription Medicines, Dr Mike Smith's First Aid Handbook* and the *Dr Mike Smith's Postbag* series.

REVISED AND UPDATED

Dr Mike Smith's Guide to Over-The-Counter Medicines

Researcher: Sharron Kerr

Greenwich Editions

This edition published 1995 by Greenwich Editions,
Unit 7, 202-208 New North Rd, London N1 7BJ

First published as *Dr Mike Smith's Handbook of Over-The-Counter
Medicines* in Great Britain in 1992 by Kyle Cathie Limited

ISBN 0 86288 040 8

A CIP catalogue record for this book is available from the British
Library.

Typeset by DP Photosetting, Aylesbury, Bucks
Printed and bound in Great Britain by
The Guernsey Press Co Ltd, Guernsey, C.I.

Contents

Acknowledgements

For her extensive research on this book, a thousand thanks go to journalist Sharron Kerr, my colleague and friend.

My thanks also go to Joan Tillott MRPhS and Nazleen Meghji MRPhS of Tillott and Tongue District Pharmacy – my local chemists – and to the pharmaceutical companies who readily sent details of their products.

Foreword –
How to Use this Book

THIS BOOK IS divided into two main sections. The first is an A-Z of common complaints, describing the symptoms and the 'self-help' measures you can take to treat them. At the end of each entry, there is a list of remedies, including homoeopathic and herbal remedies, available over the counter and suitable for the treatment of the complaint. The second section is an alphabetical list of the remedies themselves, giving details of the active ingredients and dosages recommended. A third, shorter section discusses unbranded products – those common medicines like soluble aspirin produced for the local chemist to sell 'under their own label', rather than the nationally known and advertised 'brand' products like Disprin – and a fourth the vitamins, minerals and other supplements you may want or need to add to your diet.

All the medicines listed in both sections continue to sell and be recommended by doctors and pharmacists. They have all proved themselves reliable in their own ways. But the cause of many of the conditions they are taken to relieve is unknown – cramp in a young, fit person, for example. The fact that one remedy will work for one person and that another will suit someone else better may be because, for many conditions, there is more than one cause. So it's only to be expected that there should be more than one effective remedy. A certain amount of trial and error may sometimes be required before you find the remedy that is right for you or your child.

However, to guide you further, I have whenever possible suggested my favourite or favourites among the remedies available for each complaint. I do this just because they *are* my favourites and are popular – they are the ones I will most often recommend for patients or choose for myself or my family. Although they are my first choice, the other remedies given may be equally effective in their own way for some people.

Also, time passes and medicines come and go. Just because a medicine isn't mentioned here, it doesn't mean it isn't effective and doesn't have a role. And although I've tried to be comprehensive, it is inevitable – simply because of the numbers involved – that some medicines will have been overlooked. However, if you let me know, care of the publishers, about any of your favourite medicines I've missed, I'll do my best to include them in the next reprint of the book.

Other doctors and pharmacists will have their own favourites. When these differ from mine, I hope you'll forgive me and that you will take their advice first, since they have the privilege of being able to talk to you personally and assess your individual symptoms. Their advice should also be sought about the quality and price (usually cheaper) of 'own brand' drugs.

Introduction

IN A DEVELOPED country like Britain most of the conditions the majority of us suffer from are self-limiting – they get better on their own. Among the common ones are colds, flu, gastric upsets, coughs, aches, strains, sprains, sore throats – even verrucas. While rest, possibly in bed, relaxes the body and keeps the patient at an even temperature, it's the body's own defences which deal with the infection or inflammation – the cause of almost all the conditions or their symptoms.

But even though most of us realise that it's just a matter of time before we recover from the nastiest cold or stomach upset, few can resist the temptation to try and hurry the process along or to relieve the pain or distress of the symptoms. So we treat ourselves with the tried and trusted remedies that have been used for generations and can be bought 'over the counter' (OTC). And powerful 'cures' many of them are, too. They often rely on the best of the plant-derived remedies of old. Aspirin, for example, which came originally from the bark of a certain type of willow tree, remains one of the best all purpose painkillers, temperature-reducing agents and anti-inflammatory agents available.

Some over-the-counter medicines can be bought in a supermarket, but all of them are available at the chemist's – the shop with the big difference where medicines are concerned. There, all medicines are kept or overseen by a professional pharmacist. He or she knows about and can advise on any of the medicines that are sold – or dispensed, when you hand in a doctor's prescription.

Fortunately, we are all getting healthier in Britain, so with every year that passes the pharmacist's role becomes more important. It is to the pharmacist that we should turn for everyday medical queries – as, in a way, we have done for centuries. The drug-dispensing apothecary of old was the forebear of both the modern-day family doctor and the pharmacist. While the family doctor specialises in diagnosis and takes overall professional responsibility for the care of our more serious illnesses, the pharmacist has the direct care and control of the medicines we take on a day-to-day basis.

Making the Most of your Pharmacist   A pharmacist's training involves three or four years of study, followed by a year's practical work under supervision. After this, their knowledge of the way drugs act upon the body and interact with each other – and the potential side-effects of them all – is considerable. Community pharmacists – the official name for retail pharmacists or chemists – are therefore highly qualified professionals. They are also available throughout shop opening hours, so your local pharmacist is probably the most accessible member of the healthcare team to whom you can go for free advice. Unfortunately, not many of us take full advantage of their expertise.

Most simple ailments don't need a prescription medicine. So if you don't feel well but don't think it's worth bothering your doctor, go to your local chemist and ask if you can speak to the pharmacist. He or she is trained to know when medical help is necessary, so if you are advised to go to the doctor, do so. Often, however, reassurance and an over-the-counter remedy will be all you need – and this guide is designed to help you understand the wide range of over-the-counter remedies available.

But there are certain basic precautions you must always take. Make sure you tell the pharmacist if you are already taking any medicines and if you are sensitive to anything. If you are asking advice about a child, always mention their age. If the pharmacist sells you some medicine, make sure you know how it should be taken and for how long, and follow the instructions precisely. Never exceed the recommended dose, unless it's on medical advice.

It's also worth mentioning here that the pharmacist and doctor act as a team when dealing with prescription medicines. It's part of the pharmacist's job to check that details on the prescription are correct before supplying it, make sure medicines are labelled properly and instructions fully understood. People are often nervous when they consult their doctor and may therefore not be quite clear about the treatment prescribed. They may also forget to mention any non-prescription medicines they are taking. You can always ask your pharmacist about anything you do not understand and check, if necessary, that your medicines will not react badly together. If you notice symptoms that you think may be due to a medicine's side-effects, the pharmacist will be able to tell you whether or not this is likely and advise you accordingly.

Pharmacists can also give advice on such things as immunisations for holidays abroad, headaches, stomach upsets, colds and coughs. They know, for instance, that different types of cough require quite different medicines, and will make sure you buy the right thing. Indeed, many of the more effective non-prescription medicines can only be supplied under the supervision of a pharmacist, so you need have no fear of being advised by someone who doesn't know what they're doing.

Certain medicines can be supplied either on prescription or over-the-counter. The over-the-counter price is sometimes cheaper than the prescription charge and it is worth asking your pharmacist's advice on this. New regulations mean that medicines are now often dispensed with information leaflets which include details of any side-effects that may occur. This knowledge could mean that more people expect to experience side-effects and therefore do so. In this case, the pharmacist is just the person to give advice or reassurance.

Many chemist shops now have a quiet area where you can talk to the pharmacist privately. On-the-spot pregnancy tests, blood-pressure checks and more recently, checks for cholesterol (blood fat) levels and general health and dietary advice are often available.

Most people will find it helpful to get to know their local pharmacist and build up a good relationship. To young mothers and the elderly in particular, a friendly pharmacist can be a valuable source of knowledgeable advice and support.

Homoeopathy   No one has so far been able to explain why homoeopathy works, as it does not conform to our accepted knowledge of scientific medicine. This method of giving medicines was first developed nearly 200 years ago by Dr Samuel Hahnemann, a great German physician, scholar and chemist. Appalled by the existing medical practices which he believed often did more harm than good, he sought a method of treatment which would be safe, gentle and effective. Since then many thousands of people throughout the world have had their symptoms relieved thanks to homoeopathy and even the Queen is said to carry a 'first-aid kit' of homoeopathic remedies with her on her travels. Homoeopathic medicines are widely recognised as a safe and effective alternative to conventional medicines.

Derived from the Greek word *homoios*, meaning 'like', homoeopathy's basic principle is that like cures like. Symptoms are treated by giving a minute dose of a substance which, if given in larger quantities to a healthy person, would actually cause those symptoms. Even in conventional medicine this principle is sometimes used – for instance, controlled doses of radiation are given to cure cancer which can be caused by too much radiation.

Over the years 'provings' have been carried out on many hundreds of substances by giving minute doses to healthy people and carefully noting the symptoms produced. Homoeopathic remedies are now based on these provings. The success of the treatment largely depends, homoeopaths say, on correctly matching the remedy to the individual's symptoms; other factors such as the patient's personality, home environment and work, which may have a bearing on the illness, can also play an important role in the choice of treatment. There are around 2,000 homoeopathic remedies, each with several uses, so it is fortunate that computers can now be used to help in the matching-up process.

Visiting a homoeopath can be a lengthy business. He or she needs to build up a picture not only of your illness, but also of your personality and lifestyle, down to the tiniest detail of your favourite foods and even your reaction to weather! Homoeopaths believe that symptoms – for example, a raised temperature, running nose, diarrhoea or vomiting – are the body's way of trying to rid itself of whatever is responsible for the illness. They also believe in the body's natural ability to heal itself. A homoeopath will therefore aim to give a remedy which will encourage this process, whereas conventional doctors prescribe medicines to suppress symptoms – aspirin, for instance, is used to bring down a temperature, or antihistamines to dry up a runny nose.

Some homoeopathic remedies are similar to herbal medicines in that they are derived from plants, but many come from minerals such as gold, carbon, silica (sand) and phosphorus, or animal products such as bee stings or snake venom. Another class of remedies, called nosodes, are derived from disease tissue, bacteria or viruses, and are used as a form of vaccination against allergies and some illnesses or inherited conditions.

The methods of preparing homoeopathic remedies and dosages are quite different to those used in herbal medicine (see below). In homoeopathy, different 'potencies' of medicine are achieved by diluting, to varying degrees, a 'mother tincture' made from the initial substance. At each stage of dilution the mixture is thoroughly shaken – a process known as succussion.

'Less is more' is another basic principle of homoeopathy. In other words, contrary to what one might expect, the more dilute the solution, the more powerful its action will be. Medicines are graded according to this potency. The greater the dilution, the higher the potency number given to the remedy. So, for example, a homoeopathic remedy labelled 12c, which has been diluted 1,200 times, is of a lower potency than one labelled 30c, which has been diluted 3,000 times. 200c is a higher potency still.

The bottle or tube of medicine will have a number indicating its strength. Over-the-counter preparations will probably be 6c or the stronger 30c, though homoeopaths may prescribe higher. Homoeopaths find that high potencies – when only one dose is necessary – are better for some conditions and lower potencies, perhaps used for longer, better for others. Any potency above 12c will be so diluted that no particle of the original material can be found on chemical analysis – so how, people naturally ask, can it possibly have any curative effect?

The honest answer is that no one knows, though one theory is that a form of radiation energy is released which stimulates the body's own healing mechanisms. Homoeopaths point out that we do not understand how many modern drugs work, but we do know that a few have unpleasant side-effects. Even though some of the substances from which homoeopathic remedies are made, such as arsenic and mercury, would be poisonous in larger amounts, in homoeopathic doses they are harmless. But with homoeopathic treatment the symptoms will sometimes become worse before they improve.

Homoeopathic medicines can safely be taken in pregnancy – for early morning sickness, for example – and a child could swallow a bottle of most homoeopathic pills with no ill effect. It is possible, however, to have an unpleasant reaction to some remedies if they continue to be taken once the symptoms have gone.

Many homoeopaths are qualified doctors who have done a further year's training in homoeopathy. They may become GPs or work in homoeopathic hospitals (there are only about three of these in the UK), in which case their treatment is available on the NHS, or they may consult privately.

The advantage of consulting a medically qualified homoeopath is that he or she is trained in diagnosis and able to prescribe conventional medicines such as antibiotics when necessary. Most homoeopaths agree that life-threatening conditions are better treated with conventional medicines.

If you consult a homoeopath who is not also a doctor, make sure he or she has done a full homoeopathic training at an approved college: there are some charlatans about. For books, advice, information and a list of practitioners, contact the British Homoeopathic Association, whose address is on p.293.

You can try self-treatment with homoeopathic remedies for everyday complaints. Nelsons and Weleda make a range of homoeopathic remedies, and some, including first-aid or travel kits for everyday ailments – with instructions – are available from specialist chemists such as Ainsworth Homoeopathic Pharmacy (address p.293). I've included a selection of homoeopathic remedies throughout this guide for those interested in trying alternative forms of medicine. I've used the abbreviations – Phos. for phosphorus, for example – which are conventional in homoeopathy. Don't worry if these are unfamiliar – your pharmacist or homoeopath will know what you mean.

There are, however, general instructions that should be followed when treating everyday ailments with homoeopathic remedies. These are the recommendations of the Homoeopathic Development Foundation.

Use the 6th potency, that is, remedies labelled 6c. The suggested dose is two tablets for adults or one tablet for a small child. In acute conditions, give a dose every hour for six doses, then three times a day between meals for three days. In chronic cases, give a dose three times a day between meals until relief is obtained.

Watch the response to each dose. When improvement is evident, increase the interval between doses, continue for two more days, then *stop*. Repeat only if the original symptoms recur. Stop dosing when the condition is cleared.

If the symptoms are aggravated after taking a remedy, stop the medication; when the aggravation has passed, do not repeat the medication. Repeat the medication only if the *original* symptoms recur.

Keep the medicines in a cool, dark place and away from things that smell. Tablets should not be handled. Tip the tablets into the cap of the container and drop them into the mouth. Best results are obtained by chewing or sucking the tablets.

Medicines are best taken apart from food or drink. They should be dissolved on a clean tongue when the mouth is free from the effects of tobacco or strongly flavoured toothpaste.

For more serious conditions the foundation recommends that a qualified homoeopathic physician be consulted.

Herbal Medicine   Herbs seem to get into everything these days! Of course, they have always added flavour to cooking, and herbal teas, such as rosehip and peppermint, have long been popular. Now, bath oils, shampoos, face and body lotions containing a variety of herbs sell like hot cakes as we are encouraged to believe that all things natural are good for us.

'Herbs' (which include a variety of plants, flowers and even trees) have been used for thousands of years to cure or prevent disease and even today 85% of the world's population is largely dependent on herbal medicine. For a long time no one really understood how or why herbal treatments worked, but more recently scientists have been able to separate many of the active chemical ingredients from healing plants and set up tests to observe their effects.

Some of these substances are now produced synthetically in laboratories and form the basis of modern drugs. For example, digoxin (a heart stimulant) is the synthetic form of the active ingredient of digitalis, found in foxgloves. And salicylates, derived from willow bark, are now produced synthetically as aspirin. However, medical herbalists believe that by isolating and using only the main, active ingredient of the plant, one is losing the benefits provided by the other ingredients working in harmony. They therefore always use the whole plant.

Herbalists say that medicines using the whole plant work in a similar way to foods providing, for example, essential vitamins and minerals – which help protect the body against illness – and enzymes which aid absorption of food.

Some plants have within them a natural antidote to the side-effects a medicinal ingredient could cause, were it extracted and given in isolation. For instance, ephedrine – a drug often prescribed by doctors to relieve bronchial symptoms – comes from the plant *Ephedra sineca* and can cause an increase in blood pressure. But the plant itself includes an ingredient that keeps blood pressure down.

As another example, dandelion leaves are a natural diuretic (that means they stimulate urine production and help to rid the body of excess fluid); they are also rich in potassium, an essential mineral salt. When man-made diuretics are used, the body may excrete too much potassium so that a supplement is needed to replace it. Herbalists can point to many such instances where the ingredients in the plant counterbalance each other.

The herbal remedies available from chemists, health food shops and supermarkets may be helpful for minor problems, but, if symptoms are persistent or severe, consult a registered medical herbalist for a full assessment and tailormade prescription. Looking for the initials MNIMN or FNIMH after the practitioner's name will help you avoid quacks – a professional herbalist (and many people do not realise these exist) will have done four years' training.

Herbal medicine aims not just to treat a particular symptom, but to improve the overall physical and mental well-being of the patient. Diagnosis and treatment based on this holistic approach will include advice on diet and lifestyle, as these may be partly responsible for the symptoms. In fact, herbalism takes so many factors into account that two people with apparently identical symptoms may be given quite different prescriptions. Professional herbalists are trained to use many of the same diagnostic methods as doctors and to refer people on for X-rays and other specialist investigations or treatment, if necessary.

Medicines are usually given in the form of a 'tincture' – a concentrated solution made from suitable herbs which have been soaked in water and alcohol. Sometimes the herbalist provides the actual plants from which to make an 'infusion' (similar to tea) or a 'decoction', whereby the plants are gently simmered for some time and the juices then strained off. Medicinal herbs can also be given as suppositories, ointments and poultices.

It is part of a medical herbalist's training to learn the most effective quantities of each plant to use, but the constituents of the plant can vary, depending on such factors as where it is grown and the time of year it is picked. This means it is impossible to measure accurate dosages, and is another reason that most orthodox doctors still have their doubts about herbal medicine.

Most herbal remedies are safe and mild for children as well as adults, and even the names of many healing plants sound soothing – lemon balm, comfrey, meadowsweet and speedwell, for instance. However, like anything else, they can be harmful if used incorrectly or taken in excess. One man died recently from drinking too much carrot juice – so always follow the instructions carefully.

Some of the more potentially dangerous herbs (like lobelia, an anti-asthmatic) can only be prescribed by medical herbalists and/or doctors. Some, such as devil's claw – a joint and muscle pain-reliever – should be avoided in pregnancy. If you are in any doubt, ask professional advice.

Conventional medicines usually act quickly and are therefore best for acute illness, but they can also cause side-effects. Herbal remedies often take longer to be effective but for simple, common ailments and recurrent problems such as indigestion, constipation, insomnia, eczema, ulcers and headaches, advice and treatment from a medical herbalist could bring relief. Serious side-effects are most unlikely.

Some conventional and herbal medicines work well together but others can interact badly, so always tell your doctor and herbalist about any medicines you are taking. Throughout this guide, I've listed a selection of over-the-counter herbal medicines and remedies available which may help some common ailments.

For more information about herbal medicine contact the National Institute of Medical Herbalists (address on p.293).

Dos and Don'ts of Over-the-Counter Medicines Every day, six million people in Britain visit pharmacies and a million people ask for advice about symptoms of heartburn and haemorrhoids, corns and constipation. Not only that, more than £580 million a year is now passed over the counter for cough, cold and sore-throat remedies, general and topical analgesics, indigestion and stomach-upset remedies, laxatives, acne treatments, vitamins, eye-care products, anti-diarrhoeal medicines, hay-fever treatments and so on and so on . . .

In every pharmacy an average minimum of 50 people a day will buy an over-the-counter medicine. That's almost three-quarters of a million people a day in Great Britain, so as you can see self-medication plays a major role in modern health care.

People visit a pharmacy instead of arranging a doctor's appointment for many reasons, including convenience, informality and cheapness (most OTC medicines cost less than the current prescription charge). But there are important guidelines you must follow if OTC medicines are to be used safely.

- Always ask your pharmacist for help.
- Always read the label or packet. This will tell you how much medicine it is safe to take, and when and how to take it. Taking a lot of medicine at once does not mean it will work better or faster, and it can be harmful. If you do take too much medicine, get help quickly – from your doctor, local

hospital or chemist – but don't delay. If need be, call an ambulance.

● Take extra care when you give medicine to children, and always keep medicines out of their reach. Be particularly careful when other children are in your house. Never let children play with medicines or even empty medicine bottles.

● If you are pregnant, or think you may be, never take medicines without consulting your doctor.

● Always consult your doctor or pharmacist before taking an OTC medicine if you are already taking medication or have a medical condition.

● Never take an analgesic within four hours of having taken one, even if it is of a different type or brand.

● Tablets or capsules can stick in your throat, so take them with plenty of water while sitting or standing up.

● Swallow capsules whole, unless you are told to open them up.

● If you buy a suppository, unwrap it and follow the instructions. You use it by pushing it into the anus (back passage). A pessary is for use in a woman's vagina (front passage). Remember, your pharmacist is an expert on medicines, so always ask for advice if you are not sure what to do.

● Some medicines may cause drowsiness. If affected don't drive or operate machinery and avoid alcoholic drink. Alcohol or other medicines may change the way your medicine works.

● Aspirin should not be given to children under 12 except with medical advice. There appears to be some connection between young children taking aspirin and developing Reye's Syndrome – a rare condition (affecting only about seven children in a million) which causes brain inflammation and liver damage. It is not even certain that aspirin is directly implicated, but the possibility is enough to make doctors decide that it is not normally worth the risk. Paracetamol is a safe alternative as a painkiller.

● Don't keep old medicines in your home. Flush them down the toilet, or ask the pharmacist to destroy them for you.

A–Z of Common Complaints

ACNE AND SPOTS

Acne is a disorder of the sebaceous glands in the skin which causes spots. It's probably one of the most distressing of common skin conditions and it affects almost all youngsters at some time, although severe cases are rare.

Spots usually appear first when the sufferer is anywhere between the ages of 11 and 15, and disappear when he or she is in the mid to late 20s. In rare and depressing cases they can continue into the late 30s. Acne affects the skin on the face, neck, back and chest and is generally worse in men than in women.

Spots normally occur because of an increase in the production of sebum, the skin's normal oily secretion. Sebum keeps the skin moist and supple – without it, the skin would become dry and might even crack. The over-production of sebum is due to stimulation from a male hormone, androgen, and leads to the shiny skin commonly seen in teenagers. With the increase in this skin grease, the pores in the skin can become blocked and infected by bacteria which thrive on the sebum. This in turn causes spots.

The most common types of acne spots are blackheads, pustules, papules and cysts. Blackheads are very small black spots which usually appear around the nose and chin. They are caused by dead skin cells and sebum collecting in a hair follicle and becoming discoloured by exposure to air. Pustules are inflamed spots with white centres caused by bacterial activity in sebum which has collected in a hair follicle. Papules are inflamed spots. In severe cases, cysts develop – tender, swollen lumps under the skin caused by scar tissue forming around an inflamed area of skin.

Many people, particularly adolescents, suffer deep emotional anguish because of acne. It can become the most important thing in your life, making you embarrassed to meet strangers and even causing you to shy away from friends.

However, there is good news. Help is very often at hand. All sorts of acne treatments are available from your pharmacist. And for the vast majority of sufferers, these can bring remarkable relief. The bad news is that clearing up acne nearly always needs great perseverance. There is no overnight cure and you may have to persist with treatment for several months at a time.

The OTC preparations are topical, that is, they are applied directly to the skin. They fall into various categories. Antibacterial skin-washing creams, lotions and soap can help by reducing bacterial activity in the skin. Antiseptic creams, ointments and soaps can destroy micro-organisms, and abrasives can remove blockages clogging up the skin.

The most common form of treatment available is a keratolytic skin ointment – that means it 'dissolves' the keratin (the top layer of the skin) and encourages peeling of the layer of dead and hardened skin cells that form the skin's surface. These ointments – there are a number of different brands – may contain the keratolytics benzoyl peroxide, sulphur or salicylic acid. Benzoyl peroxide and sulphur also have an antibacterial effect.

If you know you have sensitive skin, or have suffered an adverse reaction to other acne preparations in the past, it's worth applying creams or lotions to a small area of skin for the first few days. If your skin seems to tolerate it, you can then treat larger areas.

Keratolytic preparations often cause soreness of the skin, so they are available in different strengths. Benzoyl peroxide, for instance, is likely to cause a mild burning sensation on the first application, as well as a moderate reddening and peeling of the skin during the first few days. Throughout the first few weeks of treatment, most patients will experience a sudden increase in peeling. This isn't harmful and will subside within a day or two if treatment is temporarily discontinued. Then start treatment again and continue while the acne is kept at bay and the other side-effects remain at non-worrying levels.

But if discomfort such as burning, redness or excessive peeling occurs, stop the treatment temporarily or consult a doctor. Patients with a known sensitivity to this active ingredient shouldn't use products which contain it. Preparations containing benzoyl peroxide shouldn't be used for longer than three months at a time.

It's also worth noting that these products may bleach dyed clothing and fabrics, so use them with care.

If keratolytic ointments don't work for you, consult your doctor, who may recommend an alternative form of treatment such as an antibiotic, or refer you to a specialist dermatologist, who may prescribe Vitamin A-derivative tablets; if you're female the doctor may suggest the use of a contraceptive pill – either a usual one known to be beneficial to the skin or one which, while still having a contraceptive effect, is primarily prescribed for the treatment of acne.

Remember that if you suffer from acne, you should try to avoid worrying about your spots, as this will make them worse. (Easier said than done, I know.) Also restrain yourself from squeezing blackheads and pimples, as this can cause further damage and scarring of the skin, and can also make the spots spread.

Many acne sufferers try to not eat chocolate and other fatty foods, and although there is no real proof that this has any effect on acne, it's worth a try, as a healthy, well-balanced diet with plenty of fresh fruit and vegetables can generally only be good for you. Sunshine can help dry up your spots – but don't overdo it and burn yourself.

What's Available? Acetoxyl 2.5 and 5, Acnegel and Acnegel Forte, Acnidazil, Benzagel 5 and 10, Benoxyl 5 Cream, Betadine Scalp and Skin Cleanser, Biactol, Boots Mediclear Acne Cream 5, Boots Mediclear Acne Cream 10, Boots Mediclear Acne Lotion, Brasivol Fine, Cepton, Clearasil Medicated Cleansing Milk and Lotion, Clearasil Medicated Cream, DDD Medicated Lotion and Cream, Eskamel Cream, Germolene Cream, Oxy 5 and 10, Panoxyl 2.5, 5 and 10, Quinoderm, Sudocrem, TCP Antiseptic Liquid, Ultra Clearasil Acne Treatment Cream, Valderma Range

Unbranded Products   Witch Hazel

My Favourites   Biactol, Clearasil

Homoeopathic Remedies   Belladonna, Hepar. Sulph., Pulsatilla, Silicea, Sulphur

Herbal Remedies   Potter's Skin Clear Tablets, Soothene Ointment

ARTHRITIS
See RHEUMATIC PAIN p.111

ATHLETE'S FOOT
Athlete's foot (*tinea pedis*) is a fungal infection of the skin which thrives in warm, wet conditions. The skin between the toes becomes red, soggy, itchy, flaky and sometimes smelly It's not very common in children but is a frequent problem for adolescents and sporty young men and women who use communal changing rooms. The condition will persist until it's treated and, as other people can be infected, prompt attention is required.

Treatment is fairly straightforward. If you suffer from athlete's foot – or as a precaution against it – you should ensure your feet are kept dry. 'Air' them as often as possible, wash them frequently, particularly during hot weather, change socks or stockings daily and avoid walking barefoot in public changing rooms. If you have to use a changing room or communal shower, try wearing sandals to avoid any risk of infection from the floor.

Antifungal creams, sprays or powders are usually very effective. They mainly contain antifungal drugs such as tolnaftate, undecenoic acid, miconazole, dichlorophen or zinc undecenoate and need to be used morning and night after thoroughly washing your feet (always use your own flannel and towel) and removing any loose skin. Rub creams or spray sprays into and around affected skin. Sprinkle powder liberally on to feet, particularly between the toes – it's helpful, too, to dust socks and the insides of shoes before wearing them. Unless the instructions on your medicine advise you differently, continue treatment for a week after all signs of infection have disappeared.

If the condition doesn't clear up in a week or so, you may need a stronger antifungal agent than those available over the counter. Consult your doctor.

What's Available?   Daktarin Cream, Spray Powder and Powder, Germolene Medicated Footspray, Mycil, Mycota Cream, Spray or Powder, Phytocil Cream and Powder, Quinoped, Scholl Athlete's Foot Range

For other foot problems such as foot odour: Boots Super Deodorising Foot Spray and Super Absorbent Foot Powder, Tinaderm Cream, Tinaderm Plus Aerosol, Tinaderm Plus Powder

My Favourites   Mycil, Mycota Cream

BACK PAIN
Although one and a half million people in this country are suffering from some degree of back pain at any one time, the majority do get better with no more complicated

treatment than bed rest and/or painkilling drugs. In many cases, the pain isn't even bad enough to merit a visit to the doctor, but if you are suffering your first attack of back pain, or if the pain is severe, see your GP before trying any self-medication – the back is a large, complicated area with tens of thousands of nerve-endings, many of which, for different reasons, can cause pain.

When people suddenly develop back pain, they tend to think that they must have 'slipped a disc', imagining the disc to be something like a tap washer. In fact, these intervertebral discs, as they are called, are firmly attached to the side of each vertebra – the interlinked bones that make up the spine – and it is impossible for them to 'slip'. They are spongy and act as a kind of ball-bearing and shock-absorber whenever the spine moves. When a disc causes trouble it is because a split has developed in its outer layers, allowing some of the soft inner pulp to prolapse – fall – through. This can then press on nearby ligaments or nerves and cause pain which may be severe. A disc (usually in the lumbar – lower back – region) tends to prolapse following some unusual, prolonged and perhaps unaccustomed physical activity. The disc walls are weakened, the back may feel stiff for a few days, and it might then be something quite minor, like a cough or a sneeze, that ruptures the wall.

However, only a tiny proportion – less than 5% – of back pain is caused by disc problems. At some time in their lives, most people will suffer from back pain which could have been prevented. There are many possible causes, the most common being a strain or sprain of one of the ligaments which help to hold the spine together or one of the muscles responsible for its movement.

Sitting or standing for long periods in unsuitable positions can often be blamed. Repetitive work, such as digging or weeding, carried on for too long, is one cause; lifting things incorrectly – while bending at the waist and twisting at the same time, for example – is another. Hours bent over a desk or at a typewriter, especially if the chair does not provide the right back support and the desk is not the correct height, throws a great strain on the back.

It is best to change position frequently, or get up and walk around from time to time, so that the muscles and ligaments get a little exercise – they were not designed to hold the same position for long. Likewise, make sure you give yourself regular breaks from the digging and the weeding!

Sales reps and others who spend hours driving can often benefit from a specially designed car seat with extra back support. Lifting should always be done by bending at the knees like a fork-lift truck, not from the waist like a crane! And combined lifting and twisting movements should be avoided, as these are very likely to strain the back.

Various forms of arthritis also commonly cause back pain. X-rays of people's backs show that osteoarthritis – general wear and tear of the joints – affects nearly everyone over 50 and this may result in pain. Rheumatoid arthritis can sometimes be a cause of inflammation and pain in the back and young men in particular may develop another form of arthritis involving the back – ankylosing spondylitis.

Women are prone to osteoporosis – a thinning of the bones – after the menopause. This may cause one or more of the vertebrae – especially those in the neck – to crumble slightly, resulting in nerve pressure and pain.

One of the reasons for consulting your doctor when you first experience back pain is to exclude less common causes – it often helps just to be assured that there is nothing seriously wrong. But it may still be difficult to pinpoint the exact problem. Relieving the symptoms will then be a question of trial and error, but fortunately most back pain will get better of its own accord within a month – often less.

Bed rest for a few days – longer with disc problems – will help any inflammation to subside. A firm mattress, perhaps placed on the floor or with a large, person-sized board under it, is best. Corsets and collars can provide helpful temporary support, but do not wear a corset for longer than three to four weeks, unless otherwise advised by your doctor, or joints can stiffen up. Heat or ice packs will often relieve pain, but be sure to protect the skin.

Aspirin or other anti-inflammatory and pain-relieving medicines like ibuprofen are most effective, and will also help to relax the tenseness in the muscles which adds to the pain. They need to be taken regularly, as recommended, so that a constant level of pain relief is maintained in the blood and the pain is not allowed to surface. Paracetamol can also ease back pain, although it does not reduce inflammation (see PAINKILLERS p.100 for a list of OTC products containing these ingredients).

None of these medicines should be taken for more than a few days except under a doctor's advice.

Massage (with or without a liniment, or muscle rub) or a vibrator applied to the painful area can also relax the muscles and be very soothing. A form of physical therapy called the Alexander Technique aims to relax muscles and improve posture by undoing bad sitting and standing habits developed over the years – it will often relieve back ache in the process. Some people find that manipulation of the back by a registered osteopath, chiropractor or physiotherapist will bring relief, but this treatment is best begun within a few days of the onset of the pain. Acupuncture can also be effective when practised by skilled hands.

Exercise, especially swimming, walking and cycling, plays an important part in keeping the muscles and ligaments in good tone. Special exercises designed for the individual by a physiotherapist, especially once the acute pain has subsided, will usually speed recovery and help prevent a relapse.

If the pain is severe – as with lumbago, which afflicts the lower back and is often so agonising that the sufferer is stuck in a stooping position, or especially with sciatica, when the pain is radiating down the leg – stay in bed and call your doctor. If a prolapsed disc is diagnosed or suspected, specialist treatment may be needed.

What's Available?   Algipan Rub and Spray, Balmosa, Deep Heat Range, Doan's Tablets, Ibugel, Ibuleve, Ibuleve Sports Gel, Lloyd's Cream, Massage Balm, Menthol and Winter-

green Heat Rub, PR Freeze Spray, Proflex Cream,
Transvasin

My Favourites   Deep Heat Range, Algipan and PR Freeze
Spray

Homoeopathic Remedies   Aconite, Arnica, Bryonia, Calc.
Fluor., Nux. Vom., Rheumasol, Rhus. Tox.

Herbal Remedies   Potter's Sciargo

BAD BREATH

The really embarrassing thing about bad breath is that all
too often you don't become aware of it until it's pointed out
to you by somebody else. But don't worry – it can affect the
best of us, not just heavy smokers or garlic eaters.

Bad breath is medically known as halitosis. It will often be
temporary, caused by eating highly spiced foods, for example. Alcohol and cigarettes also give the breath characteristic, unpleasant smells.

But the most likely cause of recurrent bad breath is poor
dental hygiene. Plaque – a sticky film of bacteria and other
ingredients – can cause decay if allowed to build up around
the teeth. It can also cause a gum disease called gingivitis (see
GUM DISEASE p.70). The gums will then look inflamed and
bleed easily when you brush your teeth. Bad breath is a
common accompanying symptom.

Regular brushing of teeth and use of dental floss – a
special strong thread or tape which is passed through the
spaces between the teeth – combined with a mouthwash
(particularly one of the antibacterial mouthwashes containing chlorhexidine) and regular trips to the dentist, will
usually bring about a cure.

If your dentist can find nothing wrong and bad breath is
persistent, consult your doctor. He can examine you to
exclude another common cause – nasal polyps. These are
benign growths, readily removed, which can prevent proper

drainage in the nose and lead to mild infection. Sinusitis, chronic catarrh, chest infection, digestive problems and constipation are all other possible causes of bad breath.

In fact, any sudden change in diet can be responsible – would-be slimmers have found that a high-protein diet, lacking in carbohydrate and fibre, will often make their breath smell unpleasant. This is likely to be due to lack of fibre in the bowel, causing a change in the 'friendly' bacterial content and its 'cleansing' effect, though no one really knows why this should affect the breath, or if indeed it is the cause of the problem. But charcoal tablets or biscuits could help – probably by absorbing the unpleasant odours, so preventing them from being exhaled.

What's Available? Bragg's Medicinal Charcoal Tablets, Listermint, Listerine Antiseptic, Oraldene, Search Dental Rinse

Unbranded Products Hydrogen Peroxide Solution

My Favourite Listermint

Homoeopathic Remedies Kali. Phos., Merc. Sol.

BED SORES

If someone who is confined to bed is so ill or paralysed that they don't, or can't, 'turn over' as usual, they risk developing painful bed sores. The skin can crack and weep and, as a result of the continuous pressure on a certain part of the body, the tissues below the skin can 'wear away'. The problem arises because the pressure prevents an adequate amount of blood from getting through to supply the tissues with oxygen and nutrients. This doesn't happen in healthy people because the normal sensations of discomfort – which at their worst become pins and needles – make us turn over or move about, even in our sleep.

These painful areas of skin are also known as pressure

sores and usually appear on the buttocks, heels and elbows due to pressure and friction from the bed itself where it is supporting the weight of the body.

Elderly people who have to stay in bed because of illness are particularly vulnerable to bed sores. Often their skin is not as supple or resilient as it used to be and their ageing nerves are not as sensitive to the warning signals that their skin and tissues are becoming numb and they need to move. And the less a patient moves around, the more likely bed sores are to develop. So, if you're looking after an elderly person who is confined to bed, make sure he or she changes position as often as possible.

Barrier creams, zinc and castor oil cream or petroleum jelly, used frequently and well rubbed in, can help protect the skin from irritation. So can talcum powder. It's the regular rubbing that is important. In hospital, when there is any likelihood of such sores developing, the nursing staff will treat those areas already mentioned every four to six hours and turn the patient every two hours.

Should the skin look particularly sore or, even worse, if it is starting to weep, seek help from your doctor or a registered nurse immediately. Once a bed sore has started, it will need regular nursing attention several times a day to clear it up.

What's Available?   Hioxyl Cream, Morhulin, Sudocrem, Vasogen

Unbranded Products   Alum B.P., Surgical Spirit B.P.

My Favourite   Sudocrem

Herbal Remedies   Hypercal Cream (for cuts and sores)

BITES AND STINGS
Compared with people in many other countries, we in Britain are lucky in having relatively few biting or stinging

insects. Venomous snakes, spiders and such like are also thin on the ground or non-existent.

However, I did say 'relatively' few. That still leaves us with around 33 different kinds of mosquito – commonly known as gnats; about 43 types of midge, six species of wasp, several kinds of bee, not to mention biting horseflies and stinging ants. Jellyfish and poisonous fish can be a hazard too and, especially as more and more of us are taking our holidays abroad, it is important to know what to do if the need arises.

Creatures that sting do so to protect themselves, insects that bite do so to feed. With mosquitoes, midges and horseflies it is only the female that bites; she needs the blood that a good bite gives her in order to rear her young – no consolation to us as we scratch away!

But whether the attack takes the form of a bite or a sting, the result is the same – a hot, red, swollen, itchy area and sometimes, more serious consequences. In the case of a sting, the symptoms are the result of the body's reaction to the poison injected; with a bite, they are due to an anti-clotting substance in the insect's saliva which it injects to make the blood – your blood! – flow more easily as it feeds. Although it is not poisonous, this substance can provoke an allergic-type response around the bite and occasionally throughout the body. Fortunately, mosquitoes in Britain do not carry disease.

When you are bitten early in the season, you are more likely to react and find yourself scratching than later on in the summer. This is because your body gradually develops some tolerance, particularly to your local gnats and midges. However this will not help you when you visit a different area and get bitten by an unfamiliar species!

Some people seem to be more attractive to biting insects than others and individuals differ in how much they react. In general, though, insect-repellants should protect you for about two hours and, if you are bitten, iced water or witch-hazel, calamine lotion or soothing antiseptic creams will usually calm the irritation. Try your best not to scratch either bites or stings, or you may introduce infection.

A bee only stings as a last resort, as it leaves its sting behind and dies soon afterwards. Remove the sting with a fingernail by scraping it out sideways and in the direction the sting is pointing outwards, rather than pinching and pulling it out, as this can squeeze the remaining venom into the skin. To counteract the acid in a bee sting, apply ice-cold water containing a little bicarbonate of soda. Wasp stings are alkaline, so bathe them with a little vinegar in ice-cold water. It doesn't leave its sting behind, just a chemical irritant.

Remedies from the chemist are soothing. They tend to be antihistamine medicines or creams, made specifically for bites and stings, to combat any allergic reactions. They can also reduce more severe swelling and irritation and some contain local anaesthetics to ease pain or irritation. The effects of a sting will usually disappear after a few hours.

However, a few people develop an allergy to wasp or bee stings and can then have an extreme, even life-threatening reaction which may come on only seconds after the sting. The sufferer may feel dizzy and sick, have a runny, itchy nose and eyes and develop a rash. Their limbs may swell, they may have difficulty breathing and even lose consciousness. If any of these symptoms occur after being stung, it is essential to get to a hospital with an accident and emergency unit (casualty department) or to a doctor immediately.

Similarly, for stings in the mouth, multiple stings or if a child under the age of two is stung, it is best to seek medical advice without delay.

Swimming can be a risky business in some waters. If you are stung by a jellyfish you may not feel it at the time but if you develop a painful, swollen area on your body and perhaps a temperature after swimming in the sea, do consult a doctor.

Stinging fish exist even around the British coast and if you tread on one you will certainly know it – the pain is excruciating. The best treatment is to immerse the stung part in very hot – but not scalding – water. This will quickly deactivate the venom.

Snake bites in Britain are unlikely to be too serious – the adder is our only venomous snake. But common first-aid measures such as sucking the wound or making an incision with a razor blade to squeeze out the venom can do more harm than good. It's best just to immobilise the bitten limb with a splint or sling and take the person straight to hospital.

Of course, bites and stings are best avoided altogether and the following tips should help:

• Don't use perfume, hair sprays or aftershave when bees or wasps are around, as they can be attracted by the scent. Bright colours may also attract insects, so wear pale clothes that cover your arms and legs against gnats and midges, especially if you seem prone to insect bites.

• Examine food and sweet drinks before putting them in your mouth and wipe food off your lips if eating out of doors.

• Don't panic if bees or wasps buzz around you and don't hit out at them. Either ignore them or walk away.

• And a final safeguard, wear shoes in the garden and when paddling – particularly in rock pools.

What's Available? Aller-eze, Anethane Itch-Soothing Cream, Anthisan, Caladryl, Dermacort, Dettol Fresh, Eurax Hc, Germolene Cream, Hc45 Hydrocortisone Cream, Lacto Calamine, Lanacane, Lanacort, Listerine Antiseptic, Mentholatum Vapour Rub, RBC, Savlon Junior, Solarcaine, TCP Antiseptic Liquid, TCP First Aid Antiseptic Cream, Triludan, Triludan Forte, Wasp-Eze, Witch Doctor

Unbranded Products Sodium Bicarbonate B.P.

My Favourites Anthisan, Aller-Eze, Triludan

Homoeopathic Remedies Apis. Mel., Pyrethrum Liquid – applied to the area immediately

Herbal Remedies Combudoron Lotion, Dr Valnet's

Tegarome, Dr Valnet's Volarome Insect Repellant, Soothene Ointment

BRUISES

Everyone is familiar with the discolouring of the skin and its
deeper tissue as the result of a knock or injury – it often
turns blue, purple or black, then fades to yellow after a few
days. A bruise is, in fact, caused by blood leaking from
damaged blood vessels and then spreading into surrounding
tissue. The leaked blood is converted into different chemicals as it is broken down by the body's clearing-away
process, which explains the range of colours.

Some people, and especially some women, do bruise more
easily than others, even if they are fit and healthy otherwise.
This may be because their small blood vessels are easily
damaged; alternatively, their blood's ability to clot may be at
fault.

If you suffer from a painful bruise, don't rub or massage
the bruised area – pressure may make things worse. Bruises
are particularly painful if the bruised area lies over a bone.
When that's the case the clogged tissues are more tightly
stretched. An ice pack, in the form of a cold compress or a
packet of frozen peas (peas are very useful because the
packet moulds easily to the shape of your body), applied
immediately after the knock may help to reduce the
bruising; it may also help to numb the pain afterwards.

If it is your leg that is bruised, sitting with your leg resting
on something that raises it above your waist and applying a
hot water bottle at a comfortably warm temperature may
allow the blood to be absorbed back into the bloodstream
more quickly.

What's Available Chymol Emollient Balm, Hirudoid,
Massage Balm, Mentholatum Vapour Rub, Lasonil, PR
Heat Spray, PR Freeze Spray, Witch Doctor

Unbranded Products Witch Hazel

My Favourites Lasonil, Witch Doctor

Herbal Remedies Nelson's Arnica Cream, Potter's Comfrey Ointment

BURNS (MINOR) AND SCALDS

To treat minor burns, just cool the area in ordinary cold tap water – perhaps by keeping it running on the burned tissues for five or ten minutes – and cover it with a clean, dry dressing. You can also soothe the sore area with creams and sprays specially made for burns and scalds. Most contain an antiseptic and some sprays contain mepyramine maleate, an antihistamine, and benzocaine, a local anaesthetic.

Even a minor burn which is bigger than a 5 cm square should be seen by a doctor. Superficial burns may hurt more than serious, deeper ones. This is because a deeper burn may have destroyed the nerve endings, so you can no longer feel the pain. With much larger burns, the damaged – or absent – skin can no longer prevent the body's water and chemicals from seeping out and evaporating. The subsequent risk of dehydration can be a greater threat than the burn itself.

What's Available Acriflex, Betadine Dry Powder Spray, Betadine Ointment, Brulidine, Burn Aid Cream, Burneze, Drapolene Cream, Germolene Cream and Ointment, Medicaid, Morsep, Solarcaine, Sudocrem, TCP Antiseptic Liquid, TCP First Aid Antiseptic Cream, Vita-E range, Witch Doctor

Unbranded Products Witch Hazel

My Favourites Burneze, Acriflex

Herbal Remedies Combudoron Lotion, Dr Valnet's Tegarome

CALLOUSES

Callouses, areas of hard, thickened skin on the soles and heels of the feet, can be very uncomfortable and make walking quite painful. They are caused by pressure, perhaps from prolonged walking, walking unevenly or something rubbing in a shoe. No one knows why some people are more prone to callouses than others.

They're not contagious and can occur in any area subject to rubbing, such as the ball or heel of the foot. Callouses differ from corns (see p.45) in that they have no core, although in both complaints it is friction which produces the area of thickened skin.

The first step in callous relief is to change your shoes. Make sure they fit well and don't press on the sore parts of your feet. But if your callouses really do cause you discomfort, consult a chiropodist. He or she will probably pare away the hard skin with a scalpel and may recommend a special insole or pad for your shoe or shoes, to relieve any pressure and prevent the callouses recurring.

Some corn paints will soften the hard skin and speed up its removal. It might also help to remove hard skin regularly with a pumice stone and use a good emollient cream to keep your skin soft.

What's Available   Compound W, Salatac Gel

CATARRH

See SINUS PAIN, NASAL CONGESTION AND CATARRH p.113

CHAPPED OR DRY LIPS

Lips sometimes need more moisture than the rest of the face because they contain no sebaceous glands – glands which secrete sebum, an oily substance that lubricates hair and skin, as well as providing some protection against bacteria. But lips have more melanin, a brown pigment which protects skin against sun.

Melanin can help protect lips from the sun, but not against the drying effects of wind and cold weather. When your lips feel dry, it is natural to lick them to moisturise them. Saliva, in fact, contains a lipase – an enzyme that can 'dissolve' fat. This removes any skin-provided sebum protection as well as any natural moisture. The lips then feel drier than ever and the sufferer, quite reasonably, licks them again – and so the drying process goes on.

If this is happening to you, you must make a conscious effort to stop licking your lips. This may be all you need to do, though regular use of a lip salve to moisturise your lips will help.

If your lips are especially dry, lip creams containing sunscreen agents, emollients or an antiseptic are available. Ask your pharmacist about Vitamin B Complex Tablets (see VITAMINS p.281), as these may be particularly helpful to the elderly.

What's Available?   Blisteze Cream, Chapstick and Sunblock 15, Lypsyl, Uvistat Lipscreen Factor 15

My Favourite   Blisteze Cream

CHILBLAINS

Chilblains are reddish-blue discolorations of the skin resulting in burning, itching and pain and usually affecting the toes, fingers and backs of the legs. They can be accompanied by swelling and when severe can ulcerate. They're caused by exposure to cold, which is why you are more likely to develop them in the winter. They affect more women than men and more young women than old.

What appears to happen is that the blood flow through the body, especially to the extremities – fingers, toes and ears – is interrupted as the small blood vessels constrict in the tissues of the sufferer. This is a natural occurrence, as the body automatically supplies less blood to the skin surface in order to retain essential heat deep within the tissues (for the body to function properly, the kidneys, the heart and particularly the brain and the blood have to keep a constant temperature of around the normal 37°C/98.4°F mark).

But with chilblain sufferers this natural defence mechanism causes problems. Those small vessels remain closed up tightly for longer than usual. When fingers or toes are exposed to warmth, the previously under-supplied tissues come 'alive' again as the blood returns to them. Then the body's normal processes react to any damage that's been done. The normal pain that is felt when not enough oxygen gets to the tissue – as with angina of the heart – is not felt when the tissues are very cold, because the nerves are also affected by the cold and do not function properly. When they warm up again and the numbness goes, pain is experienced because the tissues have become more alkaline as they have survived in the absence of an adequate supply of oxygen. That's what causes the pain and itching of chilblains until the local 'chemistry' is restored to normality.

When you get chilblains for the first time, or if they are severe, consult your doctor in order to rule out any more serious problem. Raynaud's Phenomenon, for example, has similar symptoms to chilblains – it is a condition of the hands, fingers and feet which affects people who are unduly sensitive to cold and can result in the tissues themselves becoming permanently harmed.

Treat chilblains by covering them with a loose, dry dressing such as gauze and, if you wish, applying a soothing antiseptic cream. A vapour rub may help increase blood flow, as the rubbing stimulates the circulation. There is also some evidence that one of the B vitamins – nicotinic acid – helps to prevent chilblains (see VITAMINS p.281).

If you are prone to chilblains, take particular care in cold weather. Dress up snugly in several layers of thin clothing to help insulate your body, and always wear a hat. Probably the best preventive measure of all is to find ways of keeping the extremities warm. Cosy socks and gloves are a must. And why not try battery-heated ones? You can buy them from the Raynaud's Association Trust (address on p.293).

You can also improve the circulation in your hands by waving your arms about – movements like those of a cricket bowler are the most effective.

Even if your feet or hands become really cold, never warm them on a radiator, in front of a fire or directly on a hot water bottle – this will only cause you even more pain. Always warm your hands or feet up slowly, perhaps by putting them into lukewarm water.

What's Available?   Balmosa, Bengue's Balsam, Chymol Emollient Balm, Mentholatum Vapour Rub, Snow-fire, Sudocrem, Vitathone, Zam-Buk Ointment

My Favourite   Snow-fire

Homoeopathic Remedies   Apis. Mel., Pulsatilla, Tamus Ointment

Herbal Remedies   Soothene Ointment

COLD, THE COMMON
Each time we have a 'common cold' it could be due to one of a hundred or so different viruses. These spread from person to person by so-called 'droplet infection' – passed on when the sufferer coughs or sneezes, for example. Colds aren't caused by getting wet or cold, but infection is more likely to catch hold if the body's resistance is reduced by chronic illness, fatigue, stress or depression.

Any immunity we develop after catching a particular cold virus is short-lived and may not protect against further infection, as the viruses 'going around' tend to change constantly and none of them can be 'cured' by medicines. They can be fought and destroyed only by your body's natural defences. So those of us who mix with people regularly can expect to meet and succumb to two or three colds a year.

Typical cold symptoms will be familiar to nearly everyone

– the streaming eyes, running and/or blocked-up nose, headache and dry, tickly cough. But although, singly or in combination, they can be very unpleasant, they'll normally improve within a few days and for a straightforward cold, it's not usually necessary to consult a doctor.

If you have a cold, drink plenty of fluids, take aspirin or paracetamol to relieve feverish symptoms – paracetamol is best for children (see PAINKILLERS p.100 for products containing these ingredients). Tepid sponging may cool and soothe children. As long as they have plenty of liquids, don't worry too much if they refuse to eat – their appetites recover very quickly. But do call your doctor if your child develops a high fever, persistent coughing, wheezing, earache or sickness.

For adults, of course, there's a bewildering array of over-the-counter preparations for the common cold. While you cannot treat the virus itself and the 'cold cures' won't speed up recovery, you can get some relief from the effects by taking a mild painkiller as mentioned above, or you can try one of the many cold treatments available these days – which normally contain aspirin or paracetamol anyway. Always follow instructions strictly and never take more than one product at a time.

This is most important since a medicine like paracetamol can build up in the body if you continue to take it over many days or even weeks – you are effectively taking an overdose. And though it's very rare, such a build-up can occasionally cause a tragedy.

Both aspirin and paracetamol will bring down a temperature as well as relieving pain. Other ingredients of cold treatments are likely to be a decongestant to relieve nasal congestion or catarrh, an antihistamine to control the allergic-like symptoms of a cold – streaming eyes, for instance – and sometimes the stimulant caffeine. Many also contain Vitamin C, which some people feel is beneficial.

Many cold-sufferers take large doses of Vitamin C, but I've never seen any evidence that it does any good. In fact, I think that if you take extra Vitamin C, your cold may go in seven days. Without it, it could take as long as a week! Fortunately, it is one of the vitamins which can be taken in large doses without apparent harm, but why take the risk? It really depends on what you feel about it. You pays your money or you takes your chance, and I prefer to take my chance.

Bear in mind that some over-the-counter cold cures may be unwise for pregnant women, for people with diabetes, high blood pressure, heart or thyroid disease and stomach ulcers. As with all medicines, if you do have any medical condition, or are taking other medicines, you should check with your doctor or pharmacist before taking self-medication.

Some products may cause drowsiness, too. If you are affected, do not drive or operate machinery and avoid alcoholic drink. Children taking medicines which may make them drowsy should never be left on their own, except in a safe place – like bed.

There are occasions, however, when you may need to consult a doctor about your cold. If symptoms persist, or if you already have a chest condition – chronic bronchitis, for example – it is best to see your doctor at the first sign of a cold or flu. You may need antibiotics to prevent the development of secondary bacterial infections which could cause further lung damage.

As well as those with existing chest problems or heart disorders, the very young and the very old are especially at risk from complications as a result of a cold or similar infection. They should be watched carefully in case their symptoms worsen. The ageing immune (disease-fighting) system is less effective at combating infection and the elderly are therefore particularly vulnerable.

So how will you know when to call a doctor? Coughing up green, as opposed to clear, sputum is a sure sign that a secondary bacterial infection has developed and antibiotics may then be helpful. Likewise if the cough is very bad. Other symptoms to watch for include streaks of blood in the sputum, breathlessness, wheezing (which may indicate asthma), croup, 'tightness' or pain in the chest and blueness around the lips.

It is also wise to consult a doctor if the patient's temperature, pulse and breathing rate rise and he or she seems generally unwell. Elderly people can develop pneumonia quite untypically, by suddenly becoming confused but having only minor chest symptoms, so be on the look out for this and call the doctor without delay if you are concerned. In fact, real concern is a good criterion for asking a doctor's opinion in any circumstances – if only for reassurance – and this applies as much to symptoms associated with the 'common cold' as to anything else.

What's Available?   Actifed Cough Relief (1–12 years), Actifed Syrup or Tablets, Afrazine Nasal Spray, Beechams Hot Blackcurrant or Lemon or Lemon and Honey, Beechams Powders, Beechams Powders Capsules, Benylin Day and Night Cold Treatment, Benylin Mentholated Linctus, Boots Day Cold Comfort Capsules, Boots Night Cold Comfort, Boots Night Cold Comfort Capsules, Bronalin Dry Cough Elixir, Bronalin Paediatric Linctus, Bronchial Catarrh Pastilles, Catarrh-Ex, Coldrex Tablets and Hot Drinks, Contac 400, Cupal Baby Chest Rub, Day Nurse Capsules, Day Nurse Liquid, Dimotapp Elixir, Dimotapp Elixir Paediatric, Dimotapp L.A., Dristan Decongestant Tablets, Eskornade Spansule Capsules and Syrup, Fennings Little Healers, Flurex Bedtime Medicine, Flurex Tablets or Capsules, Junior Lemsip, Lemsip, Lemsip Cold Relief Capsules, Lemsip Flu Strength, Lemsip Menthol Extra, Lemsip Night Time, Night Nurse Capsules, Night Nurse Liquid, Odourless Garlic One-A-Day, Phensedyl Plus, Potter's Catarrh Pastilles, Potter's Cough Pastilles, Sanatogen One-A-Day Garlic Perles, Sinutab Nighttime, Snuffle Babe, Sudafed Nasal Spray, Sudafed Tablets and Elixir, Tixylix Cough & Cold, Tixylix Daytime, Tixylix Decongestant Inhalant, Tixylix Original, Vapex Inhalant, Vicks Coldcare, Vicks Inhaler, Vicks Medinite, Vicks Sinex, Vicks Vapo Rub, Zubes

Unbranded Products   Menthol and Eucalyptus Inhalation B.P. 1980

My Favourites   Benylin Day and Night Cold Treatment, Actifed, Contac 400, Vicks Vapo Rub

Homoeopathic Remedies   Aconite, Gelsemium, Merc. Sol., Nat. Mur.

Herbal Remedies   During the last few years an enormous amount of research into garlic's health-promoting properties and its chemistry has resulted in renewed interest in the way it can help the body's natural systems. Taken as a regular part of the daily diet garlic may help to maintain a healthy heart and circulation. It is also used as a herbal remedy for the relief of catarrh and symptoms of rhinitis and of the common cold.

Gardolex, Herbelix Specific, Hofels Cardiomax Garlic Pearles, Hofels Garlic Pearles and One-A-Day Garlic Pearles, Hofels Garlic Parsley Tablets, Hofels Odourless Neo-Garlic Pearles, Hofels Odourless Neo-Garlic Pearles One-A-Day, Lustys Garlic Perles, Mentholair Steam Bath, Olbas Pastilles, Shen Chinese Garlic Tablets, Cirkulin Garlic Pearls

COLD SORES

Although cold sores are not usually a serious condition in themselves, they can cause considerable embarrassment and distress – and, inevitably, they tend to arrive at the most inopportune times. The typical little blisters which develop into weeping sores usually appear in groups around the lips but may also occur on other parts of the face. If precautions are not taken, the virus responsible can also be spread to others, or to other parts of the body – the eye for example – with potentially more serious results.

Cold sores are caused by the Herpes Simplex Type 1 virus, one of the herpes group of viruses, others of which cause chicken pox, shingles and glandular fever. A slightly different strain of the same virus, known as Type II, is the one usually responsible for outbreaks of herpes blisters around the genital area, although Type I may be the culprit here, too.

These viruses have one important thing in common – after the first infection, they can lie dormant, causing no symptoms, in the nerve cells of the affected area. Under certain conditions, however, they may be reactivated and track up the same nerves to the same area of skin to produce further outbreaks of blisters. It is estimated that about half the adults in this country are carriers of Type 1 herpes. Most of them will have had their first, often symptomless and undetected infection in early childhood. Many will never have another attack, some may have one after an interval of several years and a small percentage will have recurrent episodes every few months.

Various factors can contribute to reactivating the virus – exposure to sunlight, some infections and being generally 'run down' are amongst them. For a woman, an outbreak of cold sores is more likely during menstruation. However, with each new outbreak, the body produces further anti-bodies which accumulate to fight the virus – this means that, in time, outbreaks tend to lessen in both frequency and severity.

Cold sores are highly contagious while the blisters are present. The virus is also found in the saliva of the sufferer and can be spread to others – so keep your kisses until the blisters have gone.

You can infect vulnerable parts of your own body, via the fingers, if you touch the sores and do not wash your hands afterwards. Any area of broken skin is especially susceptible. It is particularly important to avoid touching the blisters and then rubbing the eyes, as the virus may be transferred and cause an ulcer on the delicate membrane covering the eye – if this is not diagnosed and treated soon enough, it can damage the sight.

Mothers with cold sores should take extra care and wash their hands frequently, and always after applying medica-

tion – babies and toddlers are extremely vulnerable to cold
sores as they won't have had time to build up their
antibodies. It is also important to keep the flannels, towels,
eating and drinking utensils of the sufferer separate from
those of the rest of the family.

With both types of herpes, close physical contact is needed
before others are infected, so if reasonable precautions are
taken during the week or so that the blisters last, there
should be little cause for concern. The virus cannot be
passed on while it is dormant and producing no symptoms,
but whenever you're infectious it is essential to protect
others.

Many sufferers from recurrent cold sores notice definite
warning symptoms before an outbreak – a 'prickly' feeling in
the area of skin usually affected, for instance. If you apply an
antiviral ointment such as Zovirax which is now available
without a prescription you can shorten the duration of the
outbreak considerably. Cold-sore creams from the pharmacist can also help. These sometimes contain ammonia, small
doses of disinfectant, an antiseptic or local anaesthetic.

A simple old wives' remedy is to apply cold coffee to the
area on a piece of clean cotton wool every two or three
hours and allow it to dry. It may sound primitive, but it
appears to work for many people, so it is worth trying if a
doctor or pharmacist isn't available. Other than this, the
sores should just be kept clean and dry.

A regular, well-balanced diet will help maintain your
general health and may therefore prevent attacks. So too
may a good sun-blocking cream applied liberally to the lips
before and during a concentrated period of sunbathing. But
there is no cure for cold sores and if you are prone to them,
keep a supply of cream in your medicine cupboard so that
you can start the treatment when the warning symptoms
first occur. Eventually you will develop your own natural
resistance and cold sores should then become a thing of the
past.

What's Available? Betadine Antiseptic Paint, Blisteze, Bongela Oral Pain Relieving Gel, Brush Off Cold Sore Treatment, Colsor Lotion and Cream, Cupal Cold Sore Ointment and Lotion, Lypsyl Cold Sore Gel, Zovirax

My Favourite Blisteze

COLIC

Colic in babies is caused by bubbles of gas or air which become trapped in the immature digestive system. The consequent pain makes the baby cry, often inconsolably, and draw his or her legs up in pain. Problems with colic often appear when the baby is about three weeks old. They can be very wearing for the parents as well as the child, but don't despair, they usually stop of their own accord at about three months.

There are ways you can help soothe your colicky baby. Rocking or cuddling should help, and a car journey or pram ride will often send the baby off to sleep. Giving the age-old but new-formulated remedy, gripe water, has soothed many a baby's mother and sometimes the baby too!

There are new gripe mixtures available which are alcohol- and preservative-free. Gripe water can relieve the colicky pains, wind and troublesome hiccups. But always ask your health visitor or doctor for advice the first time your baby screams inconsolably.

What's Available? Dentinox Infant Colic Drops, Infacol, Nurse Harvey's Gripe Mixture, Woodward's Gripe Water

My Favourite Dentinox

Homoeopathic Remedies Chamomilla 3 × Drops or Pillules

CONJUNCTIVITIS
See STICKY EYES p.120

CONSTIPATION

With several million pounds being spent each year on laxatives, constipation is clearly a very common problem, though women are three times more likely to suffer from it than men. Yet in healthy people it is an ailment that is almost entirely preventable by simple, natural methods and laxatives should rarely be needed.

Many people consider themselves constipated if they do not 'go' regularly every day. But we all have our own natural rhythm. Some people go twice a day, some people every two or three days and both are quite normal if the habit is regular. In fact, bowel habits naturally vary and, as long as the motion is soft and well-formed and the bowel movement effortless, it doesn't matter if it occurs twice a day or twice a week.

Medically speaking, being constipated usually means passing hard, pellet-like stools with considerable effort and straining. Symptoms also include a bloated abdomen and a feeling of fullness. Being 'irregular' is not the same as constipation and is not necessarily a problem. It's only if your normal bowel habit changes for no good reason for more than a week or two, or if you notice any blood or mucus in your stools, that you should go to your doctor for advice.

Because of the straining associated with it, chronic constipation can lead to other unpleasant conditions such as piles, hiatus hernia and diverticuli – small 'blow outs' in the lining of the bowel which, if they become inflamed, develop into painful diverticulitis. So it makes sense to avoid becoming constipated if possible. The easiest way to do this is to increase the amount of fibre – roughage – in your diet.

Fibre, the undigestible part of cereals, fruit and vegetables, is nature's laxative and most of us would benefit from eating at least half as much again as we do at present. The bulk it provides gives the bowel muscles something to work on and helps to speed up the elimination of food waste after the nutrients have been absorbed during digestion. Fibre swells with the water it absorbs from the gut, so this also helps to produce a soft, well-formed motion.

Many people believe that just eating a bit of extra fruit will soon cure constipation, but this is unlikely to be enough. In fact, bran, the outer husk of cereals, is the richest source of undigestible fibre – far more so than any fruit or vegetables. Wheat bran is the richest source of all.

The refining process used to produce white bread and flour, for example, removes this husk, so an easy way to increase your fibre intake is to eat more wholemeal bread flour and pastas. A daily helping of bran breakfast cereal is another excellent way and natural, uncooked bran can also be sprinkled into soups and stews. Porridge oats, brown rice, baked beans, peas, lentils and sweet corn are high in fibre too. Fruit – unpeeled is best – vegetables and nuts contain a different kind of fibre, and for maximum benefit, eat a good variety of all types of fibre-containing foods regularly.

Expectant mothers and the elderly should avoid eating large quantities of uncooked bran as it may interfere with absorption of minerals such as iron and calcium. Other types of edible fibre can be taken as required.

Contrary to popular belief, too much fibre in your diet will not give you diarrhoea. A *sudden* increase in fibrous food, however, may cause flatulence until the body adjusts, so it is best to make changes gradually.

Remember also that putting off going to the loo can lead to a loss of your usual bowel reflexes, which in turn will cause constipation. Always make a conscious attempt to go to the loo promptly whenever you feel the need.

Many people do rely on laxatives, and although this is not particularly harmful, it is a little unwise, especially if you take them all the time. They can interfere with the normal digestive processes and essential nutrients in the diet pass straight through instead of being absorbed into the body, where they would be of benefit. The risk of vitamin and mineral deficiencies is therefore one good reason not to adopt this practice.

If you do feel the need for laxatives in cases of short-term constipation, your pharmacist can advise you and suggest a suitable one. Laxatives go to work on the large intestine either by speeding up the progress of faecal matter passing through the bowel or by increasing its bulk. Stimulant laxatives such as senna make the bowel muscle contract to hurry the faeces along and bulk-forming laxatives such as ispaghula soak up water in the bowel to increase volume and make stools softer.

The laxative phenolphthalein is often referred to as a stimulant laxative. What happens is this. As food passes down the alimentary canal, the stomach and small intestine require water in order to digest it. At this stage, the contents of the alimentary tract are fluid. There is a water conservation mechanism in the colon, where excess water is re-absorbed into the body, and this can cause constipation. The stimulant effect of phenolphthalein is that it stimulates the onward squeezing movements of the colon, which hampers water absorption because the bulk within the colon is moved on too quickly.

Other laxatives contain liquid paraffin, a lubricant which makes the faeces softer and easier to pass. These should not be taken less than two hours after a meal, since there is a theoretical risk that the liquid paraffin content could interfere with the absorption of some essential vitamins.

If your bowels are very sluggish, your doctor or pharmacist may recommend extra fibre in the form of tablets, or pleasant fruit-flavoured drinks, such as Fybogel or Regulan, made from the husk of the ispaghula plant. Plenty of watery drinks and some daily exercise will also help to keep the bowels moving.

So if you often find yourself resorting to laxatives, first check with your doctor that there is no underlying medical cause for your constipation – an underfunctioning thyroid gland is one possibility – and ask if a higher fibre diet would help you. If, with your doctor's agreement, you then start to eat considerably more of the foods I have mentioned, you should soon find you are saving money on laxatives and can spend it more enjoyably and healthily on food! You may even lose some weight, too – fibrous foods are filling but usually low in calories and therefore slimming!

What's Available?   Agarol, Alophen, Andrews Liver Salt, Bonomint, Brooklax, Califig, Correctol, Dulcolax, Ex-Lax Pills and Tablets, Fybogel, Fybogel Orange, Isogel, Jaap's Health Salt, Laxoberol, Metamucil, Milk of Magnesia, Mil-Par, Normacol, Normacol Plus, Nylax, Petrolagar, Regulan, Reguletts, Senlax, Senokot

Unbranded Products   Epsom Salts B.P., Glycerin Suppositories, Senna Laxative Tablets

My Favourites   Senlax, Ex-Lax, Dulcolax

Homoeopathic Remedies   Nux. Vom., Silicea, Sulphur

Herbal Remedies   Dual-Lax, Liminate, Lustys Herbalene, Pileabs Tablets, Potter's Cleansing Herb Tablets, Rhuaka Herbal Syrup

CORNS
Corns are small lumps of hard skin on the toes, especially over the bony prominences, or on the sides of the feet. They are caused by friction or continual pressure from poorly fitting shoes. The constant rubbing causes a layer of thickened skin to develop which is gradually pushed inwards to form a nucleus or core. It eventually becomes painful when this core presses on a nerve.

There are several types of corn, of which the most common are the hard corn, soft corn and seed corn. A hard corn is a raised shiny dome of whitish or pale yellow thickened skin with a hard cone-shaped centre. It has no root and usually develops on top of the toe joints.

A soft corn appears in the damp area between the toes

where the skin surfaces rub together. It is paler and softer than a hard corn. A seed corn is similar in structure but is found on the heel or ball of the foot where the skin can be dry and not very elastic. It is the least painful of the three and often feels like grit in the skin.

To ease discomfort you can soften the hard skin with one of the corn treatments available. Preparations for treating corns usually contain keratolytics such as salicylic acid, to encourage the layer of hardened skin cells to peel off. Be careful to keep any of these solvents off the skin surrounding the corn. If solvent accidentally gets on the normal skin, wash it off immediately.

When treating corns between the toes, hold the toes apart until the solvent has completely dried – putting cotton wool between the toes is a good way of doing this. To prevent further pressure on the corns, buy some small spongy rubber rings to put around them. Beware of corn plasters – if applied incorrectly, they can do more harm than good.

If you frequently have painful corns, it is best to visit a chiropodist. Look in the Yellow Pages for chiropodists with the letters SRCh MChS after their names.

People with diabetes should always consult their doctor about foot problems, since they are more likely to pick up infections in these sore areas. Because diabetic sufferers tend to have poor circulation, they should avoid wearing tight socks or shoes which could reduce the blood flow to the feet.

We all need to look after our feet – an incredible 90% of all foot problems are caused by wearing ill-fitting or the 'wrong' shoes, so do take time to choose new shoes carefully.

What's Available?   Carnation Corncaps, Freezone Liquid, Salatac Gel, Scholl Corn Removers, Soft Corn Removers, Callous Removers

My Favourite   Carnation Corncaps

Herbal Remedies   Lanes Balto Foot Balm

COUGHS

A cough is not an illness in itself, but a symptom. Although it can be irritating and often embarrassing, it is the body's natural response to any foreign body, congestion or irritation in the lungs or throat. The irritation may be due to things like air pollution or cigarette smoke, but in a great many cases it turns out to be the result of a cold or flu virus.

Sometimes, however, coughing signals a more serious disorder in the respiratory tract. So it is extremely important to seek medical advice for any cough that lasts for longer than a few days or if there are streaks of blood in any mucus you cough up. Coughing up green sputum probably signifies a bacterial infection.

Coughs can be treated with cough suppressants or expectorants. Cough suppressants – as the name suggests – are medicines that suppress the symptom, the cough itself, without tackling the underlying cause. They reduce the frequency and intensity of a cough by acting on the part of the brain that controls the coughing reflex, or at the site of irritation in the throat. These may help if you have a dry, hacking cough. Dry coughs occur when there is irritation but little phlegm in the larynx at the top of the windpipe, or in the pharynx, the cavern between the mouth and nose at the top and the oesophagus (gullet) and trachea (windpipe) below. This irritation stimulates the cough reflex which is the body's natural response.

Expectorants relieve chesty coughs, the type you often get as a result of a cold or flu. These medicines claim to loosen the 'debris' or phlegm in order to make it easier to cough up.

There is certainly a bewildering range of cough medicines available in any pharmacy. Some simply contain soothing substances such as honey and glycerine to act on the throat's surface, together with pleasant-tasting flavourings and tiny doses of antiseptics. Some are sugar-free so that they can be taken by those suffering from diabetes, and will not cause tooth decay. Others are specially designed for children and some are even animal fat-free! Still others contain decongestants to help clear nasal passages or antihistamines to help ease allergy-like symptoms like the nasal congestion, sneezing and watery eyes that may accompany a cough.

Some cough medicines can cause drowsiness. If a medicine makes you drowsy do not drive or operate machinery. And avoid alcoholic drink. Children being given cough medicines which may cause drowsiness should not be left on their own.

If you do have an irritating cough and want something to relieve it, describe your cough to your pharmacist and take his or her advice. You don't want to buy something that may make your cough worse. As always, you should tell your pharmacist if you are taking any other medication, have a medical condition or are pregnant or think you may be.

Despite the enormous number of cough remedies available, there is disagreement as to their value. They may give temporary relief to a tickly throat and taste pleasant, even soothing, but they may or may not be any more effective than a honey drink you have made yourself or inhaling steam to ease congestion. Doctors are sometimes reluctant to prescribe cough suppressants because coughing is a protective reflex; repeated bouts of coughing can be distressing, however, so soothing medication may be needed.

When patients are well in themselves but the troublesome cough is keeping them awake at night and to no good purpose, then I'm in favour of cough suppressants. One instance when they can really be useful is when a person is over the worst of whooping cough, but the cough is persisting after the infection has past – as it sometimes can, for weeks afterwards.

What's Available?   Actifed Compound Linctus, Actifed Cough Relief (1–12 years), Actifed Expectorant, Benylin

Range, Bronal Cough Balsam, Bronalin Decongestant Contact Cough Caps, Bronalin Dry Cough Elixir, Bronalin Expectorant Linctus, Bronalin Paediatric Linctus, Bronchial Catarrh Pastilles, Buttercup Syrup range, Children's Cough Pastilles, Copholco, Copholcoids, Covonia, Cupal Baby Cough Syrup, Do-Do Expectorant, Do-Do Tablets, Famel Honey and Lemon Cough Pastilles, Famel Expectorant, Famel Linctus, Famel Original, Franolyn Chesty Cough, Franolyn Dry Cough, Gee's Linctus Pastilles, Hill's Balsam Range, Jackson's All Fours, Lemsip Chesty Cough, Lemsip Dry Tickly Cough, Meltus Adult Dry Cough Elixir, Meltus Adult Expectorant, Meltus Baby Cough Linctus, Meltus Junior Expectorant, Night Cough Pastilles, Nirolex, Nirolex for children, Nirolex Lozenges, Pavacol-D, Phensedyl Plus, Pholcodine Cough Pastilles, Potter's Catarrh Pastilles, Potter's Cough Pastilles, Robitussin Chesty Cough Medicine, Robitussin Chesty Cough with Congestion Medicine, Robitussin Dry Cough Medicine, Robitussin Junior Persistent Cough Medicine, Sudafed Expectorant, Sudafed Linctus, Tancolin, Throaties, Tixylix Cough & Cold, Tixylix Daytime, Veno's Range, Vicks Children's VapoSyrup, Vicks Cough Syrup – Expectorant, Vicks Vaposyrup for Dry Coughs, Vicks Vaposyrup for Chesty Coughs and a Blocked Nose, Vicks Vaposyrup for Dry Coughs and a Blocked Nose, Zubes

Unbranded Products   Gee's Linctus B.P., Pholcodine Linctus B.P., Simple Linctus B.P.

My Favourite   Benylin

Homoeopathic Remedies   Aconite, Bryonia, Drosera

Herbal Remedies   Garlic (see COLD, THE COMMON p.34), Olbas Pastilles, Potter's Antibron, Potter's Chest Mixture

CRADLE CAP

Cradle cap is a harmless condition resembling dandruff that is extremely common in young babies. It usually appears during the first three months of a baby's life, but can also affect toddlers and young children. If your baby develops cradle cap, you may first of all notice a little scurf on his or her head, followed by the appearance of yellowish or brownish greasy-looking scales of thickened skin which stick to the scalp. These patches sometimes appear over the whole head, sometimes just in small areas. Some specialists believe the crusts are due to excess production of sebum – grease from the sebaceous glands – in response to the mother's hormones.

Although it can be unsightly, cradle cap is unlikely to do your baby any harm. It usually disappears on its own after a few months. To ease it you can rub the baby's head with baby oil or olive oil and leave for 24 hours. Comb the hair gently, then wash the flakes of skin away. Alternatively, treat cradle cap with specially formulated gentle, medicated shampoo until the scalp is clear.

If you are worried and the cradle cap persists despite treatment, do seek the advice of your doctor or health visitor.

What's Available?   Capasal Therapeutic Shampoo, Dentinox Infant Cradle Cap Shampoo, S.C.R. Cream

My Favourite   Dentinox

CRAMP

Cramp is a common problem which can be extremely painful. It is a sudden, violent contraction of a muscle which makes the muscle become hard and tense. It's usually caused by exercise, especially unaccustomed exercise, or a prolonged period of sitting, lying or standing in an awkward position. Some people wake at night with cramp in their feet or legs. Attacks usually occur in bouts which last from a few days to a number of weeks, and there are often several weeks between each series of attacks.

No one really knows what causes cramp. It may occasionally be the result of a poor blood supply due to the furring up of the arteries – this is especially likely with elderly sufferers. But in the majority of cases, it's worth trying all the cramp remedies, in the hope that one of them will do the trick. It is not possible to be more specific about a 'cure' when no one knows the cause of the problem.

With the most common sort of cramp, in the calf muscles, try this. Stand facing a wall and at arm's length from it. Place the flat of your hands against the wall and gently bend forward from the ankles so that your calves are gently but comfortably stretched. Do this standing 'press-up' six times on three separate occasions throughout the day and continue it for ten days. If it works, keep doing it six times once a day to keep the cramp at bay. If it doesn't work, stop after ten days. This will stop me from worrying that you are continuing forever, wearing out the wallpaper to no good effect!

What's Available?   Crampex, Massage Balm

CUTS AND GRAZES

You can treat most cuts and grazes at home quite safely, but always wash your hands first, if possible. Clean the cut by holding it under running water, or by gently wiping it with an antiseptic wipe or cotton wool soaked in warm water. It's best to use a fresh piece of cotton wool for each wipe. Some small cuts will still bleed quite profusely at first, so if this is happening after a few minutes, you'll need to apply pressure to stem the flow. Press a pad, a clean tissue for example, firmly over the cut for a few minutes.

If you like to use plasters and antiseptic ointments on cuts and grazes, fine – it will do no harm. Personally, I prefer not to use ointments and I use plasters mainly to keep dirt out of the wound. When that isn't necessary or the injury is small, it will heal up nicely if left alone.

If a cut is very large or deep, if it has rugged or gaping edges, if something is embedded in it or if it is a deep cut with only a small opening in the skin (this might happen if the culprit is a rusty nail, for example) always seek medical help.

What's Available? Acriflex Burn Aid Cream, Betadine Antiseptic Paint, Betadine Dry Powder Spray, Betadine Ointment, Brulidine, DDD Medicated Cream, Dettol Antiseptic Soap, Dettol Fresh, Dettol, Drapolene Cream, Germolene Cream and Ointment, Lanacane, Medicaid, Morhulin, Savlon, Savlon Dry, Savlon Junior, Solarcaine, Sudocrem, TCP Antiseptic Liquid, TCP First Aid Antiseptic Cream, Witch Doctor

Unbranded Products Alum B.P., Centrimide Cream B.P., Iodine Tincture B.P., Witch Hazel

My Favourite Savlon

Herbal Remedies Dr Valnet's Tegarome, Nelsons Calendula Cream (to soothe abrasions), Hypercal Cream, Soothene Ointment

CYSTITIS

Cystitis is an inflammation of the bladder lining and the urethra – the tube down which urine is excreted from the bladder. It is one of the most common complaints suffered by women, and estimates suggest that more than half the women in the UK contract cystitis at some time (though it occasionally afflicts men and children too). If you have had it, you will certainly wish to avoid a recurrence. Some women experience attacks several times a year and an unfortunate few are seldom free of the problem.

A woman's anatomy makes her particularly prone to cystitis. Unlike a man's, her urethra is very short and the normally harmless germs around the anus are easily able to track upwards to the bladder, whose natural defences may be unable to cope with them. Some people say they suffer more from cystitis when they are 'run down'. It is likely that they feel run down because there is a niggling infection there which doesn't cause local symptoms all the time, but causes the sufferer to feel under par – that is, run down. From time to time, however, the local symptoms will present themselves.

Inflammation then develops and often spreads to the urethra – a condition known as urethritis – which results in the typical burning pain as urine is passed. The urine is often dark brown and strong smelling; it may also contain traces of blood. The sufferer has a constant urge to 'spend a penny' even though there is little or nothing to pass. A slight temperature, nausea, a dragging feeling in the lower abdomen and tenderness over the bladder are also common, as is a general feeling of being unwell. However, cystitis is by no means always due to an infection. The delicate lining of the urethra and/or the bladder can, in those susceptible, react to irritants such as scented soaps, powders, vaginal deodorants, bath oils and the detergents used to wash clothes. Some people are sensitive to highly spiced foods, strong tea, coffee, alcohol and fruit juices. Friction or bruising during lovemaking can also inflame the tissues, as the urethra is just above the vaginal entrance – a lubricant jelly may then help by overcoming any dryness. Hormone replacement therapy or oestrogen cream may be more effective after the menopause.

Germs can also be inadvertently 'helped' into the urethra during intercourse. Inserting tampons can do this too, as can wiping yourself from back to front (instead of front to back) after a bowel movement. The main germ which causes trouble here and after sexual intercourse is one called *Escherichia coliform*, more commonly known as *E. coli*. It lives in the bowel, where it is harmless, but if it makes its way to the vagina or urethra it can cause problems.

Thrush infection, perhaps aggravated by wearing tight-fitting trousers, is another possible cause of symptoms. It is important, too, to pass urine as soon as you feel the need and to empty your bladder completely each time by squeezing out every last drop – a reservoir of urine can make a fertile breeding ground for germs.

So, if you are prone to cystitis, always wash around your vaginal area and 'spend a penny' both before and after making love. Having sex with a full bladder, or bowel for that matter, means bruising is more likely to occur, which can also encourage cystitis. Ask your partner to wash daily, too.

Try to drink at least three or four pints of water every day to flush out any germs and prevent them settling. It has been suggested that a glass or two of cranberry juice a day may also help to keep cystitis at bay. No one knows quite why, but some Americans swear by it.

If symptoms do develop, neutralising the acidity is a worthwhile first line of treatment, since as many as two out of three sufferers won't actually have any infection and the symptoms should therefore settle in a day or so using this method alone. Start immediately symptoms appear by drinking a pint of water with a teaspoonful of bicarbonate of soda added – unless you suffer from high blood pressure, or heart or kidney trouble, in which case consult your doctor first. Drink a pint of this mixture every hour for three hours, interspersed with other soft drinks. This will change the urine from acid to alkaline and relieve the pain, but it is not something I would recommend too often, as an excess of bicarbonate of soda, especially in a sufferer whose kidneys are not working properly, could lead to side-effects such as a rise in blood pressure.

Alternatively you could take potassium citrate or a specially formulated, pleasant-tasting medicine from the chemist. These medicines mainly contain sodium citrate to make the urine less acid and are usually meant to be taken regularly for 48 hours. Such treatments can be very helpful, but if symptoms persist after the 48 hours are up, you should see your doctor – take a specimen of urine with you in a clean, screw-topped jar. If infection is found or suspected, antibiotics are usually effective but be sure to complete the course. You should not need to repeat treatments often, either.

If your symptoms come back regularly, see your doctor for advice. Just occasionally, if cystitis is a constant problem, there may be a rarer cause for which further investigations will be necessary.

Over-the-counter treatments for cystitis should not be taken by children except on medical advice, nor if you are pregnant or breast-feeding, if you have heart disease or high blood pressure, if you have had any kidney disease or if you are on a low salt diet.

Other helpful measures include rest in bed and a hot water bottle placed over your abdomen; your preferred painkiller will also make you feel better.

What's Available?   Cymalon, Cystoleve, Cystopurin

My Favourite   Cymalon

DANDRUFF AND SEBORRHOEIC DERMATITIS

Dandruff is a condition rather like acne which, although not serious, can be acutely embarrassing to those who suffer from it and a source of amusement to those who don't. It is also the most common cause of itching of the scalp, but is not a sign of general ill health.

Normally, everyone's skin cells, including those on their scalp, are replenished about every 28 days and the top layer regularly shed in minute, usually unnoticeable pieces. In dandruff sufferers, this process may be speeded up and the particles shed are larger and easily seen. With milder forms of dandruff, sometimes known as scurf, the flakes of skin are dry and white and tend to clump together in the hair. Touching the hair – which most people do many times a day without realising it – dislodges the fragments and they fall on to the shoulders, looking like a white powder.

This type of dandruff can usually be controlled by

washing the hair two or three times a week with a medicated, anti-dandruff shampoo. These often contain tar, sulphur or salicylic acid to soften and help loosen scale and scalp debris. Other anti-dandruff shampoos for more severe cases contain zinc pyrithione or selenium sulphide to reduce the development of dandruff by slowing down the growth of skin cells, as well as having mild antifungal properties.

There is, however, a more severe form of dandruff called seborrhoeic dermatitis of the scalp, which may not respond to these shampoos. It can occur on other parts of the body, too, and may be very difficult to treat effectively.

Seborrhoeic dermatitis can affect both children and adults. On a baby's scalp it is known as cradle cap (see p.50) and the condition often also appears as a nappy rash for which your doctor can prescribe a cream. For adults and older children, Capasal Therapeutic Shampoo may help, as it 'dissolves' the skin flakes but also contains a moisturiser to protect the skin from dehydration.

When they occurred in adults, both seborrhoeic dermatitis and other forms of dandruff used to be thought to be due to over-production of sebum. Diet, hygiene, climate and stress were also thought to play a part. However, recent research has shown that it is the sufferer's over-reaction to a minute, fungus-like organism called *Pityrosporum ovale*. It is the reaction to the fungus, rather than the fungus itself, that causes the scalp's top layer of skin to flake off as dandruff, or gives rise to the symptoms of seborrhoeic dermatitis.

In this condition, which is most common in young men but can affect women, too, the flakes of skin are large, yellow and oily. The skin on the scalp becomes red, inflamed and soggy, especially around the edges, and may be infected by other germs. Eyelashes, eyebrows, skin folds on either side of the nose and behind the ears can all be affected, as can other parts of the body, such as the chest, armpits, breasts and groin.

Neither dandruff nor seborrhoeic dermatitis is catching, because, as I said, it is not the fungus itself that produces the symptoms – as it is with athlete's foot, for instance – but an over-reaction to it which only occurs in susceptible people. The fungus itself is around all the time. Why some people and not others have this susceptibility isn't known.

If you find your dandruff cannot be controlled by medicated shampoos from your pharmacist, do consult your doctor, as there are now effective treatments which he or she can prescribe. The same advice applies if you think you have seborrhoeic dermatitis. Your doctor's examination will exclude other possible skin conditions such as psoriasis and eczema, and suitable treatment can then be suggested.

If dandruff or scalp symptoms are severe, there is now some good news for sufferers. A specific antifungal shampoo called Nizoral is available on prescription and is very effective. Your doctor may suggest using this twice weekly for about four weeks, interspersed with milder medicated shampoos on other days. You may then be advised to use the antifungal shampoo less frequently to prevent symptoms recurring. Regular hair-washing with this shampoo may also help if your eyelids are inflamed and crusty, although another organism – the staphylococcus – is often involved in this case too. It causes a condition known as blepharitis, to which many people are prone from childhood. Symptoms can usually be controlled by removing crusts from the eyelids by bathing them with a cotton wool bud dipped in baby shampoo, diluted to half strength, and then applying an antibiotic ointment to the rims.

Your doctor may prescribe antifungal and/or various anti-inflammatory applications for skin rashes on other parts of the body due to seborrhoeic dermatitis; taking antibiotics by mouth may be necessary if the rash becomes infected by other germs.

So, if the usual medicated shampoos do not keep your dandruff at bay, don't feel that it is too minor a problem to bother your doctor with. Any of these conditions can be very distressing and embarrassing and there is a lot that can now be done to treat them.

What's Available?   Alphosyl 2 in 1 Shampoo, Betadine Scalp and Skin Cleanser, Betadine Shampoo, Betasept Shampoo, Capasal Therapeutic Shampoo, Ceanel, Cocois, Denorex, Gelcotar Liquid, Genisol, Lenium, Polytar Liquid, Polytar Plus

My Favourite   Polytar

Homoeopathic Remedies   Graphite, Sepia

DERMATITIS
See DRY SKIN CONDITIONS p.61

DIARRHOEA
Diarrhoea is an extremely common symptom involving loose or liquid bowel movements and frequent or speedy trips to the loo. It is also often accompanied by cramping pain in the lower abdomen. It can make you feel quite exhausted and if you're on holiday it can ruin your fun.

Most attacks of diarrhoea are caused by gastro-intestinal infections – you can think of them as the body's way of getting rid of harmful substances. If more than one member of your family suffers at the same time, it is likely the diarrhoea was caused by something you've all eaten. If you have just come back from a trip away, you might have been exposed to standards of hygiene that do not match up to what you are used to, resulting in what we know as 'holiday tummy'. If your diarrhoea is accompanied by vomiting, food poisoning is also a likely cause. Gastric flu could be the culprit, too.

Another common cause of diarrhoea is stress. A job interview or a driving test can reduce the toughest of us to a bundle of nerves. Eating large amounts of food with laxative properties, such as prunes, can have an adverse effect. Diarrhoea can be a side-effect of taking certain drugs – antibiotics, for example. Tetracycline, a commonly prescribed antibiotic, can destroy friendly bacteria which normally live in the bowel and are part of our natural defences against more harmful bacteria. Consequently, if they are destroyed, the harmful ones – perhaps resistant to the antibiotic – can thrive. But if this happens to you, don't just stop taking the antibiotics. Ring your doctor and ask for advice.

Whatever the cause, most attacks of diarrhoea usually clear up quickly and without medical attention. The best way to treat yourself is not eating for 24 hours and drinking plenty of watery drinks. Frequent bursts of diarrhoea can make you feel even more ill as your body becomes dehydrated. The greatest risk from diarrhoea, and from vomiting too, is that the body's essential minerals are lost at the same time. Mineral depletion of this nature can make you feel weak and eventually faint. In a healthy person, water is essential to maintain normal body functions. Its importance is underlined by the fact that around half our body weight is water. Normally our kidneys balance the water lost in the urine and through perspiration against our fluid intake – we feel more thirsty and therefore drink more in hot weather, for instance.

Diarrhoea or sickness causes excessive loss of fluid, but if we are feeling ill, we may not feel thirsty. This means that our water balance is upset and we will continue to feel unwell until the fluid balance is restored.

To prevent mineral loss and dehydration you can buy ready-prepared sachets to be mixed with water, which are a combination of essential salts, minerals and energy-giving glucose. (This is known as oral rehydration therapy.) When these are mixed with the correct quantity of water as instructed, they are just the right strength for quick absorption, even by an inflamed stomach.

Medicines used to treat diarrhoea include powders which form a bulky mass inside the bowel to help carry away irritant substances. Typical examples are aluminium silicate (kaolin), calcium carbonate (chalk) and pectin (a purified carbohydrate product made from citrus fruits). Preparations made with these powders contain particles that swell up as they absorb water from the large intestine. This makes the faeces firmer and less runny. It's thought that these powders may absorb irritants and harmful chemicals along with the excess water.

Other drugs act on the muscular bowel wall to slow down bowel movements, relieving the familiar griping pains caused by diarrhoea. Typical examples are drugs from the opium family like codeine phosphate or morphine, which is usually mixed with kaolin.

In normally healthy adults, diarrhoea is rarely a serious condition – children and the elderly may suffer much more. This is because they are more sensitive to the problems of dehydration and often have less body fluid to lose. Babies under six months old are at the greatest risk from dehydration – their metabolic rate is high, their kidneys don't yet retain water very efficiently and they lose a greater proportion of water compared to their weight than adults do.

But even if you're a healthy adult, you should always consult your doctor if the condition doesn't improve within 48 hours, if the faeces contain blood, if there is severe abdominal pain or vomiting, or if you've just returned from a foreign country.

To help avoid gyppy tummy and the holiday runs – or worse – be careful with the ice in those long, cool drinks. Researchers writing in the *British Food Journal* pointed out some time ago that in Central America, four harmful germs were shown to survive even when frozen for 24 hours – and were still flourishing when melted in 86% proof tequila!

In the UK, hygiene standards can sometimes be inadequate when ice-making machines are sited in dirty, poorly ventilated areas, like cellars, and are not cleaned or serviced regularly. Ice is often put into the glass with the server's fingers and, in one survey, only half the ice-buckets were found to have lids – so dust and germs could float in. The researchers found germ contamination in ice-making machines as well as ice-buckets at the bar. More than one in two samples in the survey contained germs – and a large proportion of those were of the kind that could occur if someone didn't wash their hands after using the loo.

So, in future, when you are being careful about the cleanliness of your food and drink on holiday, beware of the humble ice cube. If the only available restaurant or bar doesn't look too clean, stick to the contents of mass-produced bottled drinks and thoroughly cooked food.

What's Available   Arret, Adult Kao-C and Junior Kao-C, Diareze, Diocalm, Diocalm Replenish, Diocalm Ultra, Dior-alyte, Gluco-Lyte, Imodium, Isogel, Opazimes, Pepto-Bismol, Rapolyte, Rehidrat

Unbranded Products   Kaolin Mixture B.P., Kaolin Mixture Paediatric B.P. 1980

My Favourites   Arret

DRY SKIN CONDITIONS – ECZEMA, DERMATITIS AND PSORIASIS

Eczema and dermatitis are used as virtually interchangeable terms and generally mean inflammation of the skin. The main symptoms are itching and redness, accompanied by small blisters which often weep and form a crust. Eczema can take the form of small red patches on the limbs, or it can afflict large areas of the body. Although it is not usually a 'serious' disease, nor a contagious one, it can be severe, uncomfortable and unsightly, causing the sufferer to become exceptionally self-conscious. If you think you have eczema, see your doctor – although it is often hard to define the cause of eczema or to cure it completely, there are a number of treatments available to control it.

You can help combat the dryness, itching and flaking by preserving the moisture content of your skin. Avoid harsh or highly perfumed soaps or bath additives; instead, try using the emollient (moisturising) soaps, creams and specially made bath oils listed below, and when bathing use warm water instead of hot. These emollient products can be helpful when the skin becomes generally dry – often one of the minor complaints of pregnancy. Moisturising bath oils can make the surface of the bath slippery, so do be careful getting in and out.

Dry skin conditions can be a problem in childhood. About one child in ten suffers from infantile or atopic eczema. The symptoms are similar to those described above, but may look worse as a result of the child's scratching. Consult your doctor for treatment and advice. At home, keep the child's skin away from direct contact with wool or other rough fabrics – choose soft, pure cotton instead. Keep the child's fingernails short and use only gentle cleansing products suitable for infants.

Another form of skin complaint is known as contact dermatitis. This has similar symptoms to eczema but is specifically caused by contact with substances to which your skin is sensitive – household detergents or costume jewellery, for example. Protect your hands when using household cleansing fluids or chemicals, etc., and avoid contact with metals, dyes or even washing powders which may cause you problems. Using a cream such as Savlon Barrier Cream can protect sensitive skin as it forms a protective barrier against potential irritants such as detergents and chemicals, which can cause irritation. Codella is another protective cream for working hands. If you're not sure of the cause, consult your doctor, who may choose to carry out allergy tests. A mild hydrocortisone cream will ease discomfort by reducing inflammation and calming irritated skin.

Psoriasis can vary in severity from being a mild nuisance to, rarely, being so severe that the sufferer has to be admitted to hospital. With psoriasis, the skin cells grow much faster than usual. The skin cells divide and shed, which they normally do in any case (see DANDRUFF, p.55), but in just three to four days instead of the normal 25-28.

The precise cause isn't clear. What is known is that

psoriasis can be triggered by stress, some drugs (beta-blockers given for high blood pressure, for example) and even an infection with a virus, such as German measles. Raised red patches with thick, silvery white scales appear on the skin, usually on the knees, elbows and scalp. On the scalp it's most noticeable as a thick white encrustation around the hairline and ears.

Psoriasis seems to be linked to heredity and can appear at any age, though it most commonly attacks those in their teens or twenties, affecting men and women equally. It can be a difficult condition to treat and unfortunately there's no long-term cure. Outbreaks tend to come and go – frequency and extent vary between individuals and cannot be predicted accurately.

Although psoriasis is not often harmful to the general health and is not catching, the appearance of the skin can cause the sufferer great embarrassment and discomfort, especially when large areas are involved. The condition normally improves in the summer and gets worse again in the winter, but patches will sometimes clear up completely for years. On a day to day basis, emollient baths and creams (E45 for example) rubbed into the scaly patches can help to soothe the itching and flaking. Yoga, meditation and methods of relaxation – including holidays, especially in the sun, which is extremely beneficial for psoriasis – can all bring relief and, by encouraging a calmer outlook, may help prevent further flare-ups.

Sufferers can also benefit from eating more fish, especially oily fish like mackerel and herring. It's been suggested that one of the unsaturated fats in fish oils, EPA, is able to replace, within the body, another unsaturated fat, arachidonic acid. It is the metabolism – the body's usage – of this last acid which seems to be upset in someone who suffers from psoriasis (see VITAMINS p.281).

But despite all these possible remedies, active outbreaks should always be seen by a doctor. If the psoriasis is widespread or persistent, specialised hospital treatments will be recommended.

What's Available?   Alphosyl, Alphosyl 2 in 1 Shampoo, Aveeno, Bath E45, Codella, Cream E45, Dermacort, Dermidex, Emulave Fluid, Emulsiderm Medicaid (an antiseptic cream for tender skin areas), Eurax Hc, Gelcosal, Gelcotar, Hewletts Cream, Hydromol Cream, Hydromol Emollient, Imuderm Range of Products, Infaderm Baby Bath, Cream, Lotion and Hair Wash, Lanacane, Lanacort, Morhulin, Oilatum Cream, Oilatum Emollient and Soap, Oilatum Gel, Probase 3, Psoriderm Bath Emulsion, Savlon Barrier Cream, Savlon Dry Skin Cream, Savlon Moisturising Bath Oil, Sudocrem, Wash E45

For contact dermatitis – Hc45 Hydrocortisone Cream, Dermidex

Unbranded Products   Coconut Oil B.P., Lanolin B.P.

My Favourite   Cream E45

Homoeopathic Remedies   Graphites, Rhus. Tox., Sulphur, Nelsons Graphites Cream (for dermatitis)

Herbal Remedies   Kleer, Nelsons Calendula Cream (for sore and rough skin), Nelsons Evening Primrose Cream, Potter's Psorasolv Ointment

EAR WAX

Everyone has a certain amount of wax in their ears – it is a natural substance secreted by tiny glands in the skin of the ear similar to sweat glands. It helps protect the sensitive lining in the outer channel of the ear from infection and keeps it free of dust and flakes of skin. And just as some people sweat more than others, some people naturally produce more ear wax.

Usually the wax steadily crumbles away and is expelled from the ear as tiny flakes, to be replaced by a fresh supply of wax from within the ear. It only becomes troublesome when there is a build-up of too much wax which, if left for a long time, may harden or slip against the drum and cause hearing problems.

When you first become aware of the familiar slight 'muzziness' caused by a build-up of wax, try softening the wax with a little olive oil at body temperature dropped into the ear(s) two or three times a day. Alternatively, there are special ear-wax softening drops, sometimes medicated, which your pharmacist can recommend. The wax may then gradually slide out on its own.

However, I must urge you to take great care with your ears – never delve inside too deeply or you could damage the drum. Do not attempt to clean or unblock your ears with cotton wool buds, nor use force or instruments in the ear. And never use ear drops to soften wax if your ears are inflamed or infected.

If you do use drops and after two or three days your ears still don't feel clear, consult your doctor – your ears may need syringing with warm water.

What's Available?   Audax Ear Drops, Cerumol, Cupal Wax Aid, Earex, Exterol Ear Drops, Otex, Waxsol Ear Drops, Wax Wane Ear Drops

My Favourite   Cerumol

ECZEMA
See DRY SKIN CONDITIONS p.61

FEVER
A fever, the result of a high temperature (over 38°C/ 100.4°F) which makes you sweat or shiver, can be a symptom of any one of several illnesses, but is usually a sign that your body is fighting infection. Coughs, colds and other infections are often accompanied by aches, pains and feverishness.

To help reduce a fever, take the recommended dose of aspirin, ibuprofen or paracetamol – paracetamol for children (see PAINKILLERS p.100 for products containing these ingredients). Drink plenty of cold, alcohol-free fluids. Sponging the body with tepid water can be helpful in cases of high fever – but when the temperature is as high as 40°C/103°F, at least phone your doctor for advice.

What's Available?   For children: Calpol Infant Suspension, Calpol Six Plus, Cupanol Under 6, Cupanol Over 6, Fenning's Children's Cooling Powders, Junior Disprol Tablets, Junior Paraclear, Medised, Panadol Junior and Baby/Infant Elixir

For adults: see PAINKILLERS p.100 for list of products containing aspirin, ibuprofen or paracetamol

My Favourite   For children: Calpol Infant Suspension or Calpol Six Plus

FIBROSITIS
See RHEUMATIC PAIN p.111

FLATULENCE
The problems caused by flatulence or wind are more likely to be those of embarrassment rather than ill-health, but they are problems we all share – some of us more than others! Flatulence can be painful, too, and the symptoms can range from a generally bloated feeling to aches in the stomach, cramp-like sensations in the chest and rumbling noises in the stomach and lower bowel.

When thousands of tiny bubbles of gas become trapped in the digestive system they cause pain or discomfort. The reasons for this are numerous. Gas is occasionally produced when we swallow air as we eat, usually without our being aware that this is happening. As most of us have experienced, eating food such as baked beans or spicy curries or drinking beer can bring on attacks of flatulence. Eating too quickly, overeating or being under stress can also cause the problem – or you may simply be a person who is prone to wind.

If you find that certain foods trigger wind, you can try to avoid them. For most people these will be the pulses – peas, beans and lentils, for example. Some antacids may help, or you can buy a product such as Windcheaters which is specially designed for the relief of wind, flatulence and bloating. The capsules contain activated dimethicone, also sometimes used to relieve colic in babies, which breaks down the tiny, frothy type of bubbles that cause wind. Once broken down, these bubbles form one large bubble which is much easier to pass naturally and painlessly.

What's Available? Andrews Antacid, Boots Double Action Indigestion Tablets, Maalox Plus Suspension or Tablets, Milk of Magnesia, Rap-Eze, Windcheaters

My Favourite Windcheaters

Herbal Remedies Biobalm, Digest, Indian Brandee

GIVING UP SMOKING

It's thought that every year some 100,000 people in the UK die because of smoking-related problems. These problems are mainly lung cancer, chronic obstructive lung disease (often previously known as chronic bronchitis) or coronary heart disease. Every day around 300 Britons die as a direct result of smoking. Each time you light up, just think about those 4,000 substances in cigarette smoke (the majority poisonous) that you are inhaling.

People often tell me that they don't believe there's much point in giving up smoking because they've smoked for so many years the damage has been done. Well, that's not entirely true. As soon as you give up smoking your lungs do begin to return to normal. Within eight hours the levels of nicotine and carbon monoxide in your blood will have decreased by 50 per cent. So it really is worth a try.

There's now quite a range of products you can buy from your pharmacist and please don't hesitate to ask him or her for advice. (If you suffer from diabetes or heart disease or if you are pregnant or breast feeding you should ask your doctor's opinion before trying any of the over-the-counter products to help you give up. And you shouldn't take nicotine products and smoke as well.)

There are nicotine-containing products available, such as the new patches (Nicotinell, Nicabate, Nicorette and Niconil), nicotine gum (Nicorette), and nicotine lozenges and tablets (Stoppers, Stubit and Resolution). Nicotine products should not be used together with other nicotine-containing products, including cigarettes. And, as I said, nicotine should not be taken by anyone with severe cardiovascular disease, or in pregnancy or while breast feeding, without a doctor's advice. Side-effects can include a worstening of the symptoms of peptic ulcers and gastritis.

Nicotine patches became newly available over-the-counter at the end of 1992 and have continued to sell like hot cakes ever since, thanks to national advertising campaigns and research highlighting their efficacy. The patches are thought to be successful because most smokers are addicted to nicotine and the smoker's body likes the feeling the nicotine gives it. So when nicotine levels drop – for example when you don't have a cigarette or go to sleep the body craves for more. Nicotine patches contain a reservoir of nicotine that is slowly absorbed through your skin. The idea is that you break the habit of wanting to light up because the patch is satisfying your body's craving. You can then slowly reduce the amount of nicotine you absorb by wearing smaller patches to wean you off the drug. Nicotinell, for instance, has been designed to be worn for a full 24 hours. This means that your body is being supplied with nicotine when you are probably at your weakest and your craving the strongest – first thing in the morning.

Symptoms of nicotine withdrawal are restlessness, yearning for a cigarette, irritability, lack of concentration, wanting to eat more and interrupted sleep patterns. Nicotine patches can irritate the skin where the patch has been placed.

Nicotine gum (Nicorette) is chewed and then kept in the mouth so that it allows the nicotine to be absorbed through the cheeks. But you do need to chew the gum correctly and thoroughly. You can also buy nicotine replacement lozenges.

Some people believe that lozenges have slightly more flexibility than nicotine patches because they can be used as and when the urge to light up becomes impossible to ignore. In that way they're said to be helpful for those smokers who wish to give up or cut down, as well as those who need help to overcome the urge to smoke in places where smoking is forbidden. Each Stoppers lozenge, for example, contains 0.4g nicotine – equivalent to that contained in a mid-range cigarette. The advantage over a cigarette is that Stoppers do not contain any harmful tars and resins associated with tobacco smoking. Nicotine absorption through the buccal mucosa (mucus in the mouth and inside the cheeks) is rapid and efficient. That's why they need to be dissolved in the mouth, between the cheek and gum, allowing the nicotine to be absorbed.

There are non-nicotine products available, such as Nicobrevin which are capsules containing menthyl valerate, quinine, camphor and eucalyptus. They're supposed to help withdrawl symptoms and benefit the lungs. They probably work by exciting the lining membrane of the bronchial tubes producing a warm and comforting feeling, masking the craving for a similar feeling from a cigarette. Tabmint contains silver acetate in a chewing gum and this helps you give up smoking by making cigarettes taste more unpleasant.

There may be many new aids to smoking cessation on the market – but only you can do it. Determination is what is needed most. Studies have shown that seven out of ten smokers are likely to have tried to stop smoking and have subsequently failed. Don't be frightened to ask the help of your GP. Make a list of your reasons for wanting to stop. The list could include the facts that you'll be fitter, be rid of any morning cough, will have fresher breath, fresher smelling clothes and hair, and a sense of achievement if you succeed – and just think of all the money you'll save! You may also consider trying a 'Stop Smoking' therapist, listening to an audio tape on the subject, or trying acupuncture or hypnotherapy. Enquire at your local library for services local to you.

What's Available? Nicabate, Nicobrevin, Niconil, Nicorette, Nicorette Plus, Nicorette Patch, Nicotinell, Resolution, Stoppers, Stubit, Tabmint

GUM DISEASE – GINGIVITIS, BLEEDING GUMS

Let's start with the good news – our dental health has improved enormously over the last twenty years and continues to do so. Nevertheless, periodontal (gum) disease is still the commonest of all diseases in the world, not just in Britain, and up to one in five adults in this country will have lost all their teeth by the time they are sixty, mainly because of this condition.

Gum disease can appear as an inflammation of the gum margins (the gingival margins). Gunge – a mixture of bacteria and food debris – collects in this crevice. Initially this may cause very mild inflammation, but sometimes it will inflame the gums sufficiently to make them sore and swollen – a condition called gingivitis. More seriously, the infection can spread beneath the gums and affect the deeper tissues which attach the tooth to the jaw-bone. It is then known as periodontitis or pyorrhoea and if it goes undetected and untreated the gums gradually recede, the bone becomes eroded and the teeth loosen and eventually fall out. Fortunately, gum disease can nearly always be prevented by good dental care and if you visit your dentist regularly, he or she will spot warning signs such as 'pocketing' – a gap developing between the teeth and gums. This can be measured and advice or treatment can then be given to halt the process.

Even the severest form of gum disease can be almost symptomless and surprisingly pain free, but one of the first signs that all is not well with your gums is if they look 'spongy' and inflamed, and bleed when you brush your teeth. Nearly everyone will experience this mild form of gingivitis from time to time and it is important to treat it promptly before it becomes more serious. Often a little extra care with your teeth-cleaning routine will do the trick.

The main cause of gum problems and tooth decay is plaque. This is a thin, colourless, sticky substance, composed mainly of bacteria, which forms almost continuously around the teeth and gum margins. If not removed by regular brushing it can build up and harden into a deposit known as tartar or calculus, which attracts further plaque. Tartar, unlike plaque, can be felt with the tongue and can only be removed by a dentist or dental hygienist using special instruments to scale the teeth.

When tartar has built up, every chew and every incorrect brushing can push the tender gums against the sandpaper-like plaque, making them bleed; more harmfully, it makes them shrink back, exposing more of the tooth. Indeed, many middle-aged and elderly people who have suffered from this process for years are said to be 'long in the tooth'. But this need not happen at all.

Food – particularly sugary and starchy food – interacts with plaque on the teeth and produces acid which eats away at the enamel. This acid attack can last anything from 40 minutes up to two hours after a meal or snack, so the number of times you eat during the day is important, as well as what you eat. If you must eat sweet things, try to limit them to meal times, when the other foods being eaten will 'dilute' the acid produced.

Eating a small piece of hard cheese at the end of a meal will help to neutralise the acid, as well as providing protective calcium. Contrary to popular belief, fruit such as apples do not clean the teeth and may only produce more acid. If you can, you should also avoid eating anything shortly before bedtime – our flow of saliva decreases when we sleep and its beneficial cleansing effects will therefore be less.

Saliva has another advantage – it contains a substance which neutralises acid. A recent study has shown that the Americans may have known a thing or two all along – chewing gum for a minimum of 20 minutes after a meal or snack increases the flow of saliva considerably, reducing the time that teeth are attacked by acid from two hours to just 20 minutes. Most people could benefit from it, including anyone who suffers from a dry mouth through taking certain medicines which can have the side-effect of drying up secretions. Any long-standing lack of saliva increases the likelihood of tooth decay, gum disease and mouth infections.

Of course, regular brushing – ideally for at least three minutes after breakfast and at bedtime – is also very important in keeping teeth and gums healthy. So too is the right toothbrush, replaced every three months. Ask your dental hygienist to advise you and show you the most effective way to clean your teeth. He or she will also show you how to use dental floss, useful for removing plaque from awkward crevices between the teeth and particularly necessary if your gums become inflamed and start to bleed.

Special 'disclosing tablets' which you chew and rinse around your teeth are helpful because they stain the plaque pink and enable you to see any you may have missed. Fluoride toothpaste strengthens the enamel and some toothpastes also contain an ingredient which reduces the build-up of tartar; there is also a fluoride toothpaste called Oral-B Zendium, which contains natural enzymes to help boost the mouth's defences against plaque. Antibacterial mouthwashes are available for treating mild gingivitis.

When electric toothbrushes were first invented, I thought they were the latest useless piece of 20th century equipment. How wrong I was! They vibrate electrically while the user is able to hold the small-headed brush at just the right angle. The result is the best cleaning job you can get without visiting your dental surgeon or hygienist. I never go anywhere without mine.

What's Available?   Bocasan Mouthwash, Dettol Antiseptic Mouthwash, Merocet, Oraldene

My Favourite   Oraldene

HALITOSIS
See BAD BREATH p.23

HAY FEVER
Hay fever is an allergic reaction which occurs in people who are particularly sensitive to pollen or spores released into the air by trees, grasses or moulds. Its medical name is seasonal allergic rhinitis and it is one of the most common allergies known. It is estimated that between 6 and 12 million people suffer – most between the ages of 10 and 40, with about one in six teenagers affected. It is also estimated that four million working days are lost during June and July alone through hay fever.

Hay fever strictly refers to an allergy to grass pollen, but the term is often used to cover allergy to pollen from plants, shrubs and trees. Pollens released in spring are usually from trees, whilst in the summer flower, grass or weed pollens are released. In the autumn the symptoms are usually caused by pollen from autumn-flowering plants and the spores of some fungi. The sufferer's body reacts to pollen as though it were a dangerous threat like a germ, and does all it can to get rid of it by releasing a chemical called histamine. Histamine causes inflammation and irritation of the mucous membranes of the eyes, nose and ear passages. The eyes then water in an effort to wash away the pollen and the running nose and sneezing help eject pollen from the nose. Hay fever can also cause drowsiness.

Hay-fever sufferers are most at risk between May and September, when the 'pollen count' (the level of pollen in the air) is at its highest. So listen to the pollen count forecasts broadcast daily on television and local radio or check the weather reports in newspapers. A pollen count of 50 grains per cubic metre is enough to set most sufferers sneezing. The pollen count will be high on warm, dry and windy days because pollen released from grasses and trees is carried upwards by warm air. Also, warm, dry conditions are needed for pollen to be released in the first place.

Symptoms are often more severe in the morning, when pollen is released and carried upwards as the air temperature rises. They then become worse again in the evening as the temperature drops and the pollen grains drift back down.

There is a growing body of medical evidence which points to a new link between pollution and hay fever. Studies show that pollution has an adjuvant effect on pollen, enhancing sensitisation and in some cases actually sensitising atopic individuals to airborne allergens. (Atopic individuals are those who may already be more susceptible because of an increased level of a certain antibody in their blood which they will have inherited from one or both of their parents.)

The incidence of hay fever has increased dramatically over the last thirty years, as has the air pollution from cars. Yet other studies have shown that pollen counts have actually fallen during this time. And according to Intercare Products Limited often the symptoms of pollution-aggravated hay fever are different from normal hay fever, with an itchy throat being more prominent. However, there are a number of sufferers who may not as yet have associated pollution with their condition and are therefore not treating their symptoms on low pollen days. The company consequently has launched a new product, Aller-eze Clear, which contains the oral antihistamine terfenadine that is particularly suitable for aggravated pollution symptoms – itchy watery eyes, runny nose and itchy throat.

More good news for hay fever sufferers is that Beconase (containing the steroid beclomethasone dipropionate, a very effective hayfever treatment), which was previously available only on prescription, can now be bought from your pharmacist. It's a nasal spray which works by damping down the inflammation in the nose that causes hay fever symptoms. You need to take it regularly during the time you are likely to get hay fever and it may need two or three days to build up to its maximum protective effect.

An antihistamine called cetirizine has also now gone over-the-counter, bought as Zirtek. And another new treatment you can buy from your pharmacist is sodium cromoglycate drops. Brand names include Brol-eze, Clariteyes, Optrex Hayfever Allergy Eye Drops and Opticrom Allergy Eye Drops. These eye drops act by preventing the allergic reaction, and so provide fast relief from the discomfort of itchy, runny eyes. With regular use you get continued protection.

There's also a new nasal spray, called Resiston ONE Nasal Spray, which contains sodium cromoglycate as well as a decongestant, xylometazoline hydrochloride, to relieve stuffy noses, catarrh and nasal congestion. This decongestant can also be found in new eye drops called Otrivine Antistin, where it acts as a vasconstrictor to help reduce redness of the eyes. The drops also have an antihistamine called antazoline sulphate to relieve watering, itchy eyes.

So please don't suffer in silence when it comes to hay fever. Ask your pharmacist for advice.

But over-the-counter antihistamine tablets are one of the most popular forms of treatment. Antihistamines such as brompheniramine block the effects of histamine to stop the allergic reaction occurring and newer ones such as terfenadine produce little if any drowsiness. But care should be taken initially, as with all drugs taken for the first time, because there may be rare cases when the patient reacts badly.

For most relief, start taking antihistamines as soon as the first symptoms occur, although treatment can be started at any time. Nasal sprays containing decongestants which shrink swollen nasal tissues can provide relief from a blocked nose, but should only be used in the short term, since long-term use may actually aggravate the condition.

There are many self-help measures you can take to relieve the symptoms of hay fever. Wearing plain glasses or sunglasses can prevent much of the eye irritation, by stopping pollen grains entering the eyes. Avoid walking through grass or cutting it. Keep windows and doors closed, especially when lawns are being mowed. Stay away from pets if they have been outside. Try to plan your day to avoid being outdoors in the morning and evening when pollen counts are at their highest. Don't go on country walks and avoid parks or gardens on warm and sunny days, or, if this is impossible, wash your hair afterwards. Keep car windows and air vents closed when you're out driving. Don't smoke, because this causes further irritation to those susceptible to allergies.

A final word of hope. Most hay-fever sufferers do grow out of it eventually!

What's Available?   Actifed Syrup and Tablets, Afrazine Nasal Spray, Aller-eze, Aller-eze Clear, Aller-eze Plus, Beconase Hayfever, Benylin Children's Cough Linctus, Boots One-A-Day Antihistamine Tablets, Brol-eze, Clariteyes Eye Drops, Clarityn, Congesteze, Contac 400, Dimotapp Elixir and Tablets, Dimotapp Elixir Paediatric, Dimotapp L.A., Dristan, Eskornade Spansule Capsules and Syrup, Fenox Nasal Drops, Flurex Inhalant, Hismanal, Mucron Junior Syrup, Opticrom Allergy Eye Drops, Optrex Hayfever Allergy Eye Drops, Opticrom Allergy Eye Drops, Otrivine Drops, Otrivine-Antistin, Penetrol Catarrh Lozenges (for nasal congestion in hay fever), Penetrol Inhalant, Phenergan, Phenergan Elixir, Piriton, Piriton Tablets and Syrup, Pollon-Eze, Resiston One, Seldane, Sinutab, Sudafed Nasal Spray, Tixylix Decongestant Inhalant, Triominic, Triludan, Triludan Forte, Vicks Inhaler, Vicks Sinex, Zirtek

My Favourites   Triludan, Aller-Eze

Homoeopathic Treatments   Nelsons Hay Fever Tablets, New Era for Hayfever and Allergic Rhinitis

Herbal Remedies   Herbelix Specific

HEADACHE

Headaches are an extremely common complaint, afflicting one person in three at least once a year, though some people do tend to suffer more than others. In fact, although we tend to use the word headache to describe any pain in the head, there are probably more than 100 different types of headache and they vary in intensity and location. Some develop gradually and clear up after an hour or two or a walk in the fresh air. Others can be extremely severe and can last more than 24 hours.

Two of the commonest types of headache are migraine, a severe, recurring headache which merits its own entry in this book (see p.89) and tension headache, sometimes known as muscle contraction headache.

With migraine, the pain is usually one sided and can be accompanied by other symptoms such as loss of appetite, nausea or vomiting. In a tension headache, the whole head throbs and feels as though there's a weight on top of it or a tight band around it. The pain is usually dull and persistent, originating in the muscles of the scalp. The tension headache is the most common symptom presented to a general practitioner and no one knows the cause, or why some people get a headache when they are emotionally upset and some don't.

Different sorts of headaches can also be brought on by other factors – drinking too much alcohol, sinusitis (see p.113), anxiety or being in an overheated room or smoky atmosphere are all common triggers. They may be the result of muscle strain in your neck, especially if the headache comes on after you have been reading or doing close work like sewing – you can become tense from concentrating for too long or from sitting in an awkward position.

For most minor headaches, it is worth trying the following self-help measures. Take the recommended dose of a mild painkiller such as aspirin or paracetamol (see PAIN-KILLERS p.100 for products containing these ingredients) – for best results, take the painkiller as soon as you feel the headache coming on. Drink plenty of water or other non-alcoholic, clear drinks. Rest in a quiet, darkened room may also be soothing and a warm bath will sometimes relieve tension.

Fortunately, most headaches are not a sign of serious disease, but if your headache is particularly severe; if it's accompanied by misty or blurred vision, nausea or vomiting; if there's no satisfactory explanation for a headache that is continuous or getting worse after three days, or comes back several times in the course of a week; or if you have injured your head during the past few days, you should consult your doctor for advice.

What's Available?   See PAINKILLERS p.100

Homoeopathic Remedies   Belladonna, Ignatia, Nat. Mur.

HEAD LICE

Head lice are tiny brown insects with six short, stubbly legs. They're about the size of a pin head and live on human heads, laying six to eight eggs a day of a creamy-brown colour. They turn white when the baby louse, called a nymph, has hatched. The remaining pearly white husk is commonly known as a nit. At this stage it is a harmless shell.

The eggs are attached near the base of the hair shaft – a favourite spot is around the ears. Each louse takes two weeks to mature and lives for 20 to 30 days if undetected. The lice feed on blood, using their specially developed mouth-parts to pierce the scalp. They even inject a local anaesthetic into the scalp to prevent their host feeling any pain, and an anticoagulant to stop the blood clotting, thus making it easier for them to feed! They can eventually make your head feel very itchy because, after about 10,000 bites, your immune system becomes understandably irritated.

To check whether someone has head lice, dampen the hair and then bend the head over a plain sheet of paper. Comb the hair thoroughly to see whether any insects drop out. Quickly part the hair to look out for moving lice. A magnifying glass will help.

Head lice can sometimes be a problem among schoolchildren. That's because the head louse has never had it so good. We and our children are healthier and cleaner than we have ever been, and the head louse loves it. Clean, healthy heads provide it with the perfect environment for perpetuating its lifestyle. Every time a clean-headed child comes into contact with another child's head as they play, the head louse moves from one head to another. Head lice can't jump or fly, nor do they live in bedding, furniture or clothes. The *only* way they can be passed on is by close head contact – a single louse can visit several heads in one day just by walking from one to another.

So if you or your children have head lice, please don't worry or feel ashamed. More than a million people a year in the UK get head lice, so there's no point in being embarrassed about it. It's also pretty well impossible to prevent children catching head lice from each other, as it's nothing to do with them being dirty or neglected. Like measles, mumps and chicken pox, it's just another of those things children are likely to catch once they start mixing with others.

If you have to deal with head lice, take the advice of your school nurse, pharmacist or health visitor, and use the products they recommend. When applying a shampoo or lotion, remember to ensure that no part of the scalp is left uncovered; pay particular attention to the nape of the neck and behind the ears.

There are three main insecticides in use that kill head lice and their eggs – carbaryl, pyrethroids (phenothrin and permethrin) and malathion. They are all equally effective if used according to the directions. But health authorities change their recommendations for louse treatment preparations every two to three years to prevent the lice building up a resistance to them. Your pharmacist can tell you what is currently in use in your area.

Bear in mind, too, that should a member of your family need treatment, you must treat the whole family – parents, grandparents, even lodgers – and then check them once a week to ensure they're still clear. Make sure your children's friends don't have lice either or there could be a risk of re-infection. It's wise – if not essential – to inform your child's school if you discover head lice.

Then after treatment, encourage all your family to comb their hair thoroughly every day, since the female louse – and there are many more of them than the male – must cling on to two hairs to survive; as combing or brushing separates the hair, the louse will then die. Once dead, it falls off harmlessly.

There is a new spray called Rappell on the market which contains piperonal, produced from a natural source. This helps to keep hair free of lice when lice infections are likely, or it can be used after treatment for head lice to prevent reinfection or if other members of the family have had treatment. During a head-lice epidemic, say at your child's school, it's wise for all the family to use such a spray.

What's Available? Carylderm Lotion and Shampoo, Derbac-C Liquid and Shampoo, Full Marks Lotion, Lyclear, Prioderm Cream Shampoo, Prioderm Lotion, Rappell, Suleo-C Carbaryl Lotion and Shampoo, Suleo-M Malathion Lotion

My Favourites   Carylderm, Lyclear

HEARTBURN
See INDIGESTION AND HEARTBURN, below

HIVES
See URTICARIA p.131

INDIGESTION AND HEARTBURN

Symptoms of indigestion, usually felt just below or behind the breast bone, vary from an uncomfortable feeling of fullness to nausea, pain, belching, heartburn and wind. Most people will suffer from indigestion from time to time. Often there is no recognisable pattern to the symptoms, but they may be noticeably worse just before or after a meal. Nearly one person in ten takes a remedy for some form of indigestion every day and of these one in three will have had symptoms for ten years or more. Three out of four sufferers never consult a doctor. The problem becomes more common after middle age, particularly in those who are overweight. Sensitive, anxious people are also more prone to indigestion, as anxiety increases the output of acid secretions in the stomach.

The most common form of indigestion is called heartburn, an apt name as it well describes the symptoms – waves of burning pain behind the breast bone and sometimes a burning feeling in the throat. The pain can be mistaken for heart pain (angina), but in fact angina improves with rest, whereas heartburn is usually worse when the sufferer is lying down. It is easy to see why when we look more closely at what causes it.

The stomach produces strong acid secretions which help to digest and sterilise our food. The stomach lining has a mucous coating which protects it against the acid, but the oesophagus – the gullet down which food passes from the mouth to the stomach – does not. Normally a ring of muscle – the cardiac sphincter – at the bottom end of the oesophagus acts like a trapdoor and prevents acid rising up from the stomach. Sometimes, however – if the muscle becomes a little lax, for instance, as it often does during pregnancy – small amounts of acid will enter the lower part of the oesophagus – a process known as reflux. It is normal for this to happen occasionally and the saliva we are constantly swallowing will usually be enough to neutralise the acid without symptoms being caused. Also, contractions of the muscle walls of the gullet prevent the acid rising by keeping food and saliva moving downwards.

However, if reflux occurs too often, the oesophagus will gradually become inflamed and painful as the acid burns into the tissues. This inflammation is called oesophagitis. Without effective treatment the lining of the gullet can eventually become ulcerated and constricted by scarring so that swallowing food can be difficult. Other changes in the cells may also develop in time. It is important, therefore, to treat heartburn early on to prevent oesophagitis progressing.

Indigestion can have other causes – secretions such as pepsin (an enzyme which aids digestion) and bile from the liver (which helps digest fatty foods) are also capable of irritating the vulnerable stomach. Anxious people will often, unconsciously, swallow more air with their food and eat faster than others, causing distention, a rumbling stomach and belching. This type of indigestion may be relieved by learning techniques for relaxation (with the help of cassettes, for instance) and by eating smaller, more frequent meals, slowly.

Many people think that eating greasy, rich or spicy foods, or eating too much too quickly, are the main causes of heartburn. In fact, although these do play a part, smoking more than ten cigarettes a day and drinking heavily are the most common causes, as both of these relax the cardiac sphincter and therefore make reflux more likely. Bouts of indigestion are therefore sometimes a warning signal that the body is being abused – alcohol, especially on an empty stomach, and smoking both stimulate acid production and inflame the stomach.

Some drugs – antibiotics, iron tablets and aspirin, for example – can also inflame the oesophagus and cause heartburn, especially if they are taken with too little fluid or just before going to bed. Citrus fruits, chocolate, coffee and, perhaps surprisingly, peppermint are other possible culprits. Heartburn is also a common symptom of a hiatus hernia, whereby part of the stomach protrudes upwards at the point where the oesophagus passes through a gap in the diaphragm. A sensitivity to certain foods, such as sugar and milk, can also cause unpleasant indigestion, as can fatty foods for some people. Cutting down on stimulants and avoiding foods found to aggravate the symptoms will, in this case, usually relieve them.

Indigestion and heartburn are, of course, also common during pregnancy. Being overweight, large meals and lack of exercise are other predisposing factors. If indigestion or heartburn is worrying or persistent, a doctor's examination and perhaps some special investigations may be necessary to exclude underlying causes such as hiatus hernia, peptic ulcer or gall bladder trouble.

When no such cause can be found, and in most cases of occasional indigestion, self-help measures can help. Don't smoke or drink too much alcohol, coffee or acidic fruit drinks. Lose weight if necessary. It's better to eat several small meals a day rather than one large one and to avoid eating just before going to bed. Eat slowly, sitting upright – not slouched in front of the television – and chew your food thoroughly before swallowing. Get used to bending down from the knees rather than from the waist and avoid stooping after meals. Don't wear tight belts or corsets, as they increase pressure on the stomach.

If heartburn is troublesome at night, raise the head end of the bed about eight inches – two standard house bricks are about the right height. This helps to keep the acid down in the stomach and is much more effective than using extra pillows, because you will probably slide off these in your sleep. A glass of milk before bedtime helps, too.

Combined with these measures, a regular dose, in between meals, of an antacid medicine bought from the chemist should be all that is needed to ease indigestion. These medicines neutralise stomach acid, help prevent inflammation and relieve pain. Around £42 million were spent on indigestion remedies in the UK in 1990 and as you can imagine there are several different types – for example, aluminium hydroxide, calcium carbonate, magnesium hydroxide and sodium bicarbonate. Antacids can be combined with substances called alginates, which float on the contents of the stomach and stop the gastric juices splashing upwards (refluxing) and irritating the gullet, or with drugs to disperse wind.

Some antacids are more effective than others. Magnesium hydroxide can take a while to have any effect but relief is fairly long lasting. Some remedies – those containing calcium, for instance – wear off quickly, and by over-neutralising the existing acid in the stomach, may have the rebound effect of actually stimulating further acid production. Also, the calcium and sodium salts contained in some antacid medicines will be absorbed into the bloodstream, and this is undesirable in the longer term.

Remember that all antacids can interfere with the absorption of other drugs, so check with your pharmacist if you are taking any other medicines. You will probably find that a particular brand of antacid will work better than others for your indigestion, so it will often be a case of trial and error.

Previously only-on-prescription products containing 10mg of hyoscine butylbromide are now available over the counter for the colicky pain of smooth muscle spasm. The bowel wall, for example, contains smooth muscle – so called because of its appearance under the microscope compared with other muscles like the biceps or the heart's muscle. Consequently, this medicine can relieve the pain due to the Spastic Colon Syndrome (also called the Irritable Bowel Syndrome) when the muscles go into spasm. Hyoscine sometimes causes a dry mouth, blurred vision or palpitations.

There are two other products that are newly available over the counter rather than on prescription – though they also remain on prescription too. These are Tagamet 100 and Pepcid AC, both for the short-term relief of heartburn, dyspepsia and excess stomach acid. The maximum treatment period is two weeks. One small tablet provides up to nine hours acid control. Tagamet 100 contains cimetidine and is also licensed for the preventative treatment of nocturnal heartburn. Pepcid AC contains famotidine, clinically proven to be highly effective in acid control.

Cimetidine was first discovered in 1976 and pioneered an entirely new group of medicines which revolutionised the way doctors were able to deal with problems caused by too much acid in the stomach. In fact, both these medicines belong to a group of drugs known as H2 antagonists or blockers. Rather than neutralising stomach acid, this type of medicine controls the production of excess acid and so treats the cause of the pain and discomfort. This makes these medicines different from conventional ones which neutralise the acid once it has been formed.

Unless your doctor tells you otherwise, you shouldn't take H2 antagonists if you have unintended weight loss associated with dyspepsia, if you are middle aged or older and have dyspeptic symptoms for the first time or symptoms that have recently changed, if you have kidney or liver problems, if you have a history of ulcers, if you have any other illness, if you are taking any medicines, or are seeing a doctor regularly. Don't take it if you have difficulty swallowing or have persistent stomach pains, are pregnant or breast-feeding, and if you are allergic to the drugs or any other ingredient in the products. Headaches and dizziness are among the rare side-effects reported as a result of taking H2 antagonists. As with all other medicines if you think you are reacting badly in any way, do consult your doctor. And you must see him or her if symptoms fail to respond, if they recur after treatment or if symptoms persist after two weeks of treatment.

What's Available?   Actal, Alka-Seltzer (for headache with upset stomach), Aludrox Liquid and Tablets, Andrews Answer (for headache with upset stomach), Andrews Antacid, Andrews Liver Salt, Asilone Tablets, Bismag, Bisodol Powder and Tablets, Bisodol Extra, Boots Double

Action Indigestion Mixture and Tablets, Dijex, Eno and Lemon Eno, Gaviscon, Gaviscon 250 Tablets, Gelusil Tablets, Indigestion Lozenges, Jaap's Health Salt, Lanes Charcoal Tablets, Maalox range, Maclean Indigestion Tablets, Milk of Magnesia, Moorland, Nulacin, Pepcid AC, Pepto-Bismol, Premiums, Rap-Eze, Remegel, Rennie, Rennie Gold, Setlers, Setlers Tums, Tagamet 100

Unbranded Products   Magnesium Trisilicate Mixture B.P., Sodium Bicarbonate B.P.

My Favourites   Rennie, Actal

Homoeopathic Remedies   Carbo. Veg., Kali. Phos., Nux. Vom.

Herbal Remedies   Biobalm, Digest, Potter's Acidosis, Potter's Slippery Elm Stomach Tablets

INFLUENZA

People often say they have flu when really they have some other virus which is giving them 'flu-like' symptoms – and so-called 'gastric flu' is certainly not due to the influenza virus. But for many people the symptoms of flu – a dreadfully ill feeling, sometimes with acutely painful muscles, a high temperature and a headache – are such that the sufferer may suspect he or she has been afflicted with a very serious illness.

There are three main types of 'proper' flu virus recognisable under a microscope – A, B and C, the C variety being mild and insignificant. The A type is highly infectious and often develops into a widespread epidemic or even a worldwide pandemic – the 'Asian flu' of 1957 and the 'Hong Kong flu' of 1968 were caused by the A flu virus. Influenza B spreads less rapidly, tends to remain localised to communities or institutions such as schools and colleges and to occur at intervals of about four years.

Flu is caught by breathing in the virus through germs in the air breathed out by sufferers. The virus then attacks and inflames the lining of the nose, throat and air passages, causing symptoms similar to those of a severe cold. Joint and muscle aches and pains, headache and fever are also common, as the virus is carried by the bloodstream to other parts of the body. The worst is usually over in about a week, though an attack of flu can leave the sufferer feeling tired and depressed for some time afterwards. The very young or very old and those with chronic chest or heart problems, kidney disease or diabetes are particularly vulnerable to the more severe effects of flu and, because of the way it is spread, are more likely to catch it if living in an institution.

Although antibiotics will have no effect on the virus itself (or indeed on viruses in general), your doctor will often prescribe an antibiotic at the first sign of flu for anyone with a 'weak chest' – chronic bronchitis sufferers, for example – to prevent a secondary bacterial infection developing and causing more damage. Coughing up green or yellow sputum is an indication of this type of infection and means you should consult your doctor, as antibiotics may be necessary.

Otherwise, rest in bed, take two aspirin or paracetamol every four hours, or follow the instructions for taking your preferred painkiller (see PAINKILLERS p.100). Children with flu are not generally recommended to take aspirin, however. Drink plenty of liquid. Steam inhalations can make breathing easier and linctus should relieve any cough you may have (see COUGHS p.47 for product information). To relieve flu symptoms such as blocked sinuses, stuffed-up nose and catarrh, refer to what's available for a common cold (p.34). For feverishness in children as part of flu, see FEVER p.65. But the body's own defences – the antibodies we produce in response to infection – should do the rest.

With most viruses – measles for instance – the antibodies we develop after one attack give us a natural, lasting immunity. In other cases, a specific vaccine can protect us by stimulating effective antibodies. This is because the virus does not change. Not so with flu. The vaccine produced against flu has to be updated annually because the virus itself alters and keeps developing slightly different strains. So, although the antibodies we produced if we caught flu last year will give us resistance to some attacks in future, they will not protect us against the new strains that may have developed since. Vaccine manufacturers must keep adding to their anti-flu 'cocktail' and try to keep pace.

Immunisation against flu is becoming increasingly widespread in Britain. A vaccination given in the autumn provides about 70% protection and lasts about a year. Most doctors believe it's worthwhile for the vulnerable groups – it's estimated that several thousand people die in the UK every year from the effects of flu and around eight out of every ten of those are over the age of 65.

Anyone at special risk should consult his or her doctor for advice. The risk categories include anyone who suffers from chronic chest, heart or kidney disease or diabetes. The vaccine should also benefit elderly people or children living together – in residential homes or schools, for example. Other groups at risk include those who have conditions such as AIDS which affect the body's immune system, or those who are taking drugs that are known to dampen the natural defences.

Do I have a flu injection myself, you may ask? No, but then I'm not in the high risk category and there's little evidence that the fit population suffer too much overall disadvantage from contact with the real flu germ. We may suffer some unpleasant symptoms, but they are quite often mild, and the protection the real virus germs provoke in our bodies is stronger and more lasting than that provided by vaccination – although, as I said, the variation between the different strains of flu virus means that neither natural immunisation nor vaccination lasts forever. And do high doses of Vitamin C give you protection? Again, the answer is unclear. You pays your money or you takes your chance, and I prefer to take my chance!

There isn't really anything you can do to prevent yourself

getting a cold or flu. But when you do have a bout of flu, it is foolish and unfair to others to struggle to work, unless your presence is absolutely essential – you are almost certain to infect someone else. Rest is a natural aid to recovery, so by staying quietly at home you will be doing yourself a favour, too. If everyone, at the very first sign of flu, became a recluse for a few days, epidemics and pandemics would probably become a thing of the past!

What's Available   Beechams Hot Blackcurrant or Lemon or Lemon and Honey, Catarrh-Ex, Day Nurse Capsules, Day Nurse Liquid, Jacksons Febrifuge, Lemsip Flu Strength, Night Nurse Capsules, Night Nurse Liquid, Sinutab Nightime. See also COLD, THE COMMON (p.34), COUGHS (p.47), FEVER (p.65)

INSOMNIA
See SLEEPLESSNESS p.117

MIGRAINE
Anyone who's ever had a migraine – and you can include me in that – can understand the misery it brings. Yet migraine sufferers are often branded as 'neurotic' and made to feel guilty about their 'weakness'. This is completely unfair, as studies have shown that there is no typical 'migraine personality'. Migraine affects as many as one in ten people (mainly women) of any race, occupation, class or age, including children. More than half will have a relative – often their mother – with the same problem.

Frequency of attacks varies greatly, from only once or twice a year to several times a week. Severity and type of symptoms differ widely, too. A sufferer may find that he or she has a mild attack at one time and then a severe one next time. The severity is usually related to extra tension and strain and it is really very important to remain as calm as possible.

So what makes a migraine more than 'just a headache'? The pain is usually one sided, and in the 'common' type, there are other symptoms such as loss of appetite, nausea or vomiting. A few sufferers will have the 'classic' type of migraine, preceded, 20–30 minutes before the headache itself, by warning symptoms – called an aura – which may include flashing lights before the eyes, shimmering or double vision, slurred speech, numbness and giddiness. These symptoms are probably due to a sudden constriction in some of the blood vessels in the brain.

The headache comes on as these vessels then expand and the blood surges through, leading to the characteristic throbbing headache. Many experts believe that this constriction and dilation of the blood vessels is brought about by changing levels of certain chemicals circulating in the body, such as adrenaline – also released during stress – and prostaglandins. Adrenaline tenses the muscles, the heart and its blood vessels to prepare us for 'fight or flight'. Prostaglandins sensitise the nerve endings to make us more alert. In susceptible people, they will 'overdo' it and cause the above symptoms. Studies also suggest that there may be a slight difference – perhaps inherited – in the biochemical make-up of migraine sufferers which makes them more susceptible.

The trigger for an attack can be emotional or physical and common ones include anxiety, excitement, depression, changes in weather or routine, bending for long periods (such as when gardening), hot baths, loud noises, flashing or bright light, including that from a VDU screen. Glare filters are now available which many people find helpful. Alcohol, especially red wine, is one of the worst culprits, and certain foods, for example chocolate, cheese, fried foods, citrus fruit, onions, tea, coffee, wheat flour, pork and seafood, are other common triggers.

Irregular meals, dieting or a long lie-in can provoke a migraine, probably because of the drop in the body's blood sugar. Then a few biscuits or a sweet drink may be enough to stave off a full attack. It's extremely important to make sure you always eat properly and pay attention to your diet. If you think you'll have to go a long time without a proper meal, keep an emergency ration of a small snack of some sort with you.

Hormones can also play a part as far as women are concerned – some only have a migraine around the time of their menstrual period or if they are taking the contraceptive pill. Many find their migraines improve, or stop altogether, after the menopause.

To help you and your doctor pinpoint your special triggers, try to keep a diary, noting the day and time of your attacks, everything you eat and drink, meal times, daily activities, particular worries and, for women, the dates of your periods. If you think you are suffering from migraine or experience a migraine attack for the first time, consult your doctor for a proper diagnosis and advice on treatment. This will also reassure you that your migraines are not due to a tumour or to high blood pressure – two very common and usually quite unfounded fears.

Treatment will depend on the frequency of attacks and the apparent causes. Simply adjusting your habits may help considerably. Any medicines should be taken at the first sign of an attack, so always keep them handy. It usually helps to rest quietly in a darkened room in the early stages. During a migraine attack, the action of the gut slows down and painkillers may not be well absorbed. Some of the medicines available from your doctor speed up absorption as well as relieving the nausea and pain. Other drugs act by constricting the dilated blood vessels, but follow the instructions precisely as overuse can actually bring on a headache similar to migraine.

If migraine attacks are very frequent, your doctor may prescribe long-term preventive treatment, such as one of the drugs often used to control high blood pressure. Over the counter, you can buy painkillers (see p.100). Remember that migraine is different from other types of headache in that it's often accompanied or preceded by other symptoms already mentioned.

Anti-inflammatory medicines like aspirin and ibuprofen can prevent the release of prostaglandins and so are recommended for migraine – although paracetamol can help ease the pain of a headache, too. There are also tablets available over the counter which are especially designed to relieve a migraine headache. These can contain analgesics combined with buclizine hydrochloride or cyclizine hydrochloride – antihistamines to prevent vomiting and reduce nausea. Sufferers usually work out which treatment suits them best.

If stress or anxiety seems to be the underlying cause of your migraines, relaxation exercises or hypnotherapy may be helpful. And trying 'alternative' treatments like acupuncture is something I would recommend to anyone who has found no joy through traditional methods of coping with migraine.

You could not be blamed for wondering why acupuncture seems to have such a surprising success rate for so many completely different ailments and diseases. The reason is that it's not just some ancient superstition that's now available as a last resort. It works by triggering the brain to secrete its own chemicals, which function rather like natural painkillers or tranquillisers, so providing relief for sufferers.

Period-time migraines often respond to treatment with the hormone progesterone. Recent research has shown that a daily dose of a humble plant called feverfew (it looks like a miniature chrysanthemum and is now sold by many nursery gardens – the botanical name for the variety of feverfew you need is *Tanacetum parthenium*) helps many people to control their migraine. Two or three leaves can be eaten in a sandwich sweetened with a little honey, and feverfew capsules and tablets are available from some chemists and health-food shops.

What's Available?   Femigraine, Migraleve

Homoeopathic Remedies   Hom-Bidor 1% Tablets, Kali. Bich., Nat. Mur., Silicea

Herbal Remedies   Herbal Labs Feverfew 125, Golden Health Feverfew (English Grains)

MOUTH ULCERS

Mouth ulcers tend to be small lesions on the tongue, on the inside of the cheeks or the roof of the mouth – and like so many minor problems, they are something that everybody will suffer from at some stage. They're often called aphthous ulcers and have a pale grey base and a slightly raised yellowish edge, tinged with a narrow, inflamed border.

Some people find ulcers hurt so unbearably that eating is impossible. Fortunately, for most they're just a temporary nuisance. They may be painful, even unsightly, but they are harmless and will disappear of their own accord after a week or so.

Despite all the research that has been carried out, we still have no real idea what causes mouth ulcers. We do know, however, that a person is more likely to develop them if he or she is under stress, unwell, over-tired, depressed or suffering from any form of emotional upset. People in high-powered jobs, young mothers and toddlers with flu all seem to be prone to attacks. Many women find they suffer from mouth ulcers almost monthly, around the time of their period.

If you have ever had a mouth ulcer, you will be able to recognise the symptoms. Hours before they appear, the mouth will become over-sensitive or you'll experience a burning or tingling sensation. Pretty soon, blisters with red margins appear in your mouth. When they erupt they produce small, round ulcers with greyish or dirty white centres, which are often extra sensitive to salty and acidic foods.

Mouth ulcers may clear up within a few days or take over a week to disappear. In most cases, no treatment is needed. But if the ulcer is particularly painful, an antiseptic mouthwash or pastilles or gel containing antiseptics and local anaesthetics can ease soreness. A supplement of folic acid, one of the B vitamins, may help shorten an attack or prevent another one occurring (see VITAMINS p.281).

Newly available over the counter are Corlan Pellets, which are hydrocortisone lozenges. Hydrocortisone is a topical steroid which means it is put on the ulcer rather than swallowed. It works by helping to relieve pain and also by helping the ulcer to heal. But the pellets should only be used if your doctor has diagnosed recurrent aphthous ulceration of the mouth or he or she has recommended that you buy this medicine. Corlan Pellets should not be used to treat ulcers associated with injury, infection or irritation of the mouth, for example from dentures. You should consult your doctor before using them if you are allergic to the product, hydrocortisone or lactose, if you are pregnant, diabetic or suffer from recurrent oral infections.

Badly fitting dentures can rub against the side or roof of the mouth and sometimes this can cause an outbreak of ulcers. If that is the source of your problem, a cream called Aezodent, which is mildly anaesthetic and has a gum 'adhesive' to help hold the denture securely in place, may bring relief.

If any ulcer is abnormally large or lasts for more than two weeks, you should certainly consult your doctor. But if you find you're getting frequent attacks of ulcers, even though they heal quickly, it may well be worth taking a careful look at the way you live and trying to reduce any stress in your life. Find a method of regular relaxation that suits you and your lifestyle – that might mean taking a form of gentle exercise or listening quietly to music. Another simple way to combat stress is to try to get more sleep – a few early nights can work wonders.

What's Available?   Aezodent, Anbesol, Bioral Gel, Bonjela Antiseptic Pain-relieving Pastilles, Bonjela Oral Pain-relieving Gel, Corlan Pellets, Medijel Gel, Medijel Soft Pastilles, Pyralvex, Ress Q, Rinstead Adult Gel, Rinstead Pastilles, Teejel Gel, Ulc-Aid Gel, Ulc-Aid Lozenges

My Favourites   Rinstead Pastilles, Anbesol

MUSCULAR ACHES, PAINS, SPRAINS AND STRAINS

As more and more people are heeding advice to take regular exercise, a few are bound to suffer a so-called soft tissue (as opposed to bone) injury at some time – strains, sprains or bruising, for example, to muscles, ligaments, tendons or the capsule (lining) of a joint. The elderly and those who have taken up or returned to a sport late in life are more at risk than the young and fit.

A strain is a slight tearing of a muscle or the tendon attaching it to a bone, usually caused by overstretching it, whereas a sprain is a tear in a joint capsule or its supportive ligaments, due to twisting or forcing the joint beyond its normal range of movement.

Other soft tissue problems include capsulitis (inflammation of a joint lining due to a twisting or jarring injury), bursitis (inflammation of the fluid-filled bursae that act as cushions at points of wear and tear) and epicondylitis (inflammation where muscle tendons join the bony points of the elbow). If pain and tenderness are on the outer point, epicondylitis is commonly known as tennis elbow, if on the inner side golfer's elbow, but any activity that overuses these tendons can cause the same symptoms – painting a ceiling or hammering, for example.

Another condition, often in the news these days, is tenosynovitis or repetitive strain injury (RSI) – painful inflammation of the tendon sheaths in the hands, wrists or arms, which can be very disabling. Typists, factory workers or anyone using repetitive movements for hours on end are particularly prone. Regular rest breaks and more varied work will help prevent RSI developing.

When a strain or sprain first occurs, chemicals are released into the damaged tissues – they include prostaglandins, which sensitise nerve endings and cause pain, inflammation and swelling. Treatment which prevents or cuts down the release of prostaglandins is therefore likely to be helpful. Medicines known as NSAIDs – non-steroid anti-inflammatory drugs – such as aspirin and ibuprofen, act in this way and the sooner they can be given after an injury the better (see PAINKILLERS p.100 for product list). Ibuprofen is also available as a cream from pharmacists and on prescription – its commercial names are Proflex, Ibuleve or Ibuleve Sports Gel, and Ibugel. Studies show that it relieves the pain and other symptoms when rubbed directly into the injured area, without the risk of side-effects, nausea for example, that tablets may cause. Another type of NSAID is keto-profen which is newly available over the counter as Ourvail Gel 2.5%.

Lasonil is another cream that can help soft tissue injuries – it contains heparinoid, an anti-inflammatory agent. There are also soothing rubs, gels and sprays available to help ease muscular aches and pains. Sometimes an anti-inflammatory injection – into the tender spot of a tennis elbow, for instance – will be advised if the pain is acute.

First-aid measures in the initial 48 hours after injury can be very helpful and speed recovery. Rest the injured part as much as possible and raise it to reduce swelling (support an injured arm in a sling, for example). An ice pack will reduce bruising and swelling and will also relieve pain; contrary to popular belief, a hot bath will make matters worse, because it speeds up the flow of blood and increases swelling. Wrap the ice in a wet cloth or flannel to protect the skin from iceburn and frostbite and apply the pack to the injured part for ten minutes every few hours. A compression bandage such as tubigrip, worn continuously for at least two days, will help, too, but watch for numbness, tingling or the skin colour changing to white or blue – signs that the bandage is too tight.

Ideally, try to prevent injury occurring in the first place. Exercise, though undoubtedly good for you, should not be overdone. If you are unaccustomed to it, expert tuition is often advisable and do take things gradually to begin with.

What's Available?   Algipan, Balmosa, Cremalgin, Fiery Jack Rubbing Ointment, Germolene Ointment, Ibugel, Ibuleve, Ibuleve Sports Gel, Jackson's Febrifuge, Lasonil, Lloyd's Cream, Movelat, Oruvail Gel 2.5%, PR Spray, Proflex, Proflex Cream, Ralgex Cream, Ralgex Freeze Spray, Ralgex Low Odour Spray, Ralgex Stick, Samaritan Menthol, Transvasin, Wintergreen Cream. See also PAINKILLERS p.100.

Unbranded Products   Epsom Salts B.P. (used as a dressing), Witch Hazel

My Favourite   PR Spray

Herbal Remedies   Potter's Comfrey Ointment

NAPPY RASH

All babies suffer from a red or sore bottom from time to time, however well you look after them. For the first couple of years or so of a child's life, the area of skin around his or her bottom is constantly in contact with – and so under attack from – urine and faeces. Nappy rash can take the form of just a few spots, or a more severe rash. It can be triggered by several factors, such as diarrhoea or rawness caused by urine that's irritating the skin inside a chafing nappy. Bacteria in the faeces can react with urine to produce ammonia – not very pleasant on tender, young skin. This type of contamination often encourages a fungus similar to the one that causes thrush.

To avoid nappy rash change your baby's nappy frequently and clean and dry his or her bottom and skin creases thoroughly. It's helpful to leave your baby without a nappy on as often as possible – air is a great benefit. Use a barrier cream – zinc and castor oil cream, for example, to protect the baby's skin from constant exposure to moisture. If you use terry towelling nappies, be careful to sterilise them properly as well as ensuring that they're well rinsed – traces of detergent can also be an irritant.

If the baby's bottom already shows signs of a rash, specially formulated nappy rash creams can soothe it, help fight infection or prevent moisture irritating the skin. If the rash doesn't seem to get any better after a week of this treatment, ask the advice of your doctor or health visitor.

What's Available?   Brulidine, Conotrane, Daktarin Cream or Powder, Drapolene Cream, E45 Cream, Hewletts Cream, Kamillosan, Medicaid, Morhulin Cod-Liver Oil Ointment, Morsep, Panda Baby Cream, Savlon Nappy Rash Cream, Sudocrem, Vasogen

Unbranded Products   Cetrimide Cream B.P.

My Favourites   Sudocrem, Drapolene

Homoeopathic Remedies   Arsen. Alb., Calendula Cream

NASAL CONGESTION
See SINUS PAIN, NASAL CONGESTION AND CATARRH p.113

NETTLE RASH
See URTICARIA p.131

NEURALGIA
Pain resulting from a nerve being over-stimulated, compressed or squeezed is known as neuralgia. It can be very uncomfortable as the pain isn't just felt at the point of stimulation or pressure, but can be experienced along the full course of the nerve. It is sometimes described as an intense pain similar to the most agonising toothache.

This often excruciating pain can be felt anywhere in the body, depending on which nerve is affected. A fractured bone, severe bruising around a bone or a 'slipped' disc can press on a nerve and cause neuralgia; so, too, can an infection like shingles. This causes a different kind of pain, since it's the nerve itself which is inflamed by the nerve-specific shingles infection.

You can treat yourself with mild painkillers (see p.100 for product list) or ask your doctor to prescribe stronger ones if the pain is severe. But if the shingles pain persists for longer than a month, you will need your doctor's prescribed medicine. This is because the shingles will have developed into PHN – post-herpetic neuralgia – which won't respond to the usual painkillers.

What's Available? See PAINKILLERS p.100

ORAL THRUSH

Denture wearers may be familiar with the problem of oral thrush as a result of chafing, although it can also affect babies, people suffering from diabetes, those who are generally unwell and not at their strongest, or those taking steroid or antibiotic drugs.

It's caused by a yeast-like fungus called *Candida albicans* which is also responsible for vaginal thrush. This usually lives harmlessly in the mouth and the intestines. Bacteria are normally able to keep it under control, but sometimes it will suddenly grow very rapidly, producing soreness and white flecks inside the mouth, painful cracks in the skin in the corners of the mouth and/or creamy yellow patches inside the mouth and throat.

If you think you or your baby have oral thrush, consult a doctor, who may prescribe an antifungal medicine or lozenges. Thrush will not go away without treatment. But if the patient is your baby, you can help by sterilising dummies frequently and, if you're breast-feeding, taking extra care with nipple hygiene.

If you have suffered from oral thrush before and have had the symptoms diagnosed by your doctor, you'll be interested to know that an oral gel formerly only available on prescription can now be obtained from chemists on a pharmacist's recommendation. Daktarin Oral Gel contains miconazole, an antifungal and antibacterial drug that kills the yeast cells. It can be effective in the treatment of fungal infections of the lips, mouth and throat – and that includes oral thrush in babies and adults and the kind that is due to denture chafing. It's sugar free, has a pleasant orange flavour and is specially formulated to stick to mucous membranes for up to six hours after application. For denture chafing, it may be useful to smear a small amount of Daktarin on to the denture plate. Relief from symptoms may occur quickly, but it's important that you continue to use Daktarin for up to two days after the symptoms have cleared. If you're pregnant you should consult your doctor before using the gel.

What's Available? Betasept Gargle and Mouthwash, Daktarin Oral Gel, Oraldene

PAINKILLERS

Painkillers, or analgesics, can be used to treat pain resulting from a wide variety of symptoms. They can ease pain in headaches, migraine, neuralgia, colds and influenza and help reduce temperature, rheumatic pain, period pain, dental pain, back ache, muscular pain and sore throats. So it's hardly surprising that analgesics take up the biggest share of the market in over-the-counter medicines. In 1990 alone £145 million was spent on them!

Consequently there's a vast range of analgesics on sale in shops, supermarkets and chemists in soluble or tablet form – soluble painkillers are said to work more quickly because the active ingredient is absorbed into the bloodstream faster than solid tablets.

Over-the-counter analgesics mainly contain aspirin, paracetamol or a combination of the two, sometimes with the addition of the stimulant caffeine. Some also contain small quantities of codeine and others contain ibuprofen. If you are taking one kind of analgesic you should not take another within four hours – overdoses can be dangerous.

Aspirin – and its associated sodium salicylate compounds – is a non-narcotic (non-addictive) analgesic. It relieves pain, reduces fever and inflammation, and can improve the symptoms of arthritis. It's also thought to prevent blood clots from forming. It works by blocking the production of prostaglandins, which would pass pain signals on to the brain.

Aspirin can irritate the stomach and if it's used for a long time it can cause bleeding. That's why aspirin should be taken after food; if you must take it on an empty stomach, have a glass of milk at the same time. Avoid alcohol when you're taking aspirin, as it adds to the chances of the stomach being irritated. Do not take aspirin if you have a stomach ulcer. It is not usually recommended near the end of a pregnancy, either.

There also appears to be some connection between young children taking aspirin and developing Reye's Syndrome – a rare condition, affecting only about seven children in a million, which causes brain inflammation and liver damage. It is not even certain that aspirin is implicated in this condition, but the possibility is enough to make doctors feel that children under 12 should not generally be given aspirin. Paracetamol is a safe alternative.

Paracetamol is also a non-narcotic analgesic. It's gentler on the stomach than aspirin and won't cause bleeding. But large doses can cause serious damage to the liver and kidneys. It can be used during pregnancy, but always check with your doctor if you think you need to take it for more than an occasional dose.

Paracetamol works in a similar way to aspirin, but, unlike aspirin, it only blocks prostaglandin production in the brain, rather than elsewhere in the body as well. This means that it does not reduce inflammation, as aspirin does. For children it is available in a specially formulated suspension form – in the Calpol range, for example.

Ibuprofen is an NSAID (non-steroidal anti-inflammatory drug) which relieves pain, reduces inflammation and lowers temperature. It has been found in use to be gentler on the stomach than aspirin (though there is no obvious explanation for this as they work in similar ways) and as a result is as well tolerated as paracetamol. However, as with other pain-relievers, it shouldn't be taken if you have a stomach ulcer or other stomach disorder. Asthma sufferers and anyone who is allergic to aspirin should only take ibuprofen after consulting their doctor. It's not usually prescribed for pregnant women.

Codeine is a mild narcotic (habit-forming) drug which is mainly used in over-the-counter analgesics in combination with paracetamol, or paracetamol and aspirin in the case of Veganin. It blocks transmission of pain signals within the brain and the spinal cord, but used on its own does not have much painkilling effect. While its use in combination as mentioned above has always been popular, the benefits of this over the use of aspirin or paracetamol on their own are open to doubt. Do not take codeine-containing medicines if you are pregnant, or think you may be, as it has not been tested to prove that it is safe during pregnancy. However, do not be alarmed if you took a tablet or two before you knew you were pregnant, since it has not been specifically shown to cause any harm either.

Do not take any over-the-counter analgesics more frequently than once every four hours. Never exceed the stated dose. Consult your doctor if it is necessary to continue taking painkillers for more than three days, if symptoms persist or if they recur frequently.

What's Available? Actron, Alka-Seltzer and Andrews Resolve (both especially for headache with upset stomach), Anadin, Anadin All Night, Anadin Extra, Anadin Maximum Strength, Anadin Paracetamol, Askit Capsules and Powders, Aspro, Aspro Clear, Aspro Clear Maximum Strength, Bayer Aspirin, Beechams Lemon Tablets, Calpol Extra, Calpol Infant Suspension, Calpol Six Plus, Calpol Under Six, Coda-Med, Codanin, Codis 500, Cupanol Over Six, Cuprofen Ibuprofen Tablets, Dentogen Ibuprofen

Tablets, Disprin, Disprin Direct, Disprin Extra, Disprol, Fenning's Children's Cooling Powders, Fynnon Calcium Aspirin, Hedex, Hedex Extra, Inoven, Junior Disprol, Junior Paraclear, Medised, Medised Plain and Medised Plain 6+, Mrs Cullen's Powders, Nurofen, Nurse Sykes Powders, Panadeine, Panadol, Panadol Baby/Infant Elixir, Panadol Extra, Panadol Junior, Panadol Ultra, Paraclear, Paraclear Extra Strength, Paracetamol, Paracodol Propain, Paramol, Phensic, Phor Pain and Phor Pain Double Strength, Proflex, Powerin, Resolve, Solpadeine, Syndol, Tramiol 500, Veganin

Unbranded Products Aspirin, Co-Codamol, Co-codaprin, Ibuprofen, Paracetamol

My Favourites Nurofen, Paracetamol, Soluble Aspirin (both available from most chemists under 'own brand' labels), Solpadeine

Herbal Remedies Potter's Ana-Sed Pain Relief Tablets

PERENNIAL RHINITIS

Having a cold once or twice a year, as most of us do, is bad enough – imagine what it would be like to have cold-like symptoms all the year round. Probably about one person in ten – children and adults – suffers in this way.

Rhinitis is simply an inflammation of the mucous membrane lining the nose and there are many possible causes. Seasonal rhinitis (see HAY FEVER p.73) occurs as an allergic reaction to pollens and other allergens around at a particular time of year – in between while the symptoms disappear.

In the case of perennial rhinitis, however, the nose remains inflamed and unpleasant symptoms – which may include a constantly blocked or runny nose, itchy eyes and frequent sneezing – persist. The sense of taste and smell can also be affected and the sufferer often feels generally 'under the weather'. If he or she experiences these symptoms for more than one hour in 24 on most days of the year, a diagnosis of perennial rhinitis can be made. Children who suffer from perennial rhinitis typically develop a 'nose crease' from constantly rubbing their itchy nose upwards, nose bleeds are quite common and dark circles under the eyes may be another sign.

So what causes these continuing symptoms? In a few cases they will be due to a physical obstruction in the nose, such as polyps. Sometimes they will be a reaction to certain drugs, to changes in hormone levels – during pregnancy and at the menopause, for instance – or to changes in temperature and humidity. Irritating conditions at work, such as smoke or fumes, can also be responsible.

Most often, however, symptoms are due to an allergy – to animal fur and hair, for example, but especially to house-dust mites. These tiny creatures, invisible to the naked eye, exist in their millions in the furnishings, floors and bedding of even the cleanest home. They live on the dead skin cells that we shed constantly and each produces 40 faecal pellets a day – not a pretty thought! Fortunately, most of us co-exist quite happily with our house-dust mites, but these pellets are the trigger that provokes the allergic response and symptoms of perennial rhinitis in those susceptible.

Sufferers can minimise their problem by hoovering floors and furnishings and damp-dusting frequently, having the curtains and blankets cleaned regularly, covering mattresses with a plastic cover and using pillows and duvets made from artificial fibres rather than feathers. Polished boards or 'lino' are less of a mite trap than carpets. Mites thrive in warmth, so keep the bedroom cool and well aired. Smaller objects, such as children's fluffy toys, can be put into the deep freeze every so often – mites cannot survive at that temperature.

Many people who suffer from perennial rhinitis just put up with it – they think the symptoms are too trivial to bother their doctor with – or they try to treat themselves with medicines bought from the chemist, such as nasal decongestant sprays. Although these can be all right, used sparingly, for the short-term relief of the blocked nose at the end of a common cold, they are quite unsuitable for treating the long-term blocked nose of perennial rhinitis. Overuse of these sprays will soon damage the lining of the nose and actually make the condition worse with so-called 'rebound congestion'. Antihistamines bought over the counter will temporarily dry up a runny nose, but they will have no effect on a blocked nose and can cause drowsiness (for antihistamines to help ease rhinitis see 'What's Available?' under HAY FEVER p.73).

When nasal symptoms are persistent, it is important to consult a doctor, as there are several effective treatments that he or she can prescribe once the possible non-allergic causes already described have been excluded. Obviously, identifying the allergen so that the sufferer can avoid it as far as possible is helpful. Alternatively, anti-allergic, anti-inflammatory nasal sprays or drops, such as sodium cromoglycate or corticosteroids, if used consistently as directed, are very effective at both preventing and relieving symptoms. Sufferers often have, or have had, other allergic-type conditions, such as eczema or asthma, or these may run in the family. Successful treatment of rhinitis can also keep asthma attacks at bay.

So it is well worthwhile consulting your doctor if you seem to have a permanent head cold or 'hay fever' – these always have a limited duration. Perennial rhinitis does not, but modern treatments will relieve it.

What's Available?   Aller-Eze. See also HAY FEVER p.73

Herbal Remedies   Garlic (for the healing properties of garlic, see 'Herbal Remedies' under COLD, THE COMMON p.34), Herbelix Specific

PERIOD PAIN
When young women get painful periods it's likely to be due to the womb going into a spasm. This causes a cramp-like pain as soon as the period starts, or a dull ache in the

abdomen and back. Doctors call this primary dysmenorrhoea, to distinguish it from secondary dysmenhorroea, the
kind of period pain that mainly affects older women.

Secondary dysmenorrhoea can be caused by disorders
such as endometriosis (when the womb-lining tissue develops outside the womb), fibroids (benign tumours of the
womb's muscular wall) or a continuing infection – pelvic
inflammatory disease, for example.

In most cases painful periods are not a sign of ill health,
but women who suddenly develop them should go to see
their doctor, so that the cause can be treated appropriately.
An ultrasound scan may occasionally be needed to detect –
or rule out – any underlying disorder.

Sufferers from primary dysmenorrhoea sometimes have
more of a chemical called prostaglandin in their menstrual
flow than most women. The production of an egg, or ovum,
in the middle of the month triggers the release of this excess
prostaglandin, which sends pain signals to the brain – so
when a woman doesn't ovulate she usually doesn't experience pain. That's why many women who suffer from
painful periods are advised to take the contraceptive Pill,
which generally works by preventing ovulation – this is a
relatively straightforward form of bringing relief.

Painkillers also help you cope with period pain (see p.100
for product list). An anti-inflammatory one containing
ibuprofen can inhibit the production of prostaglandin,
which is why it can be so effective in relieving symptoms.
Aspirin has the same effect. Mefenamic acid, which is an
even more powerful prostaglandin dampener, has to be
prescribed by your doctor. There are also antispasmodic
medicines available on prescription – these will relieve
symptoms by relaxing the uterine muscles. Some over-the-
counter remedies contain antispasmodic agents – hyoscine
hydrobromide, for example – as well as a mild anti-
prostaglandin drug (paracetamol) and a mild diuretic (caffeine) to make you urinate more often. The diuretic helps
relieve congestion in and around the womb.

Hot baths and hot water can also be soothing for period

pain. Heat can help reduce muscle spasm, as can brisk exercise such as cycling, swimming and fast walking. A good, well-balanced diet with enough Vitamin B6 and other B vitamins is helpful, too (see VITAMINS p.281).

Once a woman has her first baby, the painful periods of the primary dysmenorrhoea kind will usually go for good.

What's Available?   Buscopan, Feminax, Librofem

Herbal Remedies   Potter's Raspberry Leaf Tablets

PILES

Piles, or haemorrhoids, are actually enlarged, worn-out veins – varicose veins that may feel rather like soft, spongy grapes. They're found in and around the lower rectum and anal canal at the very lowest end of the bowel, in a pad of tissue that is not unlike the lips found at the opposite end of the digestive system! Nature intended this soft tissue to be there because, when healthy, it makes a very good seal. But when the veins within it enlarge, becoming piles, a discharge of mucus from the anus can be just one of many distressing symptoms.

Doctors believe that at least half the people in Britain suffer from piles at some time in their life, although many are too embarrassed to seek advice. A susceptibility seems to run in families, perhaps due to an inherited weakness in the wall of the rectal blood vessels. The veins the walls contain, unlike veins elsewhere, do not have valves in them to aid the flow of blood. If anything increases the pressure on these rectal veins, they can become engorged and distended, just like varicose veins in the leg. So there is really no need to be embarrassed about having piles – the chances are that the doctor or pharmacist you consult will have had them too! They really are very common, even more so in men than in women. You are more likely to suffer from piles as you get older (especially if you are overweight), although quite young people can be troubled by them too.

There are many old wives' tales about the causes of piles. Despite popular belief, you do not get them by sitting on cold walls or hot radiators. Perhaps surprisingly, active sportsmen and women are prone to piles and, like varicose veins, they are a particular hazard of pregnancy. The weight of the developing baby can put pressure on the rectal veins, causing them to enlarge as the normal flow of blood is prevented. Fortunately, these piles usually subside after the baby's birth and treatment meanwhile can relieve the discomfort.

Some medicines, such as codeine and iron tablets, if taken regularly, can be constipating and so predispose to piles. However, chronic constipation, with the straining and increased pressure on the veins this brings, is one of the most common causes; as is a lack of fibre in the diet over many years.

If you have piles, the first sign you may notice is some bright red blood in the lavatory, or on the loo paper, after a bowel movement. It is always important to check with your doctor that this bleeding is caused by piles and not by some other condition.

'Internal' piles – also known as 'first degree' piles – which remain inside the anus are usually painless, but as the normal seal there is affected by the swollen veins, a constant, sometimes blood-stained, discharge may occur. There may also be itching and an uncomfortable aching feeling.

Second degree, 'external' piles, which prolapse through the anus, particularly when a motion is passed, tend to become inflamed, itchy and painful from time to time. They usually slip back, or can be gently pushed back, in between bowel movements. It may be easiest to do this while having a bath or using a bidet, when the area is lubricated with soap and your hands are clean.

If second degree piles are not treated, they may protrude permanently – when they are known as third degree piles – and cause considerable discomfort. Occasionally, a protruding pile will be gripped by the tight muscular band (sphincter) at the exit to the anus and become strangulated, which is very painful. If the blood inside the pile then clots, it will, in time, drop off – providing Nature's cure. Otherwise, rest in bed with the foot of the bed raised and an ice pack applied to the pile should relieve acute symptoms.

Less severe piles can often be cured completely by avoiding constipation and straining. So, if you have ever suffered from piles, or think you are likely to because they run in your family, do all you can to avoid becoming constipated. This means eating plenty of high-fibre foods – fresh fruit and vegetables, wholemeal bread and bran cereals, for instance. Fibre-containing tablets or drinks, such as Fybogel or Regulan, available from your chemist, can be helpful if you find it difficult to eat enough bran-type foods. Try also to cut down on salt and have plenty of watery or fruit drinks. This type of diet should keep your motions regular, well-formed and effortless. Laxatives are usually only advisable as a short-term measure.

If your symptoms persist, you can try some suppositories and/or ointments recommended by your pharmacist and follow their instructions. These mainly contain local anaesthetics such as lignocaine or cinchocaine to ease irritation, and astringents, bismuth subgallate for example, to help dry up piles and relieve inflammation. A suppository is usually inserted after each bowel movement and at night and in the morning. Suppositories should never be taken orally. Some are said to be safe to use in pregnancy, but always check this with your pharmacist. Your doctor may prescribe a short course of suppositories containing cortisone to relieve the inflammation and irritation, with perhaps an anaesthetic cream to ease the soreness. Again, sleeping with the foot end of the bed raised can also help.

If your piles keep recurring and being troublesome, your doctor will probably refer you to a surgeon for further advice. Injection treatment may be recommended for bleeding internal or less severe external piles. This involves injecting a special fluid into the dilated veins which causes them to shrink. You will be treated as an outpatient and, although the procedure may sound unpleasant, it is not painful and is usually very successful. In fact, it's one of the easiest and quickest forms of treatment.

As an alternative, cryosurgery – 'freezing' the veins – may be used, or constricting bands may be placed around the base of the veins. An operation under general anaesthetic, called 'Lord's procedure', can be very effective even for quite advanced piles. It involves a powerful stretching of the tight sphincter muscles around the anus. For severe third degree piles, however, many surgeons will advise removing them completely. This operation may cause discomfort for some time afterwards, but it should then solve the problem once and for all.

What's Available? Anacal, Anodesyn, Anusol, Germoloids Ointment, Germoloids Suppositories, Hemocane Suppositories, Nupercainol, Lasonil, Preparation H Suppositories, TCP Ointment

My Favourites Anusol, Preparation H

Herbal Remedies Heemex, Nelsons Haemorrhoid Cream, Pileabs

PRICKLY HEAT

Prickly heat is an extremely irritating skin rash which develops in hot weather. It occurs – more in some people than in others – when the small blood vessels under the skin widen as the temperature rises. The extra blood they then supply to the surface of the body acts as the body's radiator, allowing heat to escape, and the extra blood supplies the extra liquid which the sweat glands release as sweat. As the tissues swell with extra blood and tissue fluids, the skin becomes congested and the pores are squeezed and then blocked. The sweat builds up under the skin and causes a rash known as prickly heat or *Miliaria rubra*.

Sufferers from prickly heat will quickly recognise the

emergence of small red pimples or blisters. The tissues look red because the small blood vessels are open wide, while the engorged tissues cause discomfort and feel prickly.

There's no simple, quick remedy, but if you can immerse yourself in water to keep cool, you should feel better. Covering yourself with light, white clothing will help and, obviously, keeping out of direct sunlight is a good idea, too. Calamine cream or lotions will cool the skin and antihistamine tablets can bring great relief.

What's Available?   Caladryl, Eurax Cream, Mycil Powder. See also HAY FEVER p.73 for antihistamines

My Favourite   Caladryl

PSORIASIS
See DRY SKIN CONDITIONS p.61

RHEUMATIC PAIN
Rheumatism is a general term describing pain which affects the muscles and joints. It covers many conditions, including osteoarthritis, a joint disorder, usually of late middle age, triggered by wear and tear in the joints included in which the protective, shock-absorbing, rubbery substance called cartilage between the bones wears away. Osteoarthritis is thought to affect almost 90% of people over the age of 60, mainly in the hips, knees and shoulders.

Fibrositis – inflammation of white fibrous tissue, especially that of muscle sheaths – also comes under the heading rheumatism. So does rheumatoid arthritis, caused by a progressive swelling of the joints and one of the most crippling of all the rheumatic diseases.

The most widely used pain-relieving treatment is aspirin, but other anti-inflammatory painkillers, ibuprofen, for example, can help (see PAINKILLERS p.100 for list of products containing these ingredients). Rheumatic pain can also be relieved with heat from a hot water bottle, rheumatic liniments and sprays: these treatments work by a process known as counter-irritation, something that causes superficial irritation of the skin and thereby relieves deep-seated pain. For more severe symptoms, your doctor can prescribe anti-inflammatory drugs or stronger painkillers, and perhaps arrange for physiotherapy. In extreme cases, an operation may be necessary to replace the damaged joint with an artificial one.

What's Available? Algipan Rub and Spray, Balmosa, Bengue's Balsam, Cojene, the Deep Heat range of products, especially Deep Heat Intensive Therapy, Deep Heat Bath Tonic and Deep Heat Deep Freeze Cold Gel, Lasonil, Massage Balm, Menthol and Wintergreen Rub, Proflex, PR Freeze Spray, PR Heat Spray, Radian-B Range

My Favourite The Deep Heat range

Homoeopathic remedies Copper Ointment

Herbal Remedies Dr Valnet's Flexarome, Gonne Balm, Natural Olbas Oil, Nelsons Rhus Tox Cream, Potter's Tabritis Tablets, Vegetex

SHINGLES
Shingles is a rash of blisters on the skin accompanied by a severe stinging pain, caused by a virus – the *Varicella zoster* virus – which is also responsible for chicken pox. Anyone who develops shingles will have had chicken pox in the past, sometimes without realising it, as one can have what is known as a 'subclinical' attack, in which no spots appear.

Antibodies to the virus develop in the bloodstream at the first infection and prevent further attacks of chicken pox. However, the virus is able to settle and lie dormant in a non-infectious state, in the 'junction boxes' of nerves supplying a part of the skin or – less commonly – muscles. Often it will cause no further trouble, but if it does, the result will be shingles.

All manner of events can trigger an attack. If you're

emotionally or physically exhausted, or suffering from illness or injury – indeed, if your body's defences are not at their best for whatever reason, the virus can become active. The older you get, the more likely you are to develop shingles – of those who reach their eighties at least one in two will have suffered.

The first symptom is usually pain over the area of skin supplied by the nerves harbouring the virus. The most common place is around the side of the body, along a line following a rib. It can occur on both sides of the chest, but it is an old wives' tale that if it meets in the middle the outcome is fatal – that just isn't true.

To have the best chance of success any treatment should be given early on, preferably at the painful stage which can be when, or just before, the blisters appear.

Your doctor will sometimes prescribe a course of tablets which may help to lessen and shorten the attack. Antiviral applications to the affected area of skin can help and anaesthetic ointments or over-the-counter ointments containing calamine can also be soothing.

The surrounding skin should be kept clean to prevent other germs infecting the blisters, as this could interfere with healing and lead to scarring. Antibiotics may be needed if infection does occur.

What's Available?   Caladryl

SINUS PAIN, NASAL CONGESTION AND CATARRH

Nasal congestion and catarrh – nasal discharge, or phlegm in the throat – are usually present for a few days during and after many infections of the nose and sinuses, especially the common cold (see p.34). The combination is a harmless but annoying problem that can be stubborn to shift and can also result in deafness if it builds up in the eustachian tubes (the tubes on either side at the back of the nose and throat, which lead to the ears).

One of the best ways of treating it is steam inhalation to

help drainage. You can either do this by breathing the vapour being given off by plain hot – not boiling – water, or you can add decongestant capsules containing natural essential oils, such as pine or eucalyptus. Essential oils have a strong, pleasant odour and are extremely volatile. When exposed to air, they therefore give off a powerful vapour. Inhaling this helps give relief from catarrh, nasal congestion and sinus trouble and can loosen mucus. Do not let the vapour come into contact with the eyes.

You can also sprinkle the oils on to a handkerchief or tissue and breathe in the vapours that way. For older children and adults you can dab the oils on to bedding nearby, but avoiding the possibility of direct skin contact. Or for infants, a few drops in a jug of warm water placed in the room out of the child's reach, may give relief.

Tablets are also available over the counter to relieve sinus congestion and pain. These contain paracetamol and a drug called phenylpropanolamine hydrochloride which constricts blood vessels and thus helps ease congestion. Decongestant tablets and syrups can also be bought for blocked sinuses, stuffed-up nose and catarrh as part of cold and flu symptoms. These contain a decongestant such as pseudoephedrine hydrochloride.

You can also try sprays containing decongestants like oxymetazoline hydrochloride, which is used as a vasoconstrictor – a drug that causes narrowing of the walls of blood vessels to relieve congestion. But it's usually inadvisable to use nose drops for longer than seven days, as they can cause a 'rebound' swelling and damage to the nasal passages, making matters worse.

To insert nose drops, lie on your back on a bed with your head hanging over the edge and stay in that position for at least three minutes after inserting the drops. This prevents them simply running down the back of the nose into the throat and allows them to reach their destination – the sinuses.

If your symptoms become more severe and the sinuses are actually infected, the condition is then called sinusitis.

Anyone who has ever suffered from this will remember all too well the typical throbbing headache which is made worse by bending over or blowing the nose. It's estimated that one in 200 colds leads to sinusitis.

The bones of the cheeks, forehead and back of the nose contain a hidden network of small caverns and channels – the sinuses – which help to make the bones lighter and give resonance to our voice. The mucus-secreting membrane that lines the nose continues on to form an interconnecting lining for all the sinuses and there are tiny holes in it which normally allow for free drainage and circulation of air. When germs or particles of dirt are inhaled, they lodge in the mucus; minute, moving 'hairs' called cilia then waft them to the back of the nose where they evaporate, are harmlessly swallowed or are blown out on to a handkerchief.

However, if the lining membrane of the sinuses becomes inflamed – which is quite common after a heavy cold – more mucus than usual is produced, the cilia cease to function properly, infected secretions build up, the tiny drainage holes may become blocked and acute sinusitis results. The pain can be similar to that caused by toothache and the affected sinus – along the cheekbone below the eye, or just above the eyebrow, for example – may be tender to the touch. The sufferer will probably feel generally unwell and have a nasty headache and a blocked nose. He or she may also have a temperature and greeny discharge from the nose or running down the back of the throat.

An allergy – to irritant fumes or smoking, for instance – can also cause the lining membrane of the sinuses to swell and lead to a recurrent form of sinusitis. Diving and underwater swimming may have the same effect, if water is forced up into the sinuses.

An acute attack of sinusitis can usually be successfully treated by rest, painkillers and steam inhalations three times a day to relieve the congestion and help the sinuses to drain. A constant and comfortable room temperature and a humid atmosphere (keep bowls of water by the radiators) should help, too.

Some people also swear by an age-old remedy for catarrh and sinus trouble – garlic, in the form of garlic oil capsules, available from most chemists and health food shops (see 'What's Available?' under COLD, THE COMMON, p.34).

Over-the-counter decongestant medicines may help treat sinusitis, but some can make you drowsy. Nose drops, if prescribed by a doctor, can be helpful. For a severe attack of sinusitis, your doctor may also prescribe antibiotics and, if symptoms do not improve or attacks recur, referral to a specialist may be necessary. Treatment may then include washing out the infected sinus under a local or general anaesthetic and finally an operation to improve the drainage system from the sinuses.

What's Available? Actifed Syrup and Tablets, Afrazine Nasal Spray, Aller-eze Plus, Bengue's Balsam, Catarrh-Ex, Catarrh Pastilles, Cupal Baby Chest Rub, Dimotapp Elixir, Dimotapp Elixir Paediatric, Dimotapp L.A., Dristan Decongestant Tablets, Dristan Spray, Eskornade Spansule Capsules and Syrup, Famel Catarrh and Throat Pastilles, Fenox Nasal Drops, Karvol Decongestant Capsules, Lemsip Night Time, Mentholatum Vapour Rub, Mucron, Mucron Junior Syrup, Otrivine, Penetrol Catarrh Lozenges, Penetrol Inhalant, Sinex Decongestant Nasal Spray, Sinutab, Sinutab Nightime, Sudafed Co, Sudafed Elixir and Tablets, Sudafed Nasal Spray, Throaties Catarrh Pastilles, Tixylix Decongestant Inhalant, Triogesic, Triominic, Vicks Sinex

My Favourites Sudafed Tablets, Sinex Decongestant Nasal Spray

Homoeopathic Remedies Silicea, and for Catarrh, Arsen. Alb., Kali. Bich., Pulsatilla.

Herbal Remedies Garlic, Dr Valnet's Climarone Inhalant, Herbelix Specific, Natural Olbas Oil Inhalant Decongestant, Olbas Pastilles, Potter's Catarrh Pastilles, Potter's Chest Mixture, Sinotar

SLEEPLESSNESS

Sleep has been the subject of a great deal of research and the results, for insomniacs, are reassuring. It seems that, in the long run, Nature ensures that we get the sleep we need and there is no hard and fast rule on how much we should have – individuals differ considerably in this. What matters most is how you feel the next day – if you are alert and efficient, although you have had only five hours sleep, then that was enough for you and comparisons with friends can cause unnecessary worry. Remember, too, that the need for sleep lessens as we grow older.

It is also reassuring to know that even a prolonged period of unsatisfactory sleep will do no serious harm, although you may feel a bit tired and irritable and be less efficient than usual. Eventually the body will catch up on its sleep debt.

Experiments have shown that poor sleepers in fact often sleep more than they think they do, although perhaps not as deeply as others. During sleep, children grow and the body's worn-out tissues are renewed. Sleep is needed to relieve mental fatigue more than physical fatigue – just resting in bed will do this.

It is not yet known whether the sleep induced by sleeping pills is as restorative as natural sleep. Sleeping pills can be useful when taken for a short time, to re-establish a pattern of sleep after a crisis, say, or to relieve anxiety about not sleeping. But dependency can easily develop and can be difficult to break. A 'rebound' insomnia is also common after stopping the pills, making it very tempting to take them again.

Elderly people will often ask their doctor for sleeping pills just because they find lying awake boring and feel they should be asleep – not because they are suffering any ill effects. However, fitful sleep is usual as we grow older and sleeping pills may cause confusion and make falls more likely.

Nearly everyone has times when they sleep badly – a hectic day at work, a difficult time with the children, problems of all kinds leave us feeling worked up or on edge, and make it hard to relax. But for a few, sleep is a lasting problem. They may find it difficult to fall asleep, or they may wake up frequently or very early. Twice as many women suffer as men, especially those with an anxious personality.

Depression is a common cause of sleeplessness and, if severe, both can be relieved by antidepressants. Pain – from arthritis for example – can interfere with sleep (try pain-relievers before bed, not sleeping pills – see PAINKILLERS p.100 for product list); so too can breathing difficulties and some medicines. Alcohol, tea, coffee and cigarettes are all stimulants, so should be avoided before going to bed, whereas a light snack or a milky drink can help induce sleep. A warm bath before going to bed can be very relaxing. And a good read in bed will eventually lead to drowsiness.

As other aids to better sleep, establish a regular routine of meal times, of getting up early and of going to bed at about the same time every night – this helps the body's 'internal clock'. Make sure your bed is comfortable and the room warm, but not too warm. Imagine a peaceful scene and concentrate on relaxing each part of your body in turn. A special relaxation or sleep cassette can help you learn this technique. Some daily exercise in the fresh air will make sound sleep more likely and talking over any problems with a sympathetic person can relieve one cause of insomnia – worry.

If night sweats during the menopause disturb your sleep, hormone replacement therapy can help. If noise is a problem, try ear plugs. Overweight people tend to sleep better and losing weight can mean losing sleep – but obviously it's best to get the balance right here!

There are herbal remedies available for sleeplessness and these may be worth a try. Above all, remember that fear of not sleeping in itself can prevent sleep, so try not to let lying awake worry you – just sit up and read the most boring book you can find and you should soon fall asleep!

What's Available?   Nytol, Sominex

Homoeopathic Remedies   Noctura, Avena Sativa comp.

Herbal Remedies   Kalms Tablets, Natracalm, Natrasleep, Naturest, Potter's Ana-Sed Pain Relief Tablets, Potter's Nodoff Passiflora, Sunerven

SORE NIPPLES

Breast-feeding can sometimes result in painful nipples. The most common cause is incorrect positioning. You should always make sure that your baby is sucking the whole darker ring around your nipple, called the areola, rather than just the nipple itself.

There's no need to keep washing your nipples – just follow your usual washing routine, but don't use soap on your nipples as this could irritate them. Keeping your nipples dry by exposing them to the air now and again helps, as does changing breast pads frequently. Some women find that allowing a little breast milk to dry on them after each feed is useful. A little Kamillosan or Morsep ointment applied to the nipple area will also relieve soreness.

What's Available?   Kamillosan, Morsep

SORE THROAT

Sore throat remedies grab a multi-million pound share of the over-the-counter medicine market – a £71 million share, in fact! Yet there's little evidence that they reduce inflammation or shorten the duration of the infection. Nevertheless many people find the lozenges and gargles soothing and seem to be more than willing to pay for them. The medicines contain a variety of substances, including antiseptics such as domiphen bromide, local anaesthetics such as lignocaine hydrochloride, or antibacterial agents such as tyrothricin. Don't give throat lozenges to children under three, who may choke if the sweet sticks in their throat.

A sore throat is an infection making the throat red and sore, most often due to a viral infection which clears up by itself after three or four days. Pain can be relieved by taking soluble aspirin or your preferred painkiller (see PAINKILLERS p.100 for product list). Avoid smoking if your throat is very sore.

The exact cause of a sore throat can only be established as other symptoms develop. And there are many possible causes – it may be due to a virus and be the start of a cold or flu. It is also one of the first signs of German measles, pharyngitis or tonsillitis – the latter two of which may need antibiotics. So if sore throat symptoms persist, consult your doctor.

What's Available?   Antiseptic Throat Pastilles, Betadine Gargle and Mouthwash, Bradosol Sugar Free Lozenges, Bradosol Plus, Buttercup Syrup range, Coldrex Hot Blackcurrant and Lemon Drinks, Dequacaine, Dequadin, Famel Catarrh and Throat Pastilles, Famel Honey and Lemon Cough Pastilles, Meggozones, Merocaine, Merocets, Merothol, Merovit, Oraldene, Potter's Sore Throat Pastilles, TCP Antiseptic Liquid and TCP Throat Pastilles, Throaties, Tixylix, Tyrocane, Tyrocane Junior Antiseptic Lozenges, Tyrozets, Ulc-Aid Lozenges, Valda Pastilles, Vicks Ultra Chloraseptic, Zensyls, Zubes

Unbranded Products   Glycerin B.P., Thymol Glycerin Compound

My Favourite   Merocets

Homoeopathic Remedies   Aconite, Arsen. Alb., Bryonia

Herbal Remedies   Olbas Pastilles

STICKY EYES
Many of us will know what it's like to wake up in the morning with itchy, 'gritty'-feeling eyes and perhaps the eyelids stuck together. Underneath, the eyelids will be red and inflamed and the whites of the eyes probably bloodshot. Blinking may be painful and bright light distressing.

Conjunctivitis, as this condition is called, is very common and children are particularly prone to it. The symptoms are due to an inflammation of the conjunctiva – the delicate membrane that covers the whites of the eyes and the inner surfaces of the upper and lower eyelids. Where the membrane turns back on itself to cover both surfaces of the lids, sacs are formed, and small particles may collect here and irritate the conjunctiva – one cause of conjunctivitis.

Another possible cause is a viral or bacterial infection. Alternatively, the inflammation may be brought on by an allergic reaction – to pollens, animal hairs, cosmetics or the cleansing lotions used for contact lenses, for example.

It's perhaps surprising that conjunctivitis is not even more common than it is, since the eye is constantly exposed to various irritants and germs. Fortunately, the conjunctival sac is not an ideal breeding ground for germs, partly because of the cleansing effect of tear fluid. If a tear duct is blocked, then inflammation commonly develops and the duct will probably have to be unblocked.

If, as well as being red and sore, the eyes are gummed up with sticky discharge – including perhaps some yellow pus – this usually means that the conjunctivitis is due to a virus or bacteria. The discharge will be particularly noticeable first thing in the morning, having accumulated during the night. The sufferer may also have a cold or other infection such as, in the case of a child, measles. The discharge from the eyes is contagious, so keep handkerchiefs, towels, flannels and pillow cases separate to avoid spreading the germs to others. Your doctor will probably prescribe antibiotic eye drops and/ or ointment to apply several times a day – be sure to wash your hands both before and after doing so. The condition should improve within about four days – if not, referral to an eye specialist may be advised.

Another condition which causes irritating, sticky eyes is blepharitis, which I discussed earlier when talking about dandruff (see p.55).

Conjunctivitis due to an allergy such as hay fever will usually produce a watery discharge and can often be relieved by special preventive eye drops such as Opticrom, available on prescription, or other soothing eye lotions containing cooling witch-hazel and small amounts of anti-septics. Dark glasses can also help.

Sometimes town-dwellers will suffer from a persistent type of mild though distressing conjunctivitis – known as 'urban eye' – caused by irritant fumes and dust. Bathing the eyes twice a day with a solution of one teaspoonful of bicarbonate of soda dissolved in one pint of recently boiled and cooled water can relieve the symptoms. Use a separate piece of cotton wool for each eye, bathing the edges of the closed lids, working inwards towards the nose.

It's best to avoid eye make-up during any attack of conjunctivitis – in fact it's possible that make-up is the cause. Likewise, if you wear contact lenses, revert to your spectacles while your eyes are inflamed and ask your doctor's or ophthalmic optician's advice on future use. And if your eyes become painful or your vision is affected, always consult your doctor without delay. These symptoms could indicate that there was inflammation within the eye and in that case urgent examination and treatment, probably by a specialist, would be required without delay.

What's Available?   Brolene Eye Drops (and ointment), Clearine Eye Drops, Optrex Eye Lotion, Optrex Clearine Eye Drops (for minor eye irritations), Eye Dew, Sootheye Eye Drops

SUNBURN

While a small amount of sunshine on the skin is beneficial – it supplies Vitamin D and helps to keep the more harmful germs that live on the skin at bay – there is no longer any doubt that continuous and prolonged exposure to the sun or the rays of a sunbed can be harmful.

This harm is observed in all sorts of ways – the skin ages prematurely, with wrinkling and dark brown blemishes, often accompanied by an ugly thickening of patches of the top skin layers, called solar keratosis. Skin changes that we notice as we get older, wrinkles and loss of elasticity, are now believed to be mainly due to damage from the sun. About 70% of this skin damage, which may take years to show, probably occurs in childhood, as a young child's skin is thinner than that of an adult and more likely to burn.

Each time the skin is burnt, the damage accumulates and the risk of skin cancer developing in the future increases. Over-exposure to the ultra-violet rays of the sun makes the skin red, hot and sore. Higher doses lead to inflammation and swelling; even greater exposure leads to burning, blistering and peeling as the epidermis – the outer layer of skin – disintegrates. Very bad sunburn damages the skin so much that it cannot carry out its usual functions. The heat absorbed from over-exposure to the sun can stop the body's temperature gauge from working properly, resulting in sunstroke, which has been known to kill.

Yet nobody really need suffer from sunburn. Prevention is always better than cure. It's worth remembering that you can get burnt even on cloudy days – 80% of ultra-violet rays get through cloud and water. Always try to use a protective cream. Proprietary suntan products, such as the Uvistat range or the Sun E45 range, which protects against UVA/UVB rays, are labelled with SPFs – sun protection factors – devised to tell you how much protection you can expect. They work by absorbing, reflecting or scattering the sun's rays – the higher the number, the more protection.

Remember, too, that babies and young children are particularly vulnerable to the sun's harmful rays, so always use a sun protection cream designed for their delicate skins. Babies under six months old should be kept out of the sun anyway, not just because of the risk of sunburn, but because heatstroke can be even more dangerous.

Sticking to the rule of avoiding the sun between 11 a.m. and 4 p.m. – when ultra-violet radiation is at its most intense because the sun is directly overhead – may not necessarily be the best safeguard: times vary according to geography and seasonal changes. So a good tip is to watch your shadow. When it's the same height as you are, the sun's rays are at an angle of 45° and therefore less dangerous – provided, of course, that you use an adequate sunscreen. If your shadow is shorter, you're more likely to burn.

If you do suffer from sunburn, the painful effects don't normally last for more than a few days, followed by itching as the skin heals. Lotions containing calamine or aloe vera with perhaps menthol, phenol or camphor have a cooling effect on the skin. Blisters should not be burst and you should drink plenty of water just in case you have become dehydrated. If the skin is burnt or peeling, stay out of the sun until it has healed completely. If symptoms are severe, always consult a doctor.

What's Available?   Acriflex, Cal-A-Cool, Caladryl, Germolene Ointment, Lacto Calamine, Lana-Sting Spray, Medicaid, RBC, Solarcaine, Sudocrem, Sun E45 range, Uvistat range, Witch Doctor

Unbranded Product   Calamine Lotion B.P., Sodium Bicarbonate B.P.

My Favourite   Caladryl

Homoeopathic Remedies   Combudoron Lotion

TEETHING

Babies cut their first teeth, on average, at about the age of six months and don't complete their set of 20 baby or milk teeth until they're around two to three years old. The first don't usually give any trouble, but when the back teeth come through, they can cause pain. Some babies sail through teething without a murmur, while others aren't quite so fortunate.

Teething trouble is pretty easy to spot – if your baby is grizzly or upset, dribbling more than usual, has a red cheek or is gnawing everything in reach, then it's likely that teething is the cause. But if you have any doubts at all, it's best to get medical advice so as not to blame teething and overlook any real illness.

Special teething gels are available to relieve the baby's discomfort. These usually contain antiseptics such as cetyl-pyridinium chloride to prevent infection, as well as a local anaesthetic like lignocaine hydrochloride to numb any pain. Teething gel can be applied using a small pad of cotton wool or a clean finger and then rubbed gently on to the baby's gums. Repeat after 20 minutes if necessary. If your child is in great discomfort you can also use paracetamol infant suspensions to relieve the pain.

While we're talking about teeth, you may not realise that you can help look after your baby's teeth even before they appear. Don't allow sweet substances to stay in contact with his or her gums for long periods. This means not using baby drinks in bottles as a comforter and not dipping dummies in sweet syrups or honey.

What's Available? Anbesol, Bonjela Oral Pain-relieving Gel, Calgel, Calpol Infant Suspension, Cupanol Under Six, Dentinox Teething Gel, Fenning's Children's Cooling Powders, Junior Paraclear, Rinstead Teething Gel, Teejel Gel (use only under professional guidance if the child is sensitive to or is currently being prescribed aspirin), Woodward's Teething Gel

My Favourite Calpol Infant Suspension

Homoeopathic Remedies Chamomilla Granules, Chamomilla 3 × Drops or Pilules, Nelsons Teething Granules

Herbal Remedies Ashton and Parsons Infants' Powders

THRUSH
Thrush is a common vaginal infection due to the multiplication of a yeast-like fungus known as *Candida albicans*, which

occurs naturally in the vagina, mouth and digestive tract. When the body's natural balance is upset, perhaps by pregnancy, diabetes, having taken antibiotics recently, having had sex with someone who has thrush or even having a period, the fungus can multiply and cause great discomfort.

The most common symptoms are soreness, itching and occasionally swelling of the vagina and vulva. There is also often a whitish, curd-like discharge which looks a bit like cottage cheese and has no smell. Sometimes there is a burning feeling at the entrance to the vagina. Sometimes, too, your partner may carry the organism on his penis and develop an itchy rash. If he does, he too should be treated.

Many women do suffer numerous attacks of thrush – and once it has been diagnosed by a doctor it can be recognised by the sufferer. But if you experience thrush for the first time, or if you are in any doubt about the condition, always seek the advice of your doctor.

Two new, safe and effective over-the-counter medicines for the treatment of vaginal thrush are now available from pharmacies only. Both Femeron and Canesten 10% VC treat the symptoms of thrush with a convenient, single-dose application. Femeron contains miconazole and Canesten 10% VC contains clotrimazole, which are antifungal drugs and should relieve symptoms within two to three days of treatment.

To guard against further attacks of thrush, make sure you wash every day. When you go to the loo, it's particularly important that you wipe yourself from front to back (not from back to front) after a bowel movement, just as you would do to avoid cystitis. Avoid perfumed soaps, deodorants, bubble baths, etc, which could cause irritation. Vaginal douches should not be used, although some women do seem to find relief when they insert fresh, live yoghurt into the vagina. This contains 'healthy' germs – the lactobacilli which compete with and may overcome the thrush-causing micro-organisms.

Some women have found that using tampons or an intrauterine contraceptive device has put them more at risk of developing thrush. Others have found that wearing synthetic underwear or tight-fitting trousers helps the fungi to thrive because of the warm, moist environment.

If you think you have thrush, you should consult your doctor if any of the following conditions apply: if you haven't had thrush before; if you have a previous history of sexually transmitted disease or exposure to a partner with STD; if you have had more than two previous attacks in the last six months; if you have a known hypersensitivity to Canesten or Femeron; if you are pregnant or think you may be; if you are under 16 or over 60; if you experience any abnormal or irregular vaginal bleeding or blood-stained vaginal discharge, any vaginal sores, ulcers or blisters, any associated lower abdominal pain or difficulty in passing urine; if there is no improvement after seven days of treatment; if there are any adverse effects such as redness, irritation or swelling associated with the treatment.

What's Available? Canesten 1, Canesten 10% VC, Femeron Cream and Soft Pessary

TOOTHACHE
No matter how often we visit the dentist, our teeth are constantly under threat from our diet. We tend to eat more sugar than is good for us, and after every meal, snack or drink containing carbohydrates, food sugars in our mouth are converted by plaque bacteria into acids which attack tooth enamel (its protective layer) for 40 minutes or longer. This can lead to decay spreading down a tooth's root canal to the nerve, causing inflammation and pain.

As well as decay, toothache can be caused by such things as a cracked filling or fractured tooth, even an abscess, so any type of pain in a tooth or in the gums should always be checked out by a dentist. Aspirin (not for children), parace-tamol and ibuprofen can all be effective in treating dental pain if you have to wait for an appointment (see PAINKILLERS p.100 for list of products containing these ingredients). Oil of cloves applied to the aching tooth by means of a soaked piece of cotton wool can help numb the pain, too.

To help prevent further attacks of toothache, brush your teeth regularly. The use of dental floss is recommended, as I mentioned when talking about gum disease (see p.70), and you can also try a dental health gum after eating and drinking. This helps neutralise the teeth-attacking acids and so can help prevent tooth decay. Many millions of people throughout the world now drink artificially fluoridated water and millions more live in areas where the water contains natural fluoride. The addition of fluoride to water supplies is a frequent cause of confusion and controversy. Many people do not realise that some fluoride is naturally present in almost all water supplies and in most foods, so we ingest a certain amount each day. Usually, though, it is not enough to give our teeth as much protection as they need. Fluoridation of the water does not therefore involve adding a 'foreign' substance – it is simply a controlled means of adjusting the amount of fluoride to the most beneficial level. Experts now agree that although, as with most things, too much fluoride can be harmful, the recommended amount of one part per million (1 ppm) in the drinking water has no harmful effects.

Fluoride is an active ingredient in many toothpastes and you can buy fluoride drops and tablets over the counter to help protect children's teeth. So those who are against the addition of fluoride to the water supply ask why we cannot just use these products? The answer is that in order to be most effective, fluoride must be available continuously – during pregnancy for the mother-to-be and, for almost everyone, from birth through to late adolescence, so that it becomes built into the structure of the teeth as they develop and grow. However well-intentioned they may be, few parents could maintain the necessary continuity – giving each of their children a daily dose of fluoride for say 18 years, quite apart from the expense. Fluoride toothpaste, although helpful, only acts on the surface of the tooth, so is not as effective at preventing decay, though very good, nevertheless.

At present about 7,000 sets of dentures are supplied to school-age children in this country each year and one in three adults has no natural teeth left. In the few areas in Britain where the water has been fluoridated for many years – Birmingham is one example – tooth decay amongst children has been reduced by 50% and the number of extractions needed has dropped dramatically. The middle-aged who have lived in fluoridated areas since childhood also have much less decay, so the benefits are lasting.

Although avoiding sugary foods and in-between meal snacks will do much to prevent decay, our teeth are still constantly under attack from acid-producing germs. Teeth with fluoride built into their substance are undoubtedly better equipped for the fight. The earlier additional fluoride can be given, the better – preferably from soon after birth in the form of drops. Fluoride tablets can be taken when a child is older and should, ideally, be continued all the time that milk teeth and permanent teeth are growing. Dosage of drops and tablets will depend on the child's age and how much fluoride is present in the local drinking water, so consult your dentist or pharmacist first.

What's Available?   Bansor Mouth Antiseptic (for sore gums), Endekay Dental Health Gum, Endekay Fluoride Tablets and Drops, Oil of Cloves

My Favourites   For toothache: 'Own brand' Oil of Cloves. For adding fluoride: Endekay Tablets and Drops

TRAVEL SICKNESS

Travel sickness can be a misery not only for sufferers but for those travelling with them. It can easily ruin what started out as a pleasant journey or family outing. Travel sickness can last up to 72 hours on a very long journey, but it can also stop very quickly once the journey has finished.

Symptoms such as nausea and vomiting, loss of appetite,

sweating, feeling faint and looking pale, even greenish, during a car, sea or air journey are actually brought on by the disturbance to the balance mechanism of the inner ear caused by motion. The movement of the vehicle upsets the link between what the eyes see and what the balance mechanism of the inner ear feels – hence the alternative name of 'motion sickness'. The eyes adjust to the changes in the movement, whereas the inner ear doesn't, so the signals from the eyes and the ears don't quite add up.

Medicines for combating travel sickness are known as anti-emetics. They are drugs such as meclozine hydrochloride, an antihistamine, and they reduce the sensitivity of the vomiting centre in the brain. Some of the anti-travel sickness medicines cause drowsiness, so always read instructions carefully. Some aren't recommended during pregnancy, either, so do check with your pharmacist or doctor if you're pregnant and suffer from travel sickness. For most benefit, travel sickness medicines should be taken at least one hour before your journey starts.

You can reduce the risk of travel sickness by following some self-help measures. Don't have a large meal or alcoholic drink before a journey, don't allow smoking in the car and keep windows open if possible.

Children's ears tend to be sensitive, making them more prone to travel sickness than adults, so if you have children who suffer, don't talk about being sick in front of them, and provide plenty of distractions – games, toys, puzzles, etc. If possible, travel at night when they're more likely to fall asleep – and if all else fails do take some waterproof bags with you!

What's Available?   Avomine, Dramamine, Kwells, Sea-Legs, Stugeron, Q-Mazine Syrup, Phenergan Elixir, Travel Calm Tablets

My Favourite   Stugeron

Homoeopathic Remedies   Nelsons Travel Sickness Tablets

URTICARIA

More often known as hives or nettle rash, urticaria is a very common skin condition which affects one in five people at some time in their lives. Women are particularly prone, perhaps because of hormonal influences. With 'ordinary' urticaria, weals – intensely itchy raised marks on the surface of the skin – suddenly develop. They are usually short-lived, lasting for a few hours or days, but may last longer. The weals can be any size, appear anywhere on the sufferer's body and may be numerous. They are usually pale in the middle and red around the edges and are due to dilation of the capillaries – small blood vessels under the skin – which makes their walls more permeable and enables clear fluid called serum to leak out. If enough serum leaks out, blisters may form.

If deeper tissues are involved, a more severe type of urticaria known as angio-oedema may occur. Then the swellings are much larger, commonly affecting the face, eyelids, hands, forearms and throat and sometimes causing serious breathing difficulties. Joints in the arms and legs may also become inflamed and painful. About half the people who suffer from ordinary urticaria have recurrent attacks of angio-oedema too.

So what causes this reaction in the blood vessels? Often it is due to an increased circulation of histamine – a chemical normally present in the body. This increase can be triggered by many factors, including various foods, drugs and inhalants such as pollens, house dust and animal 'dander' – skin flakes which the animal sheds naturally and various chemicals which its body gives off. Two foods that are frequently responsible are shellfish and strawberries – so urticaria is a hazard of summer for those susceptible. Other foods that may produce the reaction include eggs, nuts, chocolate, tomatoes, pork, milk and yeast. Artificial colourings and preservatives can do so, too.

Aspirin can also be a cause of urticaria, or it can aggravate it. Penicillin is another possible culprit, as are the non-steroidal anti-inflammatory drugs often given to treat arthritis.

Sometimes contact with certain substances will bring the symptoms on – cosmetics are one example. Insect stings can also cause this type of reaction, which may even be life-threatening if the breathing is affected (see BITES AND STINGS p.25).

People whose urticaria occurs in response to triggers such as these are often but not always allergy-prone individuals – sufferers from hay fever, asthma or eczema for example – and the tendency can run in families. Anxiety may also play a part.

Other constituents in the body – called catechol amines – can, by irritating the tissues surrounding them, have the same effect on the blood vessels as histamine and almost anything can act as the trigger in this allergic-type of urticaria. I had it once after eating raw fish in a foreign restaurant, for example, but it may also have been due to the monosodium glutamate used as a taste-enhancer.

It can therefore be exceedingly difficult to track down – in order to avoid – the cause if the attacks are recurrent. In fact three out of four people are unable to do so, in spite of persistent detective work.

Some more unusual forms of urticaria have a physical cause. Cold winds or rain, or just immersing the hands or bathing in cold water, can cause weals to appear in susceptible people. If an ice cube on the skin produces a weal, this confirms the diagnosis of 'cold urticaria' – the type that's induced by the cold.

Some people develop weals when exposed to sunlight – 'solar urticaria'. Others may suffer from 'pressure urticaria' – deep, painful, non-itchy swellings which occur about two hours after some particular pressure on the skin. The hands may swell, for instance, after carrying a heavy shopping bag, or the balls of the feet after spending some time on a ladder.

Another strange form of urticaria is called dermographism, loosely 'translated' as skin writing. A mild, stroking pressure – with a fingernail for example – will produce a temporary, raised line with reddened edges. The skin can literally be used as a drawing board.

Fortunately, however, most cases of urticaria tend to resolve themselves in due course, and in the meantime antihistamine tablets prescribed by your doctor or recommended by your pharmacist usually relieve the symptoms and keep the condition under control. For mild cases, soothing creams containing antihistamine which stop the effects of histamine on the blood vessels beneath the skin, or creams and lotions containing calamine lotion help calm down any swelling and itching by cooling the skin, especially if these preparations contain menthol, phenol or camphor.

If angio-oedema is severe and breathing becomes difficult, emergency treatment by injection may be necessary to reduce the swelling.

Urticaria can occur as part of some other underlying condition – thyroid disease, for example. So if the cause is not immediately apparent, or you have more than one attack, or are concerned, do consult your doctor. He or she may wish to do blood tests and other investigations or refer you to a skin specialist.

What's Available? Aller-Eze, Anethane Itch Soothing Cream, Caladryl, Cal-a-Cool, Clarityn, DDD Medicated Lotion and Cream, Eurax, Lanacane, Lana-Sting Spray and Creme, Phenergan Elixir, Phenergan Tablets, RBC, Triludan, Triludan Forte. For other antihistamines, see under HAY FEVER p.73

My Favourite Caladryl

Homoeopathic Remedies Apis. Mel., Combudoron Lotion, Lycopodium, Nat. Mur., Sulphur,

VERRUCAS
Plantar warts on the feet, also known as verrucas, as opposed to common warts (see WARTS p.135), tend to grow inwards rather than outwards because of the constant

pressure on them from standing and walking. Verrucas normally occur on the sole of the foot and are moist. The skin surface is rough and the shape irregular. They often have tiny black centres, appear in groups and become painful if they press on a nerve.

Verrucas are caused by a virus entering the foot, possibly via a slight area of damage – in the same way as common warts – and are very infectious, particularly among children. The virus loves warmth and moisture – and soggy feet! – so is easily passed on in such places as swimming pools and showers. If you have verrucas, therefore, you shouldn't go barefoot until they have cleared up. Many swimming pools now provide plastic socks for children with verrucas to wear so as to avoid infecting others.

Verrucas can be treated with over-the-counter remedies which usually contain a keratolytic – salicylic acid, for example – to soften the verruca so that it can be cut out or pulled off. If possible, cover the verruca with a ring-pad plaster to protect the surrounding skin. Put a small quantity of the ointment or paint on the verruca, then cover it with a plaster for two to three days. After several applications, the verruca should separate from the surrounding healthy tissue. If this doesn't happen within about two weeks, consult your doctor or chiropodist.

After a few days of treatment, the verruca will probably appear white or blanched. This is perfectly normal and indicates that the treatment is working well.

You can also get rid of verrucas with another form of treatment which doesn't require the use of sticking plasters. Buy a non-keratolytic paint such as Glutarol which contains glutaraldehyde, a disinfectant working directly on the wart virus, inhibiting its activity. It also exerts a powerful anhidrotic, or anti-sweating effect, which reduces the tendency of warts and verrucas to spread, so helping to minimise the risk of cross-infection.

Other methods of removing verrucas if they become painful are cryotherapy – 'freezing' them with liquid nitrogen; 'burning' with an electric cautery; or scraping them out with a scalpel called a curette. Often a local anaesthetic will be given first to numb the surrounding area. A chiropodist is usually the best person to consult about recurrent or persistent verrucas.

Sufferers from diabetes should always consult a doctor about foot problems because they can more easily pick up infection.

What's Available? Carnation Verruca Treatment, Compound V, Compound W, Duofilm, Glutarol, Salactol

My Favourite Compound W

WARTS
Much folklore is associated with warts, and some intriguing forms of treatment. One 'cure' was to rub your warts with stones. The stones then had to be wrapped up and left at the crossroads on the way to church. If another person picked up the stones, he would heal your warts by acquiring them himself!

Quite simply, warts are small, dry lumps of skin often seen on the hands, knees and face and they develop when a virus invades the skin cells and causes them to multiply very quickly. They're spread through contact with skin that's been shed from a wart or by the virus coming into contact with damaged skin, particularly if it is warm and moist. That's why it's advisable to use only your own towels until your warts have cleared, to reduce the risk of spreading the condition to other members of your household.

Warts are a nuisance as they can be so ugly, but they're normally harmless and, if untreated, most of these 'common warts' will eventually disappear of their own accord – although this may not happen for many years.

The virus's incubation period varies from a few weeks to several months, as it often lies dormant for some time. That's why warts can erupt months after the initial infection. For the same reason warts can reappear after treatment has apparently been successful. Adults will usually have developed some immunity to the virus over the years and are less likely to catch warts than children.

If you find common warts unsightly or annoying, you can apply a solution or cream every day to get rid of them. Most contain a caustic such as acetic acid, which destroys any tissue it's applied to, or a keratolytic drug such as salicylic acid to soften the wart and loosen it. Keeping the wart(s) covered with a plaster may speed up the treatment process, but remember, there's no immediate cure and treatment with one of these products can still take weeks to complete. Make sure, too, that you follow instructions very carefully, because these remedies can make the skin surrounding the wart very sore. Immediately wash off any solvent accidentally applied to surrounding skin to avoid painful acid burns.

If you have a wart that doesn't respond to an over-the-counter treatment, ask your doctor for advice. Other methods of removing warts are the same as those for verrucas (see p.133).

Women can develop genital warts in or around the vagina or on the cervix and men can have them on the penis. These warts are usually transmitted during sexual intercourse but may occur for other reasons.

Although genital warts are also due to a virus infection, a slightly different strain is probably responsible for each type of wart. Most genital warts develop from a root-like base below the surface of the skin and all have their own blood supply, so this must be taken into account when treating them. Never treat any warts on the genitals or around the anus with over-the-counter remedies.

Some wart-like brown or black eruptions not due to a virus are the so-called 'seborrhoeic' or senile warts which many people develop on their body, temple or scalp as they get older. These usually cause no problems, but they can sometimes itch severely. It's best to have them examined by a doctor who may advise removing them.

In general, it's advisable to let a doctor examine any wart when it first appears and especially, as with moles, if it changes in size or colour, or begins to bleed. But usually warts remain nothing but an annoying blemish.

For advice on plantar warts on the feet, also called verrucas, see VERRUCAS p.133.

What's Available? Compound W, Duofilm, Glutarol, Salactol, Salatac Gel

My Favourite Compound W

WIND
See FLATULENCE p.66.

WORMS
Threadworms (Enterobius) are like little strands of white cotton – hence the name. They are less than 1.5 cm long and can be seen wriggling in the faeces. Horrible as they sound, they are a very common problem, particularly in children. It is estimated that up to 40% of children below the age of ten are infected with threadworms, though many may not show the 'itching' symptoms generally associated with them.

Threadworms produce large numbers of tiny eggs that cannot be seen with the naked eye. The eggs are present in house dust, they stick to clothing, carpets, towels and bed linen and can also be picked up in garden soil or on unwashed vegetables and salads. They are spread by eating contaminated food or by hand contact. If another person should touch an infected person's hands when eggs are present and subsequently put his or her hands into the mouth, then he or she will also become infected as a result of swallowing the eggs. The eggs then hatch in the lower bowel and at night a female worm starts to lay her eggs just outside the anus. She can lay up to 10,000 eggs, which can cause severe itching.

The wriggling of threadworms irritates the anus and

their presence slightly inflames it. This normally makes the sufferer scratch and so pick up eggs on the hands and under the fingernails. The most common sign of threadworms is scratching of the bottom, particularly at night and first thing in the morning. When the scratching takes place solely during the night, as sometimes happens, it may just cause a disturbance of sleep and hence daytime irritability – the itching itself may not be apparent. Some sufferers show no signs of infection, in which case it is a question of spotting the worms in the motions in order to detect their presence.

Threadworms are very common and appear even in the cleanest households, so there's no need to feel embarrassed about consulting your doctor. They only affect humans, never pets. And although they can be uncomfortable, they are generally harmless and do not usually cause any long-term damage.

You can buy a remedy from the chemist containing mebendazole, which kills threadworms, or piperazine, which is one of a number of substances that paralyse the worms so they can then be passed out in the faeces. These treatments are usually effective, but you should follow the instructions on the packet exactly. If the problem recurs, then everyone in your household should take a course of the medicine at the same time (your pharmacist will advise you on the correct dosage for each individual), as they may be harbouring worms themselves without necessarily having any symptoms. If this is the case, the worms can, in a variety of ways, be continually passed from person to person. So if, after treatment, your symptoms return, gather your courage and bring up the subject with everyone sharing your home – you may find they've been suffering silently, too.

Make sure that everyone scrubs their fingers and nails with a brush after each visit to the toilet and before each meal. Disinfect – by washing thoroughly – the toilet seat, toilet handle or chain and door handle regularly, as well as making sure you dust and vacuum bedrooms thoroughly.

Roundworms (ascariasis) can also be treated by piperazine. These worms are one of the largest parasites – they can be 10–30 cm long, look like earthworms and can block the intestine. They're transmitted by eggs found in contaminated raw food or in soil. Fortunately, they're rare. The sufferer may inexplicably lose weight or suffer other symptoms – a cough is not uncommon. When the doctor takes a blood test, the results should strongly suggest the diagnosis. Occasionally, an adult worm, not unlike an earthworm, may be passed in the faeces or even vomited up. But don't be alarmed – as I said, it's rare, thank goodness.

The roundworm is usually eradicated by a single dose of a medicine containing piperazine, whereas threadworms may need several days' treatment, as instructed, and phases of treatment may sometimes be separated by a week or more.

What's Available?   Ovex TM, Pripsen

My Favourite   Pripsen

A–Z of Over-the-Counter Medicines

To make it easy for you to find out about a medicine, I have listed them here with a short description and any relevant comments. The recommended dosages and other instructions are also given.

NOTE: where appropriate, dosages are given in millilitres (ml). One 5 ml spoonful = one teaspoonful; one 15 ml spoonful = one tablespoonful

Acetoxyl 2.5 and 5
Greaseless, odourless, antiseptic medications containing benzoyl peroxide for the treatment of acne. It may be necessary to change to Acetoxyl 5 as the skin becomes accustomed to treatment with the milder Acetoxyl 2.5. Apply once daily after washing the affected area. STIEFEL

Acnegel and Acnegel Forte
Acne gels containing benzoyl peroxide, invisible on the skin. Acnegel Forte has a higher percentage of benzoyl peroxide. Apply once a day after washing affected area. STIEFEL

Acnidazil
Treatment for spots and acne, containing miconazole nitrate and benzoyl peroxide. For the first week apply cream to the affected areas once daily every morning after washing. After the first week, apply twice daily morning and evening.

Continue until spots and pimples have cleared – this will normally take four to eight weeks. Then use two to three times a week. CILAG

Acriflex
Soothing cream with chlorhexidine – an antiseptic – for the treatment of minor burns and scalds, scratches,

cuts and abrasions, sunburn blisters and cracked skin. For general use, apply freely and smooth gently into the skin. For cuts, abrasions, burns etc., spread freely and, if necessary, cover with a dressing.

SETON HEALTHCARE

Actal

Antacid tablets containing alexitol sodium for relief from indigestion, stomach upset, heartburn or dyspepsia due to over-acidity. For adults only: allow two tablets to dissolve on the tongue as required.

STERLING HEALTH

Actifed Compound Linctus

Linctus for the relief of dry cough and other symptoms that accompany coughs and colds, such as runny nose, catarrh, nasal congestion and blocked-up sinuses. Contains an antihistamine, triprolidine hydrochloride; a decongestant, pseudoephedrine hydro-chloride; and dextro-methorphan hydrobromide, a cough-suppressant. May cause drowsiness. As with all medicines, if you're pregnant or currently taking any other medicine, consult your doctor or pharmacist before taking this product.

Dosage, three times a day: Adults and children over 12 – two 5 ml spoonfuls. Children 6–12 years – one 5 ml spoonful; 2–5 years – half a 5 ml spoonful.

WELLCOME

Actifed Cough Relief

(1–12 years)
Actifed Cough Relief has been specially formulated with dextromethorphan hydrobromide (a cough-suppressant) and triprolidine hydrochloride (an antihistamine) gently to soothe and relieve children's irritating coughs and so allow them to sleep. Also helps relieve other cough and cold symptoms such as watery eyes and a runny nose. Contains no colorants, is sugar-free and has a pleasant fruity taste.

Dosage: three or four times a day. Do not exceed the stated dose. Children 6–12 years – two 5 ml spoonfuls; children 2–5 years – one 5 ml spoonful; children 1–under 2 years – half a 5 ml spoonful. Adults and children over 12 years may find Actifed Compound Linctus more suitable.

May cause drowsiness. As with all medicines, if your child is currently taking any other medicine, consult your doctor or pharmacist before giving this product.

WELLCOME

Actifed Expectorant

An expectorant to help loosen

stubborn mucus and relieve other symptoms that accompany coughs and colds, such as runny nose, catarrh, nasal congestion and blocked sinuses. Contains an antihistamine, triprolidine hydrochloride; a decongestant, pseudoephedrine hydrochloride; and an expectorant, guaiphenesin. May cause drowsiness.

Dosage: As for Actifed Compound Linctus, above. As with all medicines, if you're pregnant or currently taking any other medicine, consult your doctor or pharmacist before taking this product.

WELLCOME

Actifed Syrup and Actifed Tablets

A syrup or tablets to help soothe and relieve cold and flu symptoms such as stuffed-up nose, catarrh, runny nose and blocked sinuses. Also relieves summer cold and hay-fever symptoms, including sneezing, watery eyes, congested nasal passages and a runny nose. Contains an antihistamine, triprolidine hydrochloride, and a decongestant, pseudo-ephedrine hydrochloride. May cause drowsiness. As with all medicines, if you're pregnant or currently taking any other medicine, consult your doctor

or pharmacist before taking this product.

Dosage – syrup: as for Actifed Expectorant, above. Dosage – tablets: adults and children over 12 only – one tablet three times a day.

WELLCOME

Actron

A soluble, effervescent painkiller containing aspirin, paracetamol and caffeine for the relief of headaches, colds, influenza, feverishness, rheumatic and muscular pains, period pains, neuralgia and toothache. Not for children under 12. Dosage: two tablets every four hours, if necessary. No more than eight tablets in 24 hours.

BAYER CONSUMER

Aezodent

A mildly anaesthetic ointment containing local pain-relievers benzocaine, chlorbutol and methyl salicylate, with analgesic, healing and antiseptic properties. Also contains eugenol and menthol. Used to combat chafing from dentures. Before inserting the denture in the mouth, squeeze a series of spots of the ointment on the denture, particularly where chafing is likely to occur.

ASSOCIATED DENTAL PRODUCTS

Afrazine Nasal Spray

Decongestant spray

containing oxymetazoline hydrochloride. Relieves the discomfort and symptoms of head colds and hay fever, giving up to 12 hours of relief.

Dosage: adults and children over 5 – two to three sprays to be instilled into each nostril in the morning and at bedtime. Prolonged use is not recommended.

SCHERING-PLOUGH CONSUMER HEALTH

Agarol

An emulsion for the temporary relief of constipation only. Particularly useful when it's not advisable to strain when opening the bowels – for those with a hernia, or convalescing after surgery, for example. Not suitable for children under 5. Contains phenolpthalein, liquid paraffin and agar, a carbohydrate obtained from seaweeds and used as a laxative.

Adult dosage: one to three 5 ml spoonfuls to be taken at bedtime. If necessary, the dose may be repeated two hours after breakfast. Children 5–12 years – one 5 ml spoonful at bedtime or two hours after breakfast. Agarol may be mixed with water, milk or fruit juices.   WARNER LAMBERT

Algipan Rub

A non-greasy cream to bring relief from muscular pain and stiffness, especially in back ache, sciatica, lumbago, fibrositis and rheumatic pain. Also available as a spray. Contains methyl nicotinate, which is used to make skin redden and is therefore warm; capiscin made from chillies; and glycol salicylate, a member of the aspirin family used in rheumatic rubs. Massage Algipan lightly into the affected part until it's completely absorbed into the skin. Repeat two or three times a day. Don't apply to broken skin or near the eyes or nose. Wash hands after use.   WHITEHALL

Alka-Seltzer

Effervescent tablets containing aspirin, and, when mixed with water, the antacids sodium citrate and sodium bicarbonate, for the relief of headache with upset stomach, particularly when due to too much eating or drinking. Alka-Seltzer is especially effective when taken before bed and again in the morning. Can also be taken for the relief of migraine, period pain and aches and pains associated with colds and flu. Not suitable for children under 12.

Dosage: two tablets in water. The dose may be

repeated every four hours, up to four doses in 24 hours.

BAYER CONSUMER

Aller.eze

Tablets for relief from hay-fever symptoms, itchy, watery eyes, perennial rhinitis, insect bites and skin allergies. Contains the antihistamine clemastine hydrogen fumarate. Brings relief without drowsiness in 90% of users, but may cause drowsiness in remaining 10%. Not to be taken during pregnancy or breast-feeding except under medical direction.

Dosage: adults and children over 12 – one tablet night and morning. Children 7–12 years – half to one tablet night and morning; 3–6 years – half a tablet night and morning. Tablets should be taken with water before meals.

INTERCARE

Aller.eze Clear

Tablets containing terfenadine for the symptomatic relief of allergic rhinitis including hay fever and allergic skin disorders.

Dosage: adults and children over 12: one tablet twice a day (or two tablets in the morning). Tests have shown that terfenadine does not cause drowsiness. However, as with all medicines, care

must be taken when first using it because there may be rare exceptions.

INTERCARE

Aller.eze Plus

Brings relief from nasal and sinus congestion, hay fever and other allergy symptoms without drowsiness for 90% of users, but may cause drowsiness. Contains an antihistamine, clemastine hydrogen fumarate, and a decongestant, phenyl-propanolamine hydrochloride. Not recommended for children. Not to be taken during pregnancy or when breast-feeding.

Dosage: one tablet every six hours. No more than four tablets a day.

INTERCARE

Alophen

Pills for the relief of constipation due to sluggishness of the lower bowel containing aloin, an irritant laxative; belladonna extract, a muscle relaxant; ipecacuanha root, used as a laxative; and phenolpthalein. Not suitable for children. Adults should take one to three pills at bedtime. Relief is usually prompt, occurring within eight to ten hours. Prolonged, continuous use is not recommended.

Alophen should not be used without a doctor's advice

when nausea, vomiting or abdominal pain are present. It shouldn't be used by patients with inflammatory bowel diseases or with glaucoma, and should be used with caution in patients with prostatic enlargement.

WARNER LAMBERT

Alphosyl
Lotion and cream containing alcoholic extract of coal tar and allantoin for the treatment of psoriasis and psoriasis of the scalp. Apply liberally two to four times daily. Rub vigorously into affected areas. STAFFORD MILLER

Alphosyl 2 in 1 Shampoo
Shampoo containing alcoholic extract of coal tar for the treatment of scalp disorders such as psoriasis, seborrhoeic dermatitis, scaling and itching (often associated with eczema) and dandruff. Use as shampoo, massaging second application for several minutes. For dandruff use once or twice weekly. For other conditions use every two or three days. STAFFORD MILLER

Aludrox
Tablets for the relief of indigestion, heartburn and acidity, containing aluminium hydroxide/magnesium carbonate co-dried gel and magnesium hydroxide. One or two tablets should be sucked or chewed four times daily and at bedtime, or as required.

CHARWELL HEALTHCARE

Aludrox Liquid
Antacid liquid containing aluminium hydroxide, for the relief of indigestion, heartburn and acidity. Take one or two 5 ml spoonfuls undiluted or with a little water, either four times daily and at bedtime, or as required. CHARWELL HEALTHCARE

Anacal
Suppositories or ointment containing mucopoly-saccharide polysulphuric acid ester (Heparinoid) and oxypolyethoxydodecane (Lauromacrogol 400) for the relief of symptoms associated with haemorrhoids, anal itching and inflammation. One suppository to be inserted once or twice daily. Ointment to be applied one to four times a day as needed.

PANPHARMA

Anadin
Analgesic tablets, containing aspirin, caffeine and quinine sulphate, for relief of headache, neuralgia, colds and flu, rheumatic pain, period pain and dental pain. Not suitable for children under 12. Take two tablets every four

hours, but no more than 12 tablets in any 24 hours. Also available in soluble form (soluble tablets do not contain quinine sulphate).   WHITEHALL

Anadin All Night

Tablets containing aspirin for the treatment of overnight pain. Adult dosage: for best results take two tablets at least one to two hours before going to bed. Do not give this product to children under 12 years. Do not take any other painkillers, including aspirin, in the evening or during the night. Do not exceed the stated dose.   WHITEHALL

Anadin Extra

Easy-to-swallow tablets, containing aspirin, paracetamol and caffeine, for the treatment of headache, migraine, neuralgia, rheumatic, period and dental pains and the symptoms of colds and influenza. Not suitable for children under 12.

Dosage: one or two tablets every four hours. No more than six tablets in any 24 hours.

Also available in soluble form.   WHITEHALL

Anadin Maximum Strength

Analgesic capsules containing aspirin and caffeine for the treatment of headache, migraine, neuralgia, rheumatic, period and dental pains and the symptoms of colds and flu. Not for children under 12.

Dosage: one to two capsules every four hours. No more than eight capsules in any 24 hours.   WHITEHALL

Anadin Paracetamol

Easy-to-swallow paracetamol tablets for the treatment of headache, migraine, neuralgia, rheumatic, period and dental pains and the symptoms of colds and flu. Not for children under 6.

Dosage: adults and children over 12 – two tablets. Children 6–12 years – half to one tablet. The dose should not be repeated more frequently than every four hours and not more than four doses should be given in any 24-hour period.   WHITEHALL

Anbesol

Sugar-free liquid for mouth ulcers, teething pains and denture irritation. It contains lignocaine hydrochloride, a local anaesthetic, and chlorocresol and cetylpyridinium, both antiseptics. Apply to the affected area with the fingertip. Two applications immediately will normally be sufficient to obtain pain relief. Repeat as often as necessary. For teething in babies: wet the fingertip with Anbesol and spread gently on to the sore area of the gum. One application will be sufficient. Don't repeat the application for at least half an hour.

WHITEHALL

Andrews Answer

An effervescent, lemon-flavoured drink to relieve headache with upset stomach. Contains a full 1 gm dose of paracetamol, so don't take other pain-relievers within four hours. Also contains the stimulant caffeine; an antacid, sodium bicarbonate, to settle the stomach; and citric acid, used as a flavouring.

Each sachet contains a complete dose. Dissolve the contents of one sachet in a glass of water, stir and drink when effervescence subsides. Don't take more than four sachets in 24 hours. Not suitable for children under 18.

STERLING HEALTH

Andrews Antacid

For fast relief of three kinds of indigestion – heartburn, acid indigestion and trapped wind. Contains calcium carbonate and heavy magnesium carbonate to neutralise excess acid. Adults should suck or chew one to two tablets as needed. Do not exceed 12 tablets in 24 hours. Not recommended for children.

STERLING HEALTH

Andrews Liver Salt

A sparkling drink containing an antacid, sodium bicarbonate, and a laxative, magnesium sulphate (Epsom Salts), as well as sucrose and citric acid flavouring. Drink freshens the mouth, settles the stomach and revives the system. Can be used as an antacid to settle an upset stomach, relieve indigestion and biliousness, or as a laxative.

Dosage: adults only – empty contents of sachet into glass of water and drink before fizziness subsides. As an antacid, or as a refreshing drink, use one sachet. As a laxative, use two sachets before breakfast or at bedtime. STERLING HEALTH

Anethaine Itch-Soothing Cream

Cream containing tetracaine hydrochloride, a local anaesthetic, to give prompt relief from insect bites, stings and nettle rash. Not for prolonged use and not suitable for infants under three. Smooth cream on to affected area. Repeat as needed two or three times daily.

SETON HEALTHCARE

Anodesyn

Triple-action ointment for piles, containing lignocaine hydrochloride, a local anaesthetic to relieve pain; ephedrine hydrochloride, a vasoconstrictor which narrows walls of blood vessels to reduce swelling; and allantoin, to promote healing.

To treat internal piles, attach the nozzle to the tube, squeeze tube until ointment starts to appear through the nozzle, then gently insert the nozzle into the rectum. Squeeze out the ointment while slowly withdrawing the nozzle. Use night and morning and after each bowel movement.

For external piles, wash the affected area with tepid water, dry and apply the ointment with gauze or lint. Repeat as required. SETON HEALTHCARE

Anthisan

Cream containing mepyramine maleate, an antihistamine, to relieve pain, itching and inflammation in nettle rash and insect bites and stings. Rub gently into affected areas two or three times daily for up to three days or as directed by your pharmacist or doctor. Discontinue should skin sensitivity occur. This cream should not be used for eczema or on extensively broken skin surfaces. If symptoms persist, consult your doctor.

RHONE POULENC

Antiseptic Throat Pastilles

Contain menthol, camphor and benzoic acid (an antiseptic) to soothe a dry, sore throat. Dissolve a pastille in the mouth as often as needed. ERNEST JACKSON

Anusol

Suppositories, cream and ointment for the relief of piles and other related ano-rectal conditions. Contain the antiseptic Balsam Peru; protective substances bismuth oxide and zinc oxide; the suppositories and ointment also contain bismuth subgallate, which has astringent properties. Said to be safe for use during pregnancy, but always consult your doctor first.

Anusol should be used night and morning and after each bowel movement. The cream is also helpful as a lubricant for use with the suppositories. The ointment should be applied on a gauze dressing. WARNER LAMBERT

Arret

Capsules for treatment of diarrhoea, containing loperamide hydrochloride which slows down gut wall muscles. Not suitable for children under 12. Adults should take two capsules initially and one capsule after every loose bowel movement. The usual dosage is three to four capsules a day (maximum eight daily). CENTRA HEALTHCARE

Ashton and Parsons Infants' Powders

Herbal powders containing tincture of matricaria for the relief of pain and gastric upset associated with teething.

Dosage: children over 6 months – one powder, dry on the tongue night and morning. Under 6 months – half a powder. If child is restless the dose may be repeated every one, two or three hours if necessary.

SMITHKLINE BEECHAM CONSUMER BRANDS

Asilone Tablets

For the relief of indigestion, acidity and heartburn, with dried aluminium hydroxide to combat excess acid and activated dimethicone to break down gas and relieve discomfort. Asilone gently soothes the stomach lining. Not suitable for children under 12.

Dosage: one or two tablets chewed or sucked before meals and at bedtime. For the relief of heartburn, the tablets should be sucked slowly. Also available in liquid form – the liquid also contains the antacid light magnesium oxide.

CROOKES HEALTHCARE

Askit Capsules and Powders

Capsules or powders containing caffeine, aspirin and aloxiprin (aluminium oxide and aspirin) for mild to moderate pain. Adults: two capsules at four-hourly intervals. Maximum 12 capsules in 24 hours. Or one powder with water every four hours as needed. Maximum six powders in 24 hours. Not recommended for children under 12 years except on medical advice.

ROCHE CONSUMER HEALTH

Aspro

Tablets containing aspirin for the relief of headache, rheumatic pain, sore throats, colds, flu, muscular aches, neuralgia, period pain, toothache, lumbago, sciatica and fibrositis. Dosage: adults only – two to three tablets every four hours as needed. No more than 12 tablets in 24 hours. ROCHE CONSUMER HEALTH

Aspro Clear

Soluble tablets containing aspirin for the relief of headache, migraine pain, neuralgia, colds, chills, flu, fibrositis, period pain, muscular pain, toothache, rheumatic pain.

Dosage: two to three tablets dissolved in half a glass of water every four hours as needed. No more than 13 tablets in 24 hours.

ROCHE CONSUMER HEALTH

Aspro Clear Maximum Strength

Soluble aspirin which contains the maximum single dose of aspirin available for self medication. For fast effective relief of migraine, headache, backache, toothache, period pain and for the symptomatic relief of colds and influenza, sore throat, feverishness, rheumatic pain and muscular aches and pains.

Dosage: adults and children over 12 years: one to two tablets every four hours as needed. Do not exceed eight tablets in 24 hours unless directed by a doctor. Not suitable for children under 12.

ROCHE CONSUMER HEALTH

Audax Ear Drops

Contain choline salicylate and glycerol for the relief of ear pain and for softening ear wax as an aid to its removal. To soften ear wax, use drops twice a day for four days. With the head tilted to one side, fill the ear canal with drops using the dropper provided. Plug the ear with cotton wool soaked in the ear drops.

Patients with ear pain should always seek medical advice.

NAPP

Aveeno

A range of cleansers and moisturisers based on oatmeal which has been used for centuries for its natural soothing and cleansing properties. All the Aveeno products are specially formulated for dry and sensitive skin and are suitable for adults, children and babies. The range includes a bath oil, powder bath additives, an all-purpose moisturiser called Aveenocream and a cleansing bar called AveenoBar.

BIOGLAN

Avena Sativa Comp.

A calming homoeopathic remedy to help you relax at night after the stresses and strains of a difficult day. With *Avena sativa, Humulus lupulus, Passiflora incarnata, Valeriana radix, Coffea tosta.* Ten to 20 drops to be taken in water half an hour before retiring. If necessary, this dose may be repeated up to a maximum of six doses a day. Children should take half the adult dose.   WELEDA

Avomine

Tablets containing promethazine theoclate (an antihistamine) for the prevention and treatment of travel sickness. Adults and children over 10 years: long journeys, one tablet the night before; short journeys: one tablet one or two hours before travelling or as soon as possible. Maximum four tablets in 24 hours. Not recommended for children under 10.   RHONE POULENC RORER

Balmosa

Analgesic cream containing levomenthol, racemic camphor, methyl salicylate and capsicum oleoresin for relief from pain associated with unbroken chilblains, muscular rheumatism, fibrositis, lumbago and sciatica. Do not apply to broken skin or near eyes and other sensitive areas. Gently rub Balmosa into the affected area and keep covered if possible.   PHARMAX

Balto Foot Balm

A natural blend of camphor, menthol, oils of pine and bladderwrack, protective zinc oxide and precipitated sulphur, a mild antiseptic. To soften hard, cracked skin, help curb excessive perspiration and cool tired, aching feet. Rub ointment into affected area night and morning.   LANES

Bansor Mouth Antiseptic

Solution containing cetrimide for the relief of symptoms of sore gums in all ages. Dosage: adults and children, apply a few drops to a clean finger and massage into affected gums.   THORNTON & ROSS

Bath E45

Dermatological bath oil to soothe and soften dry skin conditions, containing medicinal white oil to soften skin and cetyl dimethicone which acts as a barrier to protect against the irritating and drying effects of water or detergents.

Pour quarter of a capful into warm water, or apply on a wet sponge when showering. Blot skin gently with towel. Take care not to slip and, as with soap, avoid contact with the eyes.

CROOKES HEALTHCARE

Beconase Hayfever

Nasal spray containing beclomethasone dipropionate for the treatment of common symptoms of hayfever, such as sneezing and a runny, itching or blocked up nose. Dosage: adults two sprays into each nostril twice daily. Maximum eight sprays in 24 hours. Not recommended for children under 12 years.

ALLEN & HANBURYS

Beechams Hot Blackcurrant or Hot Lemon

Sachets of powder with an odour of blackcurrant or lemon containing paracetamol, the decongestant phenylephrine hydrochloride and Vitamin C for influenza, feverishness, chills and feverish colds including headache, sore throat, aches and pains, nasal congestion, sinusitis and its associated pain, and acute nasal catarrh.

Dosage: adults - one sachet every four hours in hot water, if necessary. Maximum of six sachets in 24 hours. Not for children except on medical advice.

SMITHKLINE BEECHAM CONSUMER BRANDS

Beechams Lemon Tablets

Dissolve-in-the-mouth tablets containing aspirin and glycine for the symptomatic relief of influenza, feverishness, chills and colds, including feverish colds, relief of mild to moderate pain including headache, migraine, neuralgia, toothache, sore throat, period pains, rheumatic pain and muscular aches and pains. Dosage: adults one to two tablets every three to four hours. Maximum 12 tablets in 24 hours. Not to be given to children under 12 years except on medical advice.

SMITHKLINE BEECHAM CONSUMER BRANDS

Beechams Pills

Tablets containing aloin, an irritant laxative for constipation. Adult dosage: take one to two pills with water at night.

SMITHKLINE BEECHAM CONSUMER BRANDS

Beechams Powders

Powders containing aspirin and caffeine for the symptomatic relief of influenza, chills and colds, mild to moderate pain, headache, migraine, neuralgia, toothache, sore throat, period pains, aches and pains, rheumatic pain and muscular aches and pains.

Dosage: adults one powder in water every three to four hours as needed. Maximum six powders in 24 hours. Children not recommended except on medical advice.

SMITHKLINE BEECHAM CONSUMER BRANDS

Beechams Powders Capsules

Capsules containing caffeine, paracetamol and

phenylephrine hydrochloride (a decongestant) for the symptomatic relief of influenza, feverishness, chills and colds and associated nasal congestion and difficult breathing, sinusitis and associated pain, acute nasal catarrh. Also for moderate pain.

Adults: take two capsules every three to four hours as needed. Maximum 12 capsules in 24 hours. Children 6–12: take one capsule every three to four hours as needed. Maximum 6 capsules in 24 hours. Not recommended under 6 years except on medical advice.

SMITHKLINE BEECHAM CONSUMER BRANDS

Bengue's Balsam

Topical rubefacient with menthol and methyl salicylate for easing pain due to rheumatic conditions and muscular strain. Massage up to four times a day. Can also be used as an inhalation from hot water for the symptomatic relief of congestion associated with head colds. Can be used to relieve chilblains but only on unbroken skin. Available in cream or ointment form.

CHANCELLOR

Benoxyl 5 or 10

Grease-free antiseptic medications containing benzoyl peroxide for treatment of acne. Apply daily. Also available in lotion form.

STIEFEL

Benylin

A syrup for the relief of coughs and the symptoms associated with phlegm. Works by dampening the cough and suppresses the production of phlegm to stop the runny nose. Contains an antihistamine, diphen-hydramine hydrochloride, and soothing menthol. Diphenhydramine hydro-chloride can help relieve coughs because its antitussive – cough-suppressant – and antihistaminic action neutralises the effects of histamine released by the body in allergic reactions. Benylin's anticholinergic actions block nerve impulses, especially those used to control intestinal spasm. It helps provide relief from nasal stuffiness, sneezing and watering of the eyes. It also has a local anaesthetic action which helps to relieve sore throats. May cause drowsiness. Can be taken by children, although for children from 1–4 years, Benylin Paediatric is recommended. Children from 6–12 years should take one 5 ml spoonful four times a day. Adult dosage: two 5 ml spoonfuls four times a day.   WARNER LAMBERT

Benylin with Codeine

Cough syrup for dry, irritating coughs. Combines the antitussive, antihistaminic, local anaesthetic and anticholinergic effects of diphenhydramine hydrochloride with the suppressive action of codeine phosphate. Also contains menthol. May cause drowsiness. Codeine may be habit-forming. Not recommended for children under five. Children 6–12 should take one 5 ml spoonful four times a day. Adult dosage: two 5 ml spoonfuls four times a day.   WARNER LAMBERT

Benylin Children's Cough Linctus

To give relief to the coughing child and to reduce bronchial and nasal congestion. Also beneficial in the treatment of hay fever and other allergic conditions affecting the upper respiratory tract. Combines the actions of diphen-hydramine hydrochloride (see BENYLIN, above) with the demulcent agent menthol, a soothing substance to help combat the congestive symptoms that frequently accompany the cough and reduce bronchial and nasal congestion. Not recommended for children under one year old. Dosage: children 6–12 years, two 5 ml spoonfuls four times a day; 1–5 years – one 5 ml spoonful four times a day. May cause drowsiness.

WARNER LAMBERT

Benylin Children's Coughs Sugar-Free, Colour-Free

Clear colourless syrup containing menthol and diphenhydramine hydrochloride. For the relief of coughs and congestive symptoms, hay fever, and allergic conditions affecting the upper respiratory tract.

Children 6 years and over: 10 ml four times a day. 1–5 years: 5 ml four times a day. Not recommended for children under 1 year.

WARNER LAMBERT

Benylin Day and Night Cold Treatment

A blister pack with 15 amber film-coated tablets and five blue film-coated tablets for the relief of symptoms associated with colds and flu. Amber tablets (daytime) combine the analgesic and antipyretic (fever-reducing) action of paracetamol with the decongestant action of phenyl-propanolamine hydrochloride. Blue (night-time) tablets combine paracetamol with the antihistamine, antitussive, antispasmodic and sedative action of diphenhydramine hydrochloride. May cause drowsiness. Not to be used in pregnancy. Not recommended for children under 12.

Dosage: four tablets daily, three amber during the day and one blue at night. Take only one tablet at a time and only at the times of day indicated on the pack. Do not take the night-time tablets during the day.   WARNER LAMBERT

Benylin Dry Cough Linctus

Contains diphenhydramine hydrochloride (see BENYLIN, above) to control dry, irritating coughs and the cough-suppressant dextromethorphan hydrobromide. Also contains menthol. Adult dosage: two 5 ml spoonfuls four times a day. Children 6–12 years – one 5 ml spoonful four times a day. For one to five-year-olds, Benylin Children's Cough Linctus is recommended (see above). Not recommended for children under one year old. May cause drowsiness.

WARNER LAMBERT

Benylin Dry Coughs Non-Drowsy

Amber peach flavoured syrup

containing dextromethorphan hydrobromide. For dry, persistent, irritating cough. Adults: 10 ml four times daily. Children 6–12 years: 5 ml four times daily. Not recommended for children under 6 years.   WARNER LAMBERT

Benylin Mentholated Linctus

Menthol-tasting and -smelling linctus to relieve nasal stuffiness, sneezing, watering of the eyes and sore throats. Particularly suitable for coughs associated with colds. Contains diphenhydramine hydrochloride (see BENYLIN, above), dextromethorphan hydrobromide to suppress the cough reflex and pseudo-ephedrine hydrochloride to combat the congestive symptoms that frequently accompany the cough and to reduce bronchial and nasal congestion.

Dosage: adults – two 5 ml spoonfuls four times daily. Children 6–12 years – one 5 ml spoonful four times daily. May cause drowsiness.

WARNER LAMBERT

Benylin Non-Drowsy for Chesty Coughs

A syrup to loosen phlegm and chesty catarrh making the cough more productive and aiding easier breathing without causing drowsiness. Contains the expectorant guaiphenesin and menthol.

Dosage: Adults – two 5 ml spoonfuls four times daily. Children 6–12 years – one 5 ml spoonful four times daily. Not recommended for children under 6.   WARNER LAMBERT

Benzagel 5 and 10

Gels containing benzoyl peroxide for the treatment of acne. Start treatment with Benzagel 5. Wash the affected areas with soap and water (this helps the Benzagel to penetrate the skin), dry and apply gel once or twice daily. The therapeutic response to benzoyl peroxide differs in individual patients, so you may need to use the stronger Benzagel 10.

BIOGLAN PHARMACEUTICALS

Betadine Antiseptic Paint

A solution containing povidone iodine – an antiseptic used in hospitals all over the world because of its effectiveness in killing all classes of germs – for the treatment and prevention of infection – as in cold sores, grazes, cuts, wounds or any break in the skin which needs protection from infection. Apply twice daily and cover with a dressing if desired.

Rinse the brush thoroughly after use.   SETON HEALTHCARE

Betadine Dry Powder Spray

Aerosol containing povidone iodine for use as a skin antiseptic for the treatment and prevention of infection in wounds, including ulcers, burns, cuts and other minor injuries. Shake the can well, spray the required area from a distance of 15–25 cm until coated with powder.

SETON HEALTHCARE

Betadine Gargle and Mouthwash

Solution containing povidone iodine for the treatment of infections of the mouth and pharynx. Use undiluted or diluted with an equal volume of warm water. Gargle or rinse with up to 10 ml for up to 30 seconds without swallowing. Repeat up to four times daily, for up to 14 consecutive days, or as directed. Not for use by children under 6.

SETON HEALTHCARE

Betadine Ointment

Ointment with povidone iodine – a broad spectrum antiseptic for the topical treatment or prevention of infection in minor cuts and abrasions and small areas of burns. For the treatment of infection – apply once or twice daily for a maximum of 14 days. For the prevention of infection – apply once or twice a week as necessary.

SETON HEALTHCARE

Betadine Scalp and Skin Cleanser

A solution containing povidone iodine for seborrhoeic conditions of the scalp and acne of the face and neck. Use as a shampoo, allowing cleanser to remain on the hair for at least five minutes. Repeat twice weekly until improvement is noted. Afterwards use once weekly.

For acne – apply directly or with a moistened sponge. Cleanse area thoroughly. Repeat application. Rinse with warm water and dry with a clean or sterile towel or gauze. Repeat twice daily until improvement is noted. Afterwards use once daily. Also available: Betadine Shampoo.   SETON HEALTHCARE

Betasept Shampoo

Specially formulated to control scalp conditions such as excessive dandruff, also infected sores and impetigo. Contains povidone iodine to relieve the symptoms of itching and redness, and help rid your scalp of excessive

oiliness and greasy scales, leaving your hair clean and manageable. It does not stain the skin or natural fabrics.

Before using this shampoo it is advisable to remove gold and silver jewellery since it may cause temporary discoloration. Use once as an ordinary shampoo, then after rinsing with warm water, apply shampoo again, massaging the scalp with the finger tips and work up a lather, using more warm water if needed. Leave for a few minutes, then rinse thoroughly. Repeat the treatment twice weekly until the condition improves. Afterwards, use shampoo once a week. If condition does not clear up, consult your doctor.

Regular use of this product should be avoided if you have a thyroid disorder, are pregnant, have a kidney problem or are receiving lithium treatment. As always, if in doubt consult your doctor or pharmacist. Children under 2 should not be treated with this product. Do not use if you are sensitive to iodine.

SETON HEALTHCARE

Biactol

Face wash with phenyoxylpropanol, an antibacterial, in a mild detergent base. Suitable for sensitive skin. Use daily instead of soap.

PROCTER AND GAMBLE

Bidor 1% Tablets

A course of treatment containing ferrous sulphate monohydrate and silica for the prevention of migraine. One tablet should be taken three times a day to help prevent the development of migraine attacks. Continue treatment for a period of from two to 12 weeks, according to the severity of the condition, to reduce the tendency to attacks. Bidor tablets should be swallowed with water, not chewed.

WELEDA

Biobalm

A traditional herbal remedy for indigestion, flatulence and stomach upsets. Contains slippery elm bark, marshmallow root powder and Irish moss powder.

MODERN HEALTH

Bioral Gel

Contains carbenoxolone sodium for the treatment of mouth ulcers. Carbenoxolone is thought to help soothe ulcers by provoking protective mucus production. Pat ulcer dry with a tissue and cover with a thick coating of Bioral. Apply after meals and at

bedtime. Suitable for both adults and children.

STERLING HEALTH

Bismag Tablets

Antacid tablets for the relief of indigestion, flatulence and stomach acidity, containing sodium bicarbonate and heavy and light magnesium carbonate. Take two to four tablets with water after meals and repeat in 15 minutes if necessary. A dose before going to bed is recommended.

WHITEHALL

BiSoDol Extra

Antacid tablets for the relief of heartburn, indigestion, acidity and flatulence, containing calcium carbonate, light magnesium carbonate, sodium bicarbonate and simethicone to break down gas. Take one or two tablets as required. Suck slowly or chew.

WHITEHALL

BiSoDol Powder

Mint-flavoured antacid powder for the relief of indigestion, dyspepsia, heartburn, acidity and flatulence. It contains sodium bicarbonate and heavy and light magnesium carbonate.

Dosage: one 5 ml spoonful well stirred into about one third of a tumbler of water (warm or cold) after meals or as required.

WHITEHALL

BiSoDol Tablets

Antacid digestant tablets for the relief of indigestion, dyspepsia, heartburn, acidity and flatulence. They contain calcium carbonate, light magnesium carbonate and sodium bicarbonate. Take one or two tablets, as required. Suck slowly or chew. Also available in spearmint flavour.

WHITEHALL

Blisteze Cream

For the quick relief of occasional cold sores, cracked and chapped lips. Contains a strong ammonia solution, an aromatic intended to relieve pain, and liquefied phenol, an antiseptic. Apply as soon as symptoms appear and repeat every hour if necessary. If you suffer from recurrent cold sores, consult your doctor. DDD

Bocasan Mouthwash

Bocasan is buffered sodium perborate monohydrate, an oxygenating oral rinse which supplies oxygen for the inhibition of the action of bacteria. It's also antiseptic and cleansing, used for the treatment of bleeding gums and other symptoms of gum disease and helpful in the control of dental plaque. Bocasan is suitable for use by both adults and children over five, although care should be taken to prevent children from swallowing the solution.

Use three times daily after meals. Dissolve the contents of one sachet in 30 ml of warm water – as hot as you would normally drink a cup of tea – and use immediately. Hold the rinse in the mouth for two to three minutes, swishing between the teeth. Do not swallow. After rinsing with Bocasan, do not cleanse the mouth with any other liquid for 30 minutes. Don't use for longer than seven days without consulting your doctor or dentist. ORAL-B

Bonjela Antiseptic Pain-relieving Pastilles

Soft pastilles containing lignocaine hydrochloride (a local anaesthetic) and aminacrine hydrochloride (an antiseptic) for the relief of the pain and discomfort of common mouth ulcers and denture sore spots.

Adults and children aged 6 years and over: place one pastille against the affected part and let it dissolve slowly. Repeat as necessary. Not recommended for children under 6. RECKITT & COLMAN

Bonjela Oral Pain-relieving Gel

Gel containing choline salicylate, a pain-reliever, and

cetalkonium chloride, an antiseptic, in a sugar-free base, for the relief of the pain and discomfort of common mouth ulcers, cold sores, denture spots and infant teething.

Dosage: adults – using a clean finger, massage approximately 15 mm of the gel into the sore area, not more than once every three hours. Children (from four months) – using a clean finger, massage approximately 8 mm of gel into the sore area, not more than once every three hours and not more than six doses in any 24-hour period.

For denture sore spots – apply to the gums and leave at least 30 minutes before reinsertion of the dentures. Do not apply this product directly to the dentures.

Preparations containing aspirin should not be given to children under 12 during Bonjela treatment.

RECKITT & COLMAN

Bonomint

Mint-flavoured chewing gum laxative with yellow phenophthalein. For overnight relief, chew before going to bed. It is only necessary to chew a tablet until the flavour is gone. Do not swallow.

Dosage: adults – one tablet; children over 6 – half to one tablet.

INTERCARE

Boots Day Cold Comfort Capsules

Contain paracetamol, pseudoephedrine hydro-chloride (a decongestant), and pholcodine (a cough-suppressant) to relieve major symptoms of colds and flu while avoiding drowsiness.

Dosage: adults and children over 12 – two capsules to be taken with a drink. Dose may be repeated every four hours up to a maximum of four doses in 24 hours if needed. If a dose of Boots Night Cold Comfort Capsules is taken at bedtime, then a maximum of three doses of Day Cold Comfort Capsules should be taken in 24 hours.

Children 6–12 years – one capsule to be taken with a drink. Dose may be repeated every four hours up to a maximum of four doses in 24 hours if needed. Children under 6 should not be given this medicine except on medical advice.

Do not use this medicine for long periods unless your doctor agrees. Do not take other medicines containing paracetamol while using Boots Day Cold Comfort Capsules. Do not exceed the stated dose. Patients suffering from asthma should consult their doctor before taking this product. Talk to your doctor before taking this medicine if you are receiving medical treatment or advice.

Also available in liquid form as Boots Day Cold Comfort.

BOOTS

Boots Double Action Indigestion Mixture

A combined treatment with the antacids aluminium hydroxide, magnesium hydroxide and activated methylpolysiloxane (which acts on the gas bubbles to relieve painful pressure in the stomach), to relieve the discomfort of painful wind, indigestion, heartburn and excess acidity.

Dosage: adults and children over 12 – two 5 ml spoonfuls after meals. A further dose may be taken at bedtime or whenever discomfort is felt. Children 5–12 years – one 5 ml spoonful. For children under 5, Boots Cream of Magnesia is recommended.

BOOTS

Boots Double Action Indigestion Tablets

A combined treatment with the antacids dried aluminium hydroxide gel and magnesium hydroxide for fast, effective relief from the discomfort of

painful wind, indigestion, heartburn and excess acidity. The tablets also contain activated polymethylsiloxane, which acts on the gas bubbles to relieve painful pressure in the stomach.

Dosage: adults and children over 12 – suck or chew one or two tablets after meals, at bedtime or whenever discomfort is felt; children 5–12 years – one tablet. For children under 5, Boots Cream of Magnesia is recommended.

BOOTS

Boots Mediclear Acne Cream 5 and 10

Contain benzoyl peroxide (in greater strength in Mediclear 10) to treat spots and acne. Apply cream to the affected areas. Massage gently with the fingertips until the cream vanishes. Wash hands after use. Apply once daily (with very fair skin apply once every other day). Not recommended for children under 12.

BOOTS

Boots Mediclear Acne Lotion

Treatment with benzoyl peroxide for spots and acne. Greaseless, colourless and odourless. Apply to the affected areas. Massage gently with the fingertips until the lotion vanishes. Wash hands after use. For the first week apply once daily (with very fair skin apply once every other day). After this, unless discomfort or irritation occurs, apply twice daily. Not recommended for children under 12.   BOOTS

Boots Night Cold Comfort Capsules

Contain paracetamol, pseudoephedrine hydrochloride (a decongestant), diphenhydramine hydrochloride (an antihistamine) and pholcodine (a cough-suppressant) to relieve the major symptoms of colds and flu for a restful night's sleep.

Dosage: adults and children over 12 – two capsules to be taken with a drink, at bedtime only. Do not exceed the stated dose. Children under 12 should not be given this medicine except on medical advice. Do not use for long periods unless your doctor agrees. Do not take other medicines containing paracetamol while using Boots Night Cold Comfort Capsules. May cause drowsiness.

If you suffer from asthma, consult your doctor before using this product. Talk to your doctor before taking this medicine if you are receiving medical treatment or advice.

Also available in liquid form as Boots Night Cold Comfort which also contains absolute alcohol.   BOOTS

Boots One-A-Day Antihistamine Tablets

Antihistamine tablets with terfenadine for relief from hay fever while avoiding drowsiness and not normally affecting your ability to drive or operate machinery. Also gives relief from rhinitis, insect bites and nettle rash. In tests Boots One-A-Day Antihistamine Tablets were shown not to cause drowsiness, but care must be taken when first using them because there may be rare exceptions.

Dosage: adults and children over 12 years – one tablet in the morning. Not recommended for children under 12. As with all medicines do not exceed the stated dose. If you are pregnant, talk to your doctor before taking this medicine.

                    BOOTS

Bradosol Plus

Throat lozenges containing the antiseptic domiphen bromide and the local anaesthetic lignocaine hydrochloride to numb sore throats and fight infection. Adults – one lozenge to be sucked every two to three hours, up to a maximum of eight lozenges per day. Do not use for more than four to five days. Not recommended for children under 12.   ZYMA

Bradosol Sugar Free Lozenges

Sugar-free antiseptic lozenges containing benzalkonium chloride for the relief of sore throats. Adults and children over 5 – one lozenge to be dissolved slowly in the mouth whenever required.   ZYMA

Brasivol Fine and Medium

Cleanser for acne containing scrub particles of fused aluminium oxide, an abrasive to clean the skin thoroughly. Available in two strengths. Before using, discontinue the use of all other soaps and skin cleansers. Apply to wet skin, rubbing gently in a circular motion for 15–20 seconds. Rinse with warm water and pat dry. Repeat two to three times daily or as directed by your doctor. If undue skin irritation occurs, discontinue use and consult your doctor.

STIEFEL

Brolene Eye Drops

Eye drops containing propamidine isethionate (an antibacterial agent) for the treatment of minor eye infections such as conjunctivitis and blepharitis. Children and adults: 1–2 drops up to four times daily. If no improvement after two days seek medical advice. Also available as Brolene with Autodrop.   RHONE POULENC RORER

Brolene Eye Ointment

Ointment containing antibacterial agent dibromopropamidine isethionate for the treatment of minor eye and eyelid infections such as conjunctivitis and blepharitis. Children and adults: apply once or twice daily. If no improvement after two days seek medical advice.

RHONE POULENC RORER

Brol-eze

Drops containing sodium cromoglycate for the treatment of eye problems related to allergic seasonal conjunctivitis including hay fever.   RHONE POULENC RORER

Bronalin Dry

Sugar- and colour-free elixir for the symptomatic relief of dry, tickly coughs and colds. Contains the cough-suppressant dextro-methorphan hydrobromide and pseudoephedrine hydro-chloride to fight congestion. Recommended for use by those with diabetes, but not for children under six. May cause drowsiness. Decongestant formula available without the cough suppressant.

Dosage: adults – one 5 ml spoonful four times a day; children 6–12 years – half a 5 ml spoonful four times a day.

Bronalin Expectorant Linctus

Sugar- and colour-free linctus containing the expectorants ammonium chloride and sodium citrate, and diphenhydramine hydrochloride, an antihistamine, for the symptomatic relief of deep, chesty coughs and colds. May cause drowsiness. Not for children under six. Not to be taken during pregnancy.

Dosage, to be taken three or four times daily: adults – one or two 5 ml spoonfuls; children 6–12 years, one 5 ml spoonful.

Bronalin Junior

Sugar-free, blackcurrant-flavoured linctus for the symptomatic relief of children's coughs and colds. Contains sodium citrate, an expectorant, and diphen-hydramine hydrochloride, an antihistamine. May cause drowsiness. Recommended for use by those suffering from diabetes.

Dosage, to be taken three times daily: children 5–12 years – two 5 ml spoonfuls; 1–5 years one 5 ml spoonful.

Bronchial Catarrh Pastilles

Contain soothing menthol, benzoin tincture, creosote (a disinfectant), aniseed oil, peppermint oil and capsicin (made from peppers) to relieve bronchial catarrh, coughs and colds.

Brooklax

Chocolate-flavoured laxative tablets with yellow phenolphthalein to relieve constipation. Should ideally be taken before going to bed.

Dosage: adults – half to two tablets; children over 6 – a quarter to one tablet.

Brulidine

Cream containing dibromopropamidine isethionate (an antibacterial agent) for first aid and treatment of minor burns, scalds, abrasions and other open injuries as well as superficial fungal infections, and also nappy rash. Adults apply to affected area two to three times daily.

Brush Off Cold Sore Treatment

A solution of povidone iodine to help limit the size and duration of a cold sore by killing the cold sore virus. Apply twice daily to the affected area and allow to dry. Do not use this product in rare cases of suspected iodine sensitivity. SETON HEALTHCARE

Burn Aid Cream

Soothing cream containing aminacrine hydrochloride, an antiseptic, for first-aid treatment of minor burns and scalds, cuts and abrasions. Apply to sore area and cover with a dressing if appropriate. Do not use repeatedly. Prolonged use may delay healing. SETON HEALTHCARE

Burneze

First-aid spray for minor burns and scalds, containing the local anaesthetic benzocaine. If the burn is extensive, seek medical help immediately. To reduce pain and blistering, use spray as quickly as possible. Spray 2.5 cm (1 in) from skin until all the pain has gone – this may take up to five seconds. If white frost appears, stop. Repeat after 15 minutes if necessary. Do not apply lint, bandage or other dressing.

Don't spray near eyes, and don't apply to broken skin.

SETON HEALTHCARE

Buscopan

Tablets containing hyoscine-n-butylbromide for stomach cramps and period pain.

Dosage: adults and children over 12 take two tablets swallowed whole with water four times daily. Take two days before period is due. Children 6–12: one tablet swallowed whole with water three times daily. Caution: not for use by patients with glaucoma. WINDSOR HEALTHCARE

Buttercup Blackcurrant Syrup

Syrup containing menthol, liquid glucose and ipecacuanha liquid extract (an expectorant) for chesty, bronchial and dry or tickly coughs. Soothes sore and irritated throat membranes, eases and relieves congestion. Adults two 5 ml spoonfuls every 2–3 hours. Children under 12 years one 5 ml spoonful every 2–3 hours.

LRC PRODUCTS

Buttercup Honey and Lemon Syrup

Syrup containing menthol, liquid glucose, purified honey and ipecacuanha liquid extract (an expectorant) for chesty, bronchial and dry or tickly coughs. Soothes sore and irritated throat membranes, eases and relieves congestion. Adults two 5 ml spoonfuls every 2–3 hours. Children under 12: one 5 ml spoonful every 2–3 hours. LRC PRODUCTS

Buttercup Syrup (Traditional Flavour)

Syrup containing squill liquid extract and capsicum tincture for coughs, colds, sore throats, hoarseness. Adults two 5 ml spoonfuls three times a day and before bedtime when the cough is troublesome.

LRC PRODUCTS

Caladryl

Soothing cream or lotion for the relief of irritation associated with hives, shingles and other minor skin complaints. Also helpful in the relief of sunburn, prickly heat, insect bites and nettle stings. Contains protective agent zinc oxide, antihistamine diphenhydramine hydrochloride and cooling camphor.

The lotion can be dabbed on the affected skin using a pad of cotton wool. The cream can be smoothed on lightly. But Caladryl shouldn't be put on raw skin or mucous membranes. If a burning sensation or rash develops, or if the condition persists,

treatment should be discontinued. WARNER LAMBERT

Calendula Lotion

A healing lotion containing calendula for cuts, abrasions or minor wounds and skin infections. May be used as a mouthwash. Add one 5 ml spoonful to a glass of cooled boiled water to cleanse wound or to use as a compress; one 5 ml spoonful to half a glass of lukewarm boiled water for a mouthwash. WELEDA

Calgel

A herbal-flavoured sugar-free gel for teething pain, containing lignocaine hydrochloride and cetylpyridinium chloride. Apply directly to the affected gums. Repeat after 20 minutes if necessary, up to six times in one day. WELLCOME

Califig

California Syrup of Figs with senna, a natural irritant laxative, for relief from constipation for all the family. To be taken at bedtime.

Dosage: adults – one to two 15 ml spoonfuls. Children 6–15 years – one and a half to three 5 ml spoonfuls; 3–6 years – one to two 5 ml spoonfuls; 1–3 years – half to one 5 ml spoonful.

STERLING HEALTH

Calpol Infant Suspension

Paracetamol suspension to relieve pain, including teething pain and feverishness such as accompanies colds and flu, without irritating the stomach. Most suitable for babies and children from three months to six years. Also available in sugar-free form.

Dosage: children 1–6 years – one to two 5 ml spoonfuls; babies 3 months to 1 year – half to one 5 ml spoonful. Don't give more than four doses in 24 hours. Don't repeat doses more frequently than every four hours, and don't continue treatment for more than three days without consulting a doctor. For babies under 3 months, a 2.5 ml dose (half a 5 ml spoonful) is suitable if fever develops following vaccination at two months; in other cases, use only under medical supervision. WELLCOME

Calpol Six Plus

Paracetamol suspension for pain associated with headaches, toothache and fever relief for children over six years old.

Dosage, to be taken four times a day: adults and children over 12 – two to four 5ml spoonfuls. Children 6–12 years – one to two 5 ml spoonfuls. For children three months to under six years, Calpol Infant Suspension is recommended (see above). The safety advice given for Calpol Infant Suspension also applies to this product. WELLCOME

Canesten 1

A vaginal tablet containing clotrimazole. A single dose pack is a full course of treatment. One tablet to be inserted into vagina at night. Not suitable for children. Canesten cream also available.

BAYER

Canesten 10% VC

A pre-filled applicator of vaginal cream wrapped in foil; contains clotrimazole. The single-dose pack is a full dose. Carefully following instructions included in pack, insert the pre-filled applicator of cream into the vagina at night before going to sleep. The vaginal cream is for external use and should not be put into your mouth or swallowed. The symptoms of thrush such as burning, soreness or itching of the vagina and surrounding area should disappear within three days of treatment. If no improvement is seen after seven days, tell your doctor. Canesten 10% VC may rarely cause side-effects in some people. The side-effects are very similar to the symptoms of thrush. If the burning, irritation or swelling get worse, see your doctor as soon as possible.   BAYER

Capasal Therapeutic Shampoo

For the treatment of dandruff, scalp psoriasis, seborrhoeic dermatitis and cradle cap. Contains salicylic acid, whose keratolytic action loosens and removes scalp scale and scalp debris; coconut oil, an effective emollient to soften and moisturise the scalp; and coal tar, an antipruritic (itch-soothing) and therapeutic agent. Use as a shampoo, daily if necessary. Leave lather on for a few minutes before washing out. Apparently safe for use in pregnancy and for children – there are no known side-effects in either case.

DERMAL LABORATORIES

Carnation Corn Caps

Corn caps with a ring of felt to relieve pressure on the corn and give immediate relief. Also contain salicylic acid to reduce the size of the corn. Packs contain five corn caps for a ten-day treatment.

CUXSON GERRARD

Carnation Verruca Treatment

Each pack of Carnation Verruca Treatment contains a complete course of treatment for one verruca. It consists of four medicated plasters and one protective plaster each packed in a labelled sachet. The active constituent is salicylic acid.

Make sure that the skin around the verruca is clean, dry and intact. Do not apply the treatment if the skin is inflamed or broken. Remove the white paper from one of the medicated plasters and apply it centrally to the verruca. Leave it in place for two days. During this time there is no need to restrict walking, sports or bathing, although violent activity may dislodge the plaster.

After two days remove the plaster, gently scrape away any loose skin from the verruca and clean the surrounding skin. After making sure the skin is dry, apply a fresh medicated plaster and leave for another two days. Repeat this treatment until all the medicated plasters have been used. The time from the start to the finish of treatment should be about eight days. Finally, in order to allow healing and to prevent infection, cover the treated area with the protective plaster. If the verruca has not disappeared after four weeks, repeat treatment. Not recommended for use by those suffering from diabetes. Do not treat more than three verrucas at the same time.

The treatment may cause some mild pain and soreness. If pain is severe, remove the medicated plaster, clean the skin and cover with the protective plaster. In these cases treatment should not be repeated. If you are over 50 or under six years old, consult your doctor to make sure that it is a verruca you are treating.   CUXSON GERRARD

Carylderm Lotion

Contains carbaryl for the treatment of head lice infestations. Sprinkle lotion on the hair and rub gently on to the head until the entire scalp is moistened. Pay special attention to the back of the neck and the area behind the ears. Take care to avoid the eyes. Allow hair to dry naturally – use no heat. The hair may be shampooed after two hours. While still wet, comb the hair with an ordinary comb. Then use a nit comb to remove the dead lice and eggs. Treatment should be carried out in a well-ventilated room to avoid any discomfort from the alcohol fumes. Can also be used to treat pubic lice.

Children under the age of six months should be treated under medical supervision. The lotion also contains isopropyl alcohol which may cause wheezing in patients suffering from asthma or cause stinging or inflammation of the skin in patients with severe eczema. In either case it may be more appropriate to use Carylderm Shampoo.   NAPP

Carylderm Shampoo

Contains carbaryl for the treatment of head lice. Wet the hair thoroughly and apply shampoo. Work up a lather and ensure that no part of the scalp is left uncovered. Pay special attention to the back of the neck and the area behind the ears. Take care to avoid the eyes. Leave for at least five minutes. Rinse thoroughly with clean, warm water and repeat. While the hair is still wet, comb with an ordinary comb. Then use a nit comb to remove the dead lice and eggs. This treatment should be carried out a total of three times at three-day intervals. Children under the age of six months should be treated under medical supervision. Can also be used to treat pubic lice.   NAPP

Catarrh-Ex

Tablets with paracetamol and the decongestant pseudo-ephedrine hydrochloride for the relief of congestion associated with pain and fever. Relieves the symptoms of nasal congestion, blocked sinuses, feverishness, aches, pains, colds and flu.

Dosage, to be taken three times a day: adults and children over 12 – one tablet. Children 6–12 years – half a tablet. THOMPSON MEDICAL

Catarrh Pastilles

Contain soothing menthol, abietis pine oil, sylvestris pine oil and creosote (a disinfectant) to ease the symptoms of catarrh and an irritating cough. Dissolve one pastille slowly in the mouth when required. ERNEST JACKSON

Ceanel Concentrate

Liquid containing undecenoic acid (an antifungal agent), cetrimide (an antiseptic) and phenylethyl alcohol (an antibacterial agent) for use as an adjunct in the management of psoriasis of the scalp, seborrhoeic dermatitis, dandruff and psoriasis of the trunk and limbs. Adults: use three times in the first week. Twice weekly thereafter.

QUINODERM

Cepton Medicated Skin Wash, Lotion and Gel

For the treatment of acne. Contain the antiseptic chlorhexidine gluconate.

Use Wash morning and night. Wash hands and face in the normal way. Wash with undiluted skin wash, rinse and repeat. For maximum effect, leave the second wash on the skin for one minute before rinsing.

Use Lotion morning and night. After washing, moisten a cotton wool pad with lotion and apply to the face, particularly around the nose, forehead and chin. Do not rinse off. After shaving, pour lotion on to the hands and splash on to the face. During the day, moisten a pad or tissue with lotion and apply to oily areas to cleanse, tone and remove greasy patches as they appear.

Use Gel morning and night. After washing the face, apply a thin coating of the gel to the affected area and work in thoroughly. ZYMA

Cerumol

Ear drops for the loosening and removal of ear wax. They contain paradichlorobenzene, an insecticide, chlorbutol, which has antibacterial properties, and arachis oil. Insert five drops into the ear

when the head is inclined,
preferably when lying down.
This may cause a harmless
tingling sensation. If the drops
run out when the head is held
up, a small plug of cotton
wool moistened with Cerumol
may be applied. Repeat two or
three times daily for up to
three days. Unless the ear wax
is unusually hard it should
run out of its own accord. If
not, consult your doctor for
possible syringing. You are
advised to consult your doctor
in all cases of ear disorder
before using any ear drops.
Use this product within six
months of opening.

LABORATORIES FOR APPLIED BIOLOGY

Chamomilla 3 × Drops or Pillules

Third homoeopathic potency
of *Matricaria chamomilla* for the
relief of colicky pain and
teething troubles in infants.

Dosage – drops: five to ten
drops to be taken in a little
water three times a day, or, if
necessary, five drops can be
taken every half hour until
the condition improves, for up
to four hours. Dosage –
pillules: one to five pillules to
be dissolved in the mouth
every half hour until the
condition improves. For
children under six months,
the pillules may be crushed.

WELEDA

Chapstick and Sunblock 15

Moisturiser for chapped lips.
Available in original, mint,
orange, cherry and strawberry
flavours as well as a Sunblock
15. All variants contain a
sunscreen. Apply as required.

WHITEHALL

Charcoal Tablets

Said to absorb excess gas in
the intestinal tract, relieving
flatulence and heartburn and
also thought to be helpful in
treating dyspepsia and
occasional diarrhoea.   LANES

Chilblain Cream

Cream containing methyl
nicotinate, a vasodilator – it
helps bring blood to the
surface of the skin and can
help improve circulation, for
the symptomatic relief of
aches associated with
chilblains. Gently bathe
affected parts in warm water.
Dry carefully. Apply cream
sparingly morning and night
and more frequently if
needed.   J. PICKLES & SONS

Children's Cough Pastilles

Contain honey, ascorbic acid,
squill liquid extract and
ipecacuanha liquid extract –
expectorants, to ease a child's
persistent cough. Pastilles can
be taken as needed, but
limited over a 24-hour period
as follows: children over

8 years – 12 pastilles;
6–8 years – ten pastilles;
3–5 years – eight pastilles.

ERNEST JACKSON

Chymol Emollient Balm

Ointment balm containing
eucalyptus oil, terpineol,
methyl salicylate, and phenol
for chapped and sore skin,
chilblains, bruises and sprains.
To be applied to the affected
areas as required.   ROSMARINE

Cirkulin Garlic Pearls

Contain organically grown
Chinese garlic. May help
relieve colds and maintain a
healthy heart and circulation.
Take two tablets three times a
day with a little water, ideally
before meals. Swallow whole.

CEDAR HEALTH

Clariteyes Eye Drops

New eye drops containing
sodium cromoglycate for extra
relief from itchy, runny eyes
in hay fever.   SCHERING PLOUGH

Clarityn

Antihistamine tablets
containing loratadine for fast
relief from the symptoms of
hay fever, allergic rhinitis,
some skin allergies and
urticaria.

  Dosage: adults and children
over 12 – one tablet daily
when symptoms require
treatment. The effect of each
tablet lasts 24 hours. Do not
exceed the stated dose. Do not
use during pregnancy.

SCHERING-PLOUGH CONSUMER HEALTH

Clearasil Medicated Cleansing Milk and Lotion

Antibacterial cleansing milk
for combination skin and
lotion for oily skin to help
prevent spots. Wash face and
neck with a mild soap,
moisten cotton pad with
lotion or milk and cleanse.
Repeat with fresh cotton pads
until no trace of dirt remains.
Do not rinse once cleansing is
complete. Use morning and
night.   PROCTER AND GAMBLE

Clearasil Medicated Cream

For treatment of spots and
blackheads. Contains triclosan,
an antibacterial agent, and
precipitated sulphur, an
antiseptic; it works by killing
the bacteria that can cause
spots. Ultra Clearasil, with
benzoyl peroxide, is also
available. Spread over problem
areas, or directly on to spots.

PROCTER AND GAMBLE

Clearasil Medicated Cream Colourless

A colourless cream containing
the same active ingredients as
the skin-tinted medicated
cream above. Adults and
children: wash affected areas
and apply twice daily.

PROCTOR AND GAMBLE

Cocois

A specially formulated ointment for the treatment of scaly scalp caused by psoriasis, eczema, seborrhoeic dermatitis and dandruff. It is based on a tried and trusted formulation and contains coal tar solution, salicylic acid, and sulphur in a coconut oil emollient base. It contains no steroids.

Apply daily to the affected area as initial treatment, then as frequently as needed to control the condition. Cocois should be massaged in gently and left for an hour, then washed out with a mild shampoo. BIOGLAN

Coda-Med

Tablets with paracetamol, codeine phosphate and caffeine for the symptomatic relief of tension headache, rheumatic pain, toothache, neuralgia, period pain, flu and colds. Also help to lower the temperature in mild feverish conditions. Not to be given to children under eight except on medical advice. No more than four doses to be taken in 24 hours.

Dosage: adults – one or two tablets every four hours. Children 8–14 years – one tablet every four hours.

THOMPSON MEDICAL

Codanin

Strong analgesic tablets containing paracetamol and codeine for the relief of bad headaches, migraine, period pains, neuralgia, rheumatic pains and dental pain. Not suitable for children under six except on medical advice.

Dosage: adults – two tablets with water at three- to four-hour intervals as required. Don't exceed eight tablets in 24 hours. Children 6–12 years – half a tablet with water as above. Don't exceed four doses in 24 hours. WHITEHALL

Codella

A non-greasy cream for dry, cracked skin and torn cuticles. Contains glycerin, kaolin and the antiseptic povidone iodine to act as a barrier to protect the skin, leaving it soft and supple. Use a small amount and rub well into the skin until absorbed. NAPP

Codis 500

Analgesic tablets containing aspirin and codeine phosphate for the relief of mild to moderate pain including headache, migraine, neuralgia, toothache, period pains, aches and pains and the symptoms of colds, influenza and feverish conditions. Also for the symptomatic relief of sprains, strains, rheumatic pain, sciatica, lumbago, fibrositis, muscular aches and pains, joint swelling and stiffness.

Dosage – adults and children over 12: one to two tablets as directed, dissolved in water. The dose may be repeated after four hours. Maximum eight tablets in 24 hours in divided doses. Not for children under 12 except on doctor's advice.

RECKITT & COLMAN

Cojene

Tablets containing aspirin, codeine phosphate and caffeine to relieve rheumatic pain and a painkiller. Dosage: adults and children over 12 years – one to two tablets. Maximum six tablets in 24 hours. The single dose may be repeated after four hours if needed. If symptoms persist for more than three days consult your doctor. Prolonged use, except on medical advice, may be harmful. Not for children under 12 years.

ROCHE CONSUMER HEALTH

Coldrex

Available as tablets, blackcurrant-flavoured drink or real lemon-flavoured drink, for relief from the symptoms of colds and flu, and to soothe sore throats. Tablets contain paracetamol; phenylephrine hydrochloride to clear a stuffy nose; the stimulant caffeine; terpin hydrate, a cough expectorant; and Vitamin C. Drinks do not contain expectorant or caffeine. Take tablets at first signs of a cold or flu every four hours.

Dosage – tablets: adults – two tablets up to four times a day. Children 6–12 years – one tablet up to four times a day. Not to be given to children under six. Dosage – drink: adults – one sachet up to four times a day. Empty contents into a tumbler and fill with very hot water. Stir until dissolved and sweeten if desired with honey or sugar. Not to be given to children under 12.

Some medicines don't combine with these products. If you are pregnant or already taking medicines, ask your doctor's advice before taking Coldrex.

STERLING HEALTH

J. Collis Browne's Tablets

Peppermint-flavoured tablets containing light kaolin, morphine hydrochloride and calcium carbonate to treat diarrhoea in colic, mild forms of gastro-enteritis, mild food poisoning and 'holiday tummy'. Not suitable for children under six.

Dosage: adults and children

over 10 – two to three tablets at once, followed by two to three tablets every four hours. Chew tablets before swallowing. Children 6-10 years, one tablet at once, followed by one tablet every four hours.

NAPP

J. Collis Browne's Mixture

For the relief of diarrhoea and tummy upsets. Contains anhydrous morphine to slow down the movement of the bowel wall.

Dosage: adults and children over 12 – two to three 5 ml spoonfuls once or twice at four-hourly intervals if required. Children 6–12 years – one 5 ml spoonful as above. Not suitable for children under six.

NAPP

Colsor Lotion and Cream

For cold sores. Both contain phenol, menthol and tannic acid (an astringent). J. PICKLES

Combudoron Lotion

Homoeopathic lotion with extracts of *Urtica urens*, *Herba*, *Arnica montana* and *Planta tota*, for the relief of sunburn, insect bites, minor burns and minor rashes, including nettle rash. Use one 5 ml spoonful to a cup of boiled water. Soak a piece of lint in the solution and apply as a compress. Keep moist. Use the lotion undiluted on insect bites.

WELEDA

Compound V

Liquid verruca remover containing salicylic acid. Treatment kit includes verruca cushions, plasters and abraders. Apply a drop at a time until the verruca is covered. Place a cushion around the verruca, then apply a plaster over the cushion. Repeat daily for up to four weeks, rubbing off the top layer of dead skin with an abrader before each application. Anyone suffering from diabetes should consult their doctor before using.

WHITEHALL

Compound W

Liquid wart- and verruca-remover containing salicylic acid. Not to be used for children under six. Apply a drop at a time until the wart or verruca is covered. Cover with a waterproof plaster. Repeat daily for up to four weeks, removing and replacing or changing the plaster each day until the wart or verruca disappears. WHITEHALL

Conotrane

Medicated cream with dimethicone, a water-repellent, and benzalkonium chloride, a mild but effective antiseptic, for the treatment and prevention of nappy rash. Apply to the affected area several times a day as necessary or after every nappy change.

BOEHRINGER INGELHEIM

Contac CoughCaps

Capsules containing dextromethorphan hydrobromide (a cough suppressant) for an unproductive cough. Adults: take one capsule twice daily at eight-hourly intervals. Maximum of two capsules in 24 hours. Children not recommended except on medical advice.

SMITHKLINE BEECHAM CONSUMER BRANDS

Contac 400

Capsules containing phenylpropanolamine hydrochloride, which constricts blood vessels to ease congestion, and chlorpheniramine maleate, an antihistamine. Gives up to 12 hours' relief from cold and allergy symptoms such as runny nose, sneezing and congestion.

SMITHKLINE BEECHAM CONSUMER BRANDS

Copholco

Cough syrup for the relief of ticklish coughs with

pholcodine (a cough-suppressant), terpin hydrate (an expectorant), menthol and aromatic cineole.

Dosage: adults – two 5 ml spoonfuls without water to be sipped slowly four to five times daily. Children over 8 years – one 5 ml spoonful taken as above. As with any medicine, if you are pregnant or breast-feeding, consult your doctor before taking this product. ROCHE CONSUMER HEALTH

Copholcoids

Cough pastilles for the relief of ticklish coughs with the same active ingredient and safety advice as Copholco syrup, above. Adults should suck one or two pastilles three or four times daily according to the severity of the condition. Children over 8 years – suck one pastille three times daily at four-hourly intervals. ROCHE CONSUMER HEALTH

Copper Ointment

For the relief of muscular rheumatic pain containing a copper salt in a base with yellow soft paraffin. Apply thinly and massage well into the affected area once or twice a day. WELEDA

Corlan Pellets

Newly available over-the-counter Corlan Pellets are

hydrocortisone lozenges for use in recurrent aphthous ulceration of the mouth. Children under 12 years should receive medical advice before treatment. Adults: one pellet four times a day to be kept in the mouth near the ulcer. Do not exceed the stated dose. If symptoms persist, consult your doctor.

EVANS

Correctol Laxative

Gentle laxative with dioctyl sodium sulphusuccinate to soften intestinal waste that has become too dry and hard, and yellow phenolphthalein, a laxative. Not to be used during pregnancy or breast-feeding. Not recommended for children under 12.

Dosage: adults and children over 12 – one tablet as needed at bedtime or on waking.

SCHERING-PLOUGH CONSUMER HEALTH

Covonia Bronchial Balsam

Linctus containing guaiphenesin, menthol, dextromethorphan hydrobromide (a cough suppressant) for symptomatic relief in non-productive coughs such as those associated with the common cold and bronchitis.

Adult dosage: three 5 ml spoonfuls repeated after four hours. Elderly: two 5 ml

spoonfuls repeated after four hours with caution. Children 6–12 years: two 5 ml spoonfuls repeated after four hours. Not recommended for children under 6 years.

THORNTON & ROSS

Covonia for Children

Sugar-free linctus with no artificial colourings containing dextromethorphan hydrobromide (a cough suppressant) for the relief of symptoms of non-productive coughs such as those associated with the common cold. Children 2–5 years: one 5 ml spoonful repeated every four to six hours as needed; 6–12 years: one to two 5 ml spoonfuls repeated every 4–6 hours as needed. Not recommended for children under 2.

THORNTON & ROSS

Crampex

Tablets containing nicotinic acid – one of the Vitamin B group; calcium in the form of calcium gluconate; and cholecalciferol – Vitamin D3; for the relief of muscle cramp at night. Not recommended for children.

Dosage: adults, including the elderly – one or two tablets with a drink, preferably before retiring. If symptoms persist, consult your doctor.

NAPP

Cream E45

Unperfumed, non-greasy, dermatological cream for dry skin conditions. Contains the emollients white soft paraffin, light liquid paraffin and hypoallergenic anhydrous lanolin. Helpful in treatment of sunburn, flaking, chapped skin, nappy soreness, 'detergent hands', dermatitis, the dry stage of eczema and certain cases of psoriasis. Also helps soften rough, hard skin on other parts of the body.

CROOKES HEALTHCARE

Cremalgin Balm

Balm containing glycol monosalicylate, methyl nicotinate and capsicum oleoresin for the symptomatic relief of rheumatism, sciatica, lumbago, fibrositis and muscular stiffness. Adults: massage into affected area two to three times daily.

RHONE POULENC RORER

Cupal Baby Chest Rub

Menthol, eucalyptus and turpentine oil rub for babies and young children, for symptomatic relief of nasal catarrh and congestion due to colds. Rub on the chest, throat and back morning and night. Leave bedding and clothes loose to allow easy inhalation of the vapours. Don't apply directly to the nostrils and keep away from the eyes.

SETON HEALTHCARE

Cupal Baby Cough Syrup

A blackcurrant-flavoured, sugar-free syrup to relieve and soothe the irritating and distressing coughs often accompanying colds. Specially prepared for babies over three months and young children, it contains dilute acetic acid, an expectorant.

Dosage, to be given slowly: three months to a year – half a 5 ml spoonful. Over 1 year – one 5 ml spoonful. Over $2\frac{1}{2}$ years – two 5 ml spoonfuls. Repeat as necessary every two or three hours.   SETON HEALTHCARE

Cupal Cold Sore Lotion

Contains the antiseptic povidine iodine for the treatment of skin infections caused by bacteria and viruses, especially cold sores. Apply twice daily to the affected area and allow to dry. Avoid use in rare cases of iodine sensitivity.

SETON HEALTHCARE

Cupal Cold Sore Ointment

Soothing antiseptic for the treatment of cold sores containing diperodon hydrochloride, a local anaesthetic; allantoin to encourage healing; cooling camphor; and protective zinc oxide. Apply the ointment to cold sores on the lips, five or six times a day. SETON HEALTHCARE

Cupanol Over Six

Sugar-free, colour-free, animal-fat-free paracetamol suspension for the relief of mild to moderate pain including headache, migraine, neuralgia, toothache and sore throat in children over six. Also for the symptomatic relief of flu, feverishness and colds.

Dose to be taken no more frequently than every four hours, and no more than four doses in 24 hours. Adults and children over 12 – two to four 5 ml spoonfuls. Children 6–12 – one to two 5 ml spoonfuls.

SETON HEALTHCARE

Cupanol Under Six

Sugar-free, colour-free, paracetamol oral suspension for the relief of pain and feverish conditions in children over three months old.

Dose to be taken four times daily – don't repeat more frequently than every four hours. Children over 5 years – three or four 5 ml spoonfuls. Children 1–5 years – two 5 ml spoonfuls. Three months to one year, half to one 5 ml spoonful. SETON HEALTHCARE

Cuprofen Ibuprofen Tablets

For the relief of headaches, migraine, neuralgia and fibrositis, backache and lumbago, rheumatic and muscular pains, period and dental pains. Also for the symptomatic relief of colds, flu and feverishness. Not suitable for children under 12. Maximum strength also available.

Dosage: adults and children over 12 – initial dose, two tablets to be taken with water. May be followed by further doses of one or two tablets every four hours. Do not exceed six tablets in 24 hours.

Also available in soluble form. SETON HEALTHCARE

Cymalon

A 48-hour course of soluble granules to relieve the symptoms of cystitis. Contains sodium citrate and sodium bicarbonate to make urine less acid. Also contains citric acid.

Empty one sachet into a glass of cold water. Stir until dissolved, then drink. Take one sachet in water three times daily over 48 hours. You should take all six sachets to complete the treatment.

STERLING HEALTH

Cystoleve

A 48-hour treatment for cystitis containing sodium citrate to make urine less acid. Directions – as for Cymalon, above.   SETON HEALTHCARE

Cystopurin

A 48-hour course for relief of cystitis, containing potassium citrate to make urine less acid. Take one sachet dissolved in water three times daily over 48 hours. All six sachets must be taken to complete the course. Do not take Cystopurin without first consulting your doctor if you are pregnant or have had any kidney disease. Not for children under six.

ROCHE CONSUMER HEALTH

Daktarin Cream

Contains miconazole nitrate – an antifungal and antibacterial drug which destroys fungus and its spores. Used to treat minor fungal and some bacterial infections of the skin, such as athlete's foot, 'dhobie itch', intertrigo and infected nappy rash. Apply to affected area twice a day. Relief from symptoms may occur quickly, but it is important that you continue to use cream for up to ten days after the symptoms have cleared.

JANSSEN PHARMACEUTICAL

Daktarin Oral Gel

Sugar-free gel containing miconazole (see Daktarin Cream, above) to treat fungal infections of the lips, mouth and throat such as oral thrush in babies and adults and due to denture chafing. Specially formulated to adhere to mucous membranes for up to six hours after application.

Dosage: adults and children over 6 – squeeze a small amount of gel on to a clean finger and apply to the affected area four times a day after food. Children under 6 – use twice a day. For oral thrush caused by denture chafing, it may be useful to smear a small amount of gel on to the denture plate. For best results, keep the gel in contact with the affected area for as long as possible before you have to swallow, and then swallow it. Relief from symptoms may occur quickly, but it's important that you continue to use gel for up to two days after the symptoms have cleared. If you are pregnant, consult your doctor before using the gel.

JANSSEN PHARMACEUTICAL

Daktarin Powder

Medicated talc with miconazole (see Daktarin Cream, above) for the treatment of fungal infections such as infected nappy rash, intertrigo and athlete's foot. It is particularly useful where a drying effect is needed and may be used on broken skin. Apply to affected area twice daily. Also available in spray powder form to cool and soothe. JANSSEN PHARMACEUTICAL

Day Nurse Capsules
Capsules containing dextromethorphan hydrobromide (a cough suppressant), paracetamol and phenylpropanolamine hydrochloride (for nasal congestion) for colds and influenza.

Adults: take two capsules every four hours as needed. Maximum eight capsules in 24 hours. Children 6–12 years: take one capsule every four hours as needed. Maximum four capsules in 24 hours. Not recommended for children under 6 except on medical advice.

SMITHKLINE BEECHAM CONSUMER BRANDS

Day Nurse Liquid
Liquid containing the same active ingredients as Day Nurse Capsules for colds and influenza. Adults take 20 ml every four hours as needed. Maximum 80 ml in 24 hours. Children 6–12 years take 10 ml every four hours as needed. Maximum 40 ml in 24 hours. Not for children under 6 except on medical advice.

SMITHKLINE BEECHAM CONSUMER BRANDS

DDD Medicated Cream
Cream containing thymol, menthol, methyl salicylate, chlorbutol and titanium dioxide for cuts and grazes, spots and pimples and minor rashes. For minor skin problems, cuts and grazes clean the affected area with warm water to remove all dirt. Rub cream well into the skin at least each morning and evening to help speed healing. For spots, pimples and minor rashes use cream regularly.

DDD

DDD Medicated Lotion
Lotion containing thymol, menthol, salicylic acid, chlorbutol, methyl salicylate, glycerin and ethanol for spots and pimples, and minor rashes. For spots use night and morning, for minor rashes apply three times daily.

DDD

Deep Heat Bath Tonic
Bath tonic with oils of juniper, eucalyptus, patchouli and thyme to help ease aches and pains. Add one to two capfuls into hot running water.

MENTHOLATUM

Deep Heat–Deep Freeze Cold Gel

A menthol rub for tired muscles, after sports, gardening or exercise. Combines the benefits of muscle massage with the soothing sensation of coldness. Also helpful for rheumatic pain and stiff limbs and joints. Apply liberally to the required area. Massage until gel is completely absorbed into the skin. Use as needed. Also available in spray form for painful muscular spasms.   MENTHOLATUM

Deep Heat Massage Liniment

Available in a new shatter-proof bottle. Contains menthol and methyl salicylate. Massage with the liniment can help stimulate the blood flow, soothe away pain and relax stiffness, so this product is ideal as a pre-sport warm-up. Gently massage the liniment into the affected area until penetration is complete. Apply three to four times daily. Do not use on children under 5.   MENTHOLATUM

Deep Heat Maximum

A soothing rub with menthol and the counter-irritant methyl salicylate, for the relief of nagging muscular aches and rheumatic pain. Not suitable for young children. Massage into affected area until penetration of the cream is complete. Apply two or three times daily.   MENTHOLATUM

Deep Heat Rub

A warming, pain-relieving rub to provide effective relief from rheumatic pain and all muscular aches, pains and strains. Contains soothing menthol, eucalyptus and turpentine oil, and the counter-irritant methyl salicylate, to stimulate the blood flow and relax stiffness. Massage into affected area until penetration of cream is complete.

Deep Heat Spray is also available.   MENTHOLATUM

Denorex

Anti-dandruff shampoo to clear dandruff and soothe irritation, scaling, itching and flaking. Also suitable for treatment of psoriasis of the scalp and seborrhoeic dermatitis. Contains coal tar to stop itching and to moisturise, and soothing menthol. Apply every other day for first ten days (or daily if necessary), then two to three times a week until signs of dandruff disappear. Repeat once a week after that. Use as ordinary shampoo, but leave on the hair for two to three minutes.

New Denorex Plus Conditioner is also available.

WHITEHALL

Dentinox Cradle-Cap Shampoo

A treatment shampoo for infant cradle cap and general care of the scalp and hair. Contains sodium lauryl ether sulpho-succinate and sodium lauryl ether sulphate, both medicated cleansers. Wet baby's head with warm water, massage a little of the shampoo gently but firmly over the entire scalp. Rinse off and repeat. Rinse thoroughly and dry. Repeat at each bath until the scalp is clear and then use as necessary. Avoid contact with the eyes. DDD

Dentinox Infant Colic Drops

An alcohol-free suspension for the relief of wind and griping pains in infants, caused by the accumulation of ingested air. Helps to bring up wind. Can be used from birth onwards. Contains activated dimethicone (to break down wind). DDD

Dentinox Teething Gel

A sugar-free gel to relieve the pain of baby teething, containing lignocaine

hydrochloride and cetylpyridinium chloride. Application can be repeated after 20 minutes if necessary.

DDD

Dequacaine

Lozenges to treat severe sore throats, containing a local anaesthetic, benzocaine, and an antibacterial agent and antifungal drug, dequalinium chloride. Not suitable for children under 12.

Dosage: adults and children over 12 – one lozenge to be sucked every two hours or as needed. No more than eight lozenges in any 24-hour period. CROOKES HEALTHCARE

Dequadin

Antibacterial lozenges with dequalinium chloride (see above) for treatment of infections of the mouth and throat. Dosage for adults and children – one lozenge to be sucked slowly and repeated as necessary, or as directed by your doctor. CROOKES HEALTHCARE

Derbac-C Liquid

Carbaryl liquid to eradicate head lice. Keep the head upright and rub the liquid well in until the scalp and all the hair are thoroughly moistened. Allow hair to dry naturally. Shampoo next day in the normal way. While the hair is wet use a nit comb to remove dead eggs.　NAPP

Derbac-C Shampoo
Shampoo with carbaryl to eradicate head lice. Wet hair and massage into the scalp. Rinse out thoroughly. Re-apply shampoo and work into a lather. Leave on the head for at least five minutes and then rinse off with clean water. Comb out hair with a nit comb and then dry. Apply as directed at three-day intervals for a total of three applications. Not to be used on infants less than six months old.

NAPP

Derbac-M Liquid
Malathion liquid to eradicate head lice, crab lice and the scabies mite. A gentle formula ideal for use if asthma or sensitive skin is a problem. Not for infants less than six months old. For head lice – keep head upright and rub the liquid well in until the scalp and all hair are thoroughly moistened. Pay particular attention to the area around the ears and at the back of the neck. Allow hair to dry naturally. Shampoo next day with an ordinary shampoo. Use a nit comb to remove dead eggs.　NAPP

Dermacort
Hydrocortisone cream for effective relief from skin irritations, dermatitis and rashes caused by plants, insect bites, jewellery, detergents and toiletries such as deodorants and soaps. Dosage: adults and children over 10 only – apply sparingly over a small area once or twice a day. Rub gently into the skin until the cream disappears. Do not use for longer than a week.

PANPHARMA

Dermidex
Dermatological cream to soothe the irritation of itching skin and fight infection. Useful for itching, chapped hands, minor vulval and anal irritations, after-shave soreness, chafed skin, painful skin and deodorant irritation. Contains the local pain-relievers lidocaine and chlorbutanol; an astringent, aluminium chlorhydroxy-allantoinate; and cetrimide, an antiseptic.　SETON HEALTHCARE

Dettol
Liquid antiseptic/disinfectant containing chloroxylenol for antiseptic wound cleansing and disinfection of skin lesions and abrasions, cuts, bites and insect stings. Can also be used as a germicidal agent for dandruff, spots and pimples.

Should not be used in eczematous conditions. For wound cleansing and disinfection, dilute by 50 ml to one litre of water. Also available as cream and mouthwash.   RECKITT & COLMAN

Dettol Antiseptic Soap
An antiseptic soap containing trichlorocarbanilide which helps against hand-borne infection.   RECKITT & COLMAN

Dettol Fresh
Liquid antiseptic/disinfectant containing benzalkonium chloride for antiseptic wound cleansing and disinfection of skin lesions, including abrasions, cuts, bites and insect stings. Can also be used as a bath additive and as a germicidal agent for spots and pimples. Should not be used in eczematous conditions. For first aid dilute by 50 ml to one litre of water.

RECKITT & COLMAN

Diareze
Capsules containing loperamide hydrochloride which slows down gut-wall muscles – an effective ingredient for the symptomatic relief of diarrhoea.
   Dosage: adults and children over 12 – take two capsules initially, followed by one

capsule after each loose bowel movement up to a maximum of eight per day. Not recommended for children under 12. Diareze is for the symptomatic relief of diarrhoea only and is not a substitute for rehydration therapy.   BOOTS

Digest
A traditional herbal remedy containing parsley, centaury and marshmallow root for the symptomatic relief of indigestion and flatulence. Acts by gently decreasing stomach acidity. Sodium- and aluminium-free.   MODERN HEALTH

Dijex
Indigestion tablets containing the antacids aluminium hydroxide and magnesium carbonate co-dried gel. Liquid available.
   Dosage: adults and children over 12 – one or two tablets every two to four hours as required. Chew or swallow with a little water or milk. For nocturnal symptoms, two tablets may be taken at bedtime. Children 5–12 years – half the above dose.

SETON HEALTHCARE

Dimotapp Elixir
Sugar-free nasal decongestant with the antihistamine brompheniramine maleate and

decongestants phenylephrine hydrochloride and phenylpropanolamine hydrochloride. May cause drowsiness.

Dosage, to be taken three times daily: adults – one or two 5 ml spoonfuls. Children 6–12 years – one 5 ml spoonful; 2–6 years – half a 5 ml spoonful. In no instance should the interval between doses be less than four hours. If you are under the care of a doctor, are taking continual prescribed medication or you think you may be pregnant, consult your doctor before taking Dimotapp Elixir.

WHITEHALL

Dimotapp Elixir Paediatric

Dimotapp Elixir for the treatment of colds, hay fever and nasal congestion in children. May cause drowsiness.

Dosage, to be taken three times daily: children 6–12 years – two 5 ml spoonfuls; 2–6 years – one 5 ml spoonful. In no instance should the interval between doses be less than four hours. WHITEHALL

Dimotapp L.A.

Tablets to help stop a runny nose caused by colds, hay fever, catarrh or nasal congestion, with the same active ingredients and safety

warnings as Dimotapp Elixir, above. Not recommended for children under 12.

Dosage: one tablet night and morning. WHITEHALL

Diocalm

Tablets containing attapulgite, and morphine hydrochloride for diarrhoea. Adults: two tablets every 2–4 hours as needed. Maximum 12 tablets in 24 hours. Replace lost fluids. Children 6–12 years: one tablet every two to four hours as needed. Maximum six tablets in 24 hours. Not for children under 6.

SMITHKLINE BEECHAM CONSUMER BRANDS

Diocalm Replenish

Sachets containing glucose, potassium chloride, sodium chloride and sodium citrate to prevent and correct dehydration, in particular to replace the fluid and electrolytes lost during diarrhoea.

Dosage: adults take one or two sachets dissolved in 200 ml water as soon as possible after start of diarrhoea, repeated after each bowel movement. Children under 12 years: one sachet in 200 ml water taken as above. Children under 6: do not exceed nine sachets in 24 hours. Infants (bottle-fed): substitute equivalent volume in place of normal feed in first 24 hours. Gradually reintroduce milk after 24 hours, beginning with half-strength milk feeds.

For breast-fed babies substitute half of each breast-feed with solution in feeding bottle, alternating for equal periods. Continue for 24 hours then gradually re-introduce normal breast-feeding during second day. Discontinue treatment once diarrhoea has stopped.

SMITHKLINE BEECHAM CONSUMER BRANDS

Diocalm Ultra

Capsules containing loperamide hydrochloride (which slows down the movement of the gut wall) for diarrhoea. Adults: two capsules at once and one at each loose bowel movement. Maximum eight capsules in 24 hours. Not recommended for children under 12 years.

SMITHKLINE BEECHAM CONSUMER BRANDS

Dioralyte

Sachets in plain and effervescent tablets in blackcurrant flavour containing sodium bicarbonate, citric acid, glucose anhydrous, sodium chloride, and potassium chloride for the correction of fluid and electrolyte loss in infants, children and adults. Adults

two or four tablets or one or two sachets dissolved in 200 ml or 400 ml fresh drinking water after each motion. Children half adult dose.

RHONE POULENC RORER

Disprin

Soluble aspirin for the relief of headache, toothache, neuralgia, period pain, rheumatic pain, lumbago, sciatica and to relieve the symptoms of colds, influenza and sore throat. Dissolve tablets in water before taking. Adults and children over 12 years: two to three tablets every four hours as needed. Do not take more than 13 tablets in 24 hours. As with other pain relievers, do not take if you have a stomach disorder. Consult your doctor before taking Disprin if you are asthmatic, allergic to aspirin or are receiving regular medical treatment.

RECKITT & COLMAN

Disprin Direct

Tablets containing aspirin which disperse on the tongue without water for the relief of mild to moderate pain in headaches, including tension and migraine headaches, toothache, neuralgia, period pains, rheumatic pain, lumbago and sciatica. Also relieves the symptoms of influenza, feverishness and feverish colds, and eases sore throats. Adults and children over 12: one to three tablets every four hours. No more than 13 tablets to be taken in any 24-hour period. Not to be given to children under 12 except on a doctor's advice.

RECKITT & COLMAN

Disprin Extra

Tablets containing aspirin and paracetamol for the treatment of mild to moderate pain, including headache, migraine, neuralgia, toothache, sore throat, aches and pains. Also for symptomatic relief of rheumatic aches and pains, influenza, feverishness, feverish colds. Adults and children over 12: one to two tablets every four hours. Maximum six tablets in 24 hours. Not for children under 12 except on medical advice.

RECKITT & COLMAN

Disprol

Paracetamol tablets for the treatment of mild to moderate pain, including headache, migraine, neuralgia, toothache, sore throat, period pains, aches and pains such as muscle pains and back ache. Also for symptomatic relief of rheumatic aches and pains, influenza, feverishness and feverish colds.

Dosage – adults and children over 12: one to two tablets every four hours. Maximum eight tablets in 24 hours. Children 6–12 years: half to one tablet every four hours. Maximum four tablets in 24 hours. Not to be given to children under 6 except on a doctor's advice.

RECKITT & COLMAN

Junior Disprol Suspension

A sugar-free suspension of paracetamol in a banana-flavoured liquid for the treatment of mild to moderate pain, including headache, migraine, neuralgia, toothache, pain in teething, sore throat, aches and pains. Also for symptomatic relief of rheumatic aches and pains, influenza, feverishness and feverish colds.

Dosage: children 3–12 months: half to one 5 ml spoonful every four hours. One year to under 6 years: one to two 5 ml spoonfuls every four hours. 6–12 years: two to four 5 ml spoonfuls every four hours. No more than four doses in any 24-hour period. Dosage for children under three months at the physician's discretion.

RECKITT & COLMAN

Junior Disprol Tablets

Contain paracetamol for the

treatment of mild to moderate pain, including headache, migraine, neuralgia, toothache, pain in teething, sore throat, aches and pains. Also for the symptomatic relief of rheumatic aches and pains, flu, feverishness and feverish colds.

Dosage: children 6–12 years – two to four tablets; 1–under 6 years – one to two tablets; 3–12 months – half to one tablet. Dosage for children under 3 months is at your doctor's discretion. Dosage to be taken every four hours, but not more than four doses should be given in any 24-hour period.

Junior Disprol Tablets should be dissolved in water or a fruit drink. For more than two tablets, dissolve in at least half a glass of liquid.

RECKITT & COLMAN

Doan's
Tablets containing paracetamol and sodium salicylate, a mild pain-reliever, for the relief of back pain.

Dosage: two to three tablets every four hours. Maximum 16 tablets in 24 hours. ZYMA

Dr Valnet's Climarome
A natural inhalant with essential oils of lavender, niaouli, pine, mint and thyme. Spray on a clean handkerchief or tissue and breathe in as required through the day. Alternatively, spray on to a pillow before going to sleep, or use in a bowl of hot water and inhale vapours. CEDAR HEALTH

Dr Valnet's Flexarome
Soothes muscular fatigue and sensitive joints. Contains ginger tincture and essential oils of origanum, common juniper, cypress, turpentine and rosemary.

LABORATOIRE COSBIONAT

Dr Valnet's Tegarome
Natural first-aid treatment for minor abrasions, bites, burns and stings. Contains essential oils of lavender, niaouli, cypress, rosemary, sage, geranium, thyme and eucalyptus. LABORATOIRE COSBIONAT

Dr Valnet's Volarome
Insect-repellent with essential oils of lavender, geranium, sage, citronella, eucalyptus and mint. Apply to exposed parts of the body.

LABORATOIRE COSBIONAT

Do-Do
Tablets for the relief of chest congestion, containing ephedrine hydrochloride, a decongestant; the stimulant caffeine; and theophylline sodium glycinate, used to treat bronchial asthma.

Dosage: one tablet every four hours with a maximum of four tablets in any 24 hours. ZYMA

Do-Do Expectorant

Linctus with expectorant guaiphenesin for the relief of bronchial cough.

Dosage: adults and children over 12 – one or two 5 ml spoonfuls every two to four hours; children 6–12 years – one or two 5 ml spoonfuls every four hours. Not recommended for children under 6 unless advised by a doctor. ZYMA

Dramamine

Tablets containing dimenhydrinate (an antihistamine) to prevent travel sickness in adults and children. Take the first dose half an hour before starting your journey.

Dosage: adults and children over 12 – one to two tablets, two to three times daily; children 7–12 years – half to one tablet, two to three times daily; 1–6 years – quarter to half a tablet, two to three times daily. Do not take during pregnancy except under medical supervision. May cause drowsiness. SEARLE

Drapolene Cream

A cream for the prevention and treatment of nappy rash that won't block the action of one-way nappy liners or disposable nappies. Can also be used for minor burns and wounds. Contains the antiseptics benzalkonium chloride solution and cetrimide.

For nappy rash – apply evenly at every nappy change, paying particular attention to the folds of the skin. For minor burns and wounds – apply liberally to the affected area as necessary. It's important to ensure that the affected area is free from all traces of soap. WELLCOME

Dristan

Nasal spray for the relief of symptoms of head colds and hay fever. Contains the decongestant oxymetazoline hydrochloride to give relief from stuffed-up nose, catarrh and nasal congestion. Also contains camphor, menthol and eucalyptus. Use only as directed. With head upright, place nozzle loosely into each nostril. Spray once or twice into each nostril, repeat every eight to ten hours as necessary. For children 6–16 years, spray lightly once into each nostril. WHITEHALL

Dristan Decongestant Tablets

To clear congestion and relieve pain and for the relief of colds, sinus congestion and catarrh. Contain aspirin to relieve the aches and pains associated with the common cold and flu; the decongestant phenylephrine hydrochloride; the antihistamine chlorpheniramine maleate; and the stimulant caffeine. May cause drowsiness.

Dosage: adults – two tablets every four hours. No more than eight tablets in 24 hours. Children 6–12 years, half the adult dose. Not recommended for children under 6 years except on medical advice.

WHITEHALL

Dual-Lax

Herbal laxative tablets for the relief of temporary constipation. Based on senna and cascara sagrada, herbs with a long tradition of use to relieve constipation. Available in normal strength and extra strong. Suitable for vegetarians. Gluten free. Do not use during early pregnancy or if breast-feeding.

LANES

Dulcolax

Tablets containing the laxative bisacodyl for the relief of constipation. Also available in suppository form.

Dosage: adults and children over 10 – one to two tablets swallowed whole at night; children under 10 – consult your doctor. Suppositories available for adults and also Dulcolax Suppositories for Children. One to be inserted rectally in the morning. Caution: do not take antacids within one hour of taking Dulcolax tablets.

WINDSOR HEALTHCARE

Duofilm

A clear paint for the treatment of plantar and mosaic warts containing the keratolytics salicylic acid and lactic acid. Warts should be soaked in hot water for five minutes. Dry with your own towel. Rub surface of warts with a pumice stone or emery board. Apply Duofilm to the warts. Allow to dry and cover with plaster if wart is large or on the foot. Continue treatment once or twice daily until the wart is completely cleared and the ridge lines of the skin have been restored.

STIEFEL

Earex

Ear drops containing arachis, almond and rectified camphor oil to remove excess ear wax. To use, tilt the head to one side. Put four drops into the ear using the dropper. Gently place a piece of cotton wool into the ear and leave for about 30 minutes. Repeat night and morning for up to four days until wax is softened. SETON HEALTHCARE

Emulave Fluid
A liquid cleanser for delicate, irritated and dry skin. Ideal for washing and bathing babies. Emulave Bar, a non-soap cleansing bar made from compressed oatmeal, is also available. BIOGLAN

Emulsiderm
An emollient containing the moisturisers liquid paraffin and isopropyl myristate, with a mild antiseptic, benzalkonium chloride. Used to treat dry skin conditions such as eczema, dermatitis and psoriasis. Contains no lanolin, perfume or steroids. Can be used in the bath or as an in-shower moisturiser. Alternatively, apply directly on to the skin to treat localised dry patches. Suitable for adults and children.

DERMAL LABORATORIES

Endekay Dental Health Gum
Chewable gum to neutralise plaque acid. Contains urea, a mild diuretic. No sugar, added

colouring or preservatives. Recommended for everyone with natural teeth, both adults and children. STAFFORD-MILLER

Endekay Fluoride Tablets and Drops
For strengthening tooth enamel to resist decay in children. Drops for children under 2; tablets available in two strengths, for 2 to 4-year-olds and for children over 4.

Dosage – drops: serve seven drops on a spoon or mixed with food or drink. Tablets, for children 2–4 years – one tablet to be sucked or slowly dissolved in the mouth. Tablets for 4 years and over – as above. STAFFORD-MILLER

Eno
Sachets of powder containing citric acid, sodium bicarbonate and sodium carbonate for indigestion, flatulence and nausea. Adults: one sachet in water every two to three hours if needed. Maximum six sachets in 24 hours. Not recommended for children except on medical advice.

SMITHKLINE BEECHAM CONSUMER GOODS

Eskamel Cream
Cream with mild antiseptic, keratolytic and exfoliative properties containing sulphur and resorcinol for the treatment of acne. Apply once

a day but if you have very oily skin the cream may be applied more often.   GOLDSHIELD

Eskornade Spansule Capsules and Eskornade Syrup

Capsules or syrup containing a combination of an oral nasal decongestant and an antihistamine – phenylpropanolamine hydrochloride and diphenylpyraline hydrochloride – for the relief of congestion and hyper-secretion in the nose and sinuses in association with the common cold, rhinitis, sinusitis and influenza.

GOLDSHIELD

Eurax

Cream and lotion containing crotamiton, which relieves itching, used to treat skin irritations, except areas of dermatitis. Apply as required but only on small areas of skin in babies and infants.   ZYMA

Eurax Hc

Cream combining the anti-itching properties of crotamiton and anti-inflammatory and anti-allergic properties of hydrocortisone for the relief of inflammation and itching in contact dermatitis and insect bite reactions. Adults and children

over 10 years: apply sparingly over a small area twice a day for a maximum period of one week. Not recommended for children under 10 years.   ZYMA

Ex-Lax Pills

Laxative pills containing yellow phenolphthalein. Take with a glass of water at bedtime. Adults and children over 6 years – one pill.   INTERCARE

Ex-Lax Tablets

Chocolate tablets with yellow phenolphthalein to relieve constipation. Take with a glass of water at bedtime. Adults one tablet. Children over 6 years – half to one tablet.

INTERCARE

Exterol Ear Drops

A solution containing urea hydrogen peroxide to soften and effervesce within the ear wax – helping to break down its structure and expel it naturally. This special action may be heard as a slight bubbling in the ear. Squeeze five to ten drops into the ear. Retain in the ear for a few minutes by keeping the head tilted. Repeat once or twice a day for at least three or four days.   DERMAL LABORATORIES

Eye Dew

Blue and clear eye drops containing distilled witch hazel

and naphazoline for clearer whites of the eye. One or two drops put into both eyes. Not suitable for use with soft lenses. If you suffer from glaucoma, high blood pressure, heart disease, diabetes or hyperthyroid, consult a doctor before use.

CROOKES HEALTHCARE

Famel Catarrh and Throat Pastilles

Pastilles containing creosote, a disinfectant, and soothing menthol, for the relief of sore, infected throats, catarrh and coughs. Suck one pastille as required. SETON HEALTHCARE

Famel Expectorant

Linctus with the expectorant guaiphenesin and liquid glucose for the relief of tight, chesty coughs.

Dosage: adults and children over 12 – four 5 ml spoonfuls. Children 5–12 years – two 5 ml spoonfuls; 1–5 years – one 5 ml spoonful. Take the dose every four hours up to four times daily. SETON HEALTHCARE

Famel Honey and Lemon Cough Pastilles

Pastilles to soothe coughs and sore throats, containing the expectorant guaiphenesin. Not recommended for children under five.

Dosage: adults and children over 10 – one every hour as required. Children 5–10 years – one every two hours.

SETON HEALTHCARE

Famel Linctus

For the relief of dry, tickly coughs. Containing pholcodine, a cough-suppressant, and papaverine hydrochloride, used to treat spasm of smooth muscle.

Dosage: adults and children over 12 – two 5 ml spoonfuls; children 5–12 years – one 5 ml spoonful. Not suitable for children under five, except on medical advice. SETON HEALTHCARE

Famel Original

Syrup for the symptomatic relief of dry, troublesome coughs. Contains creosote, a disinfectant often used in small doses in cough mixtures, and codeine phosphate, a cough-suppressant. May cause drowsiness.

Dosage: adults and children over 12 – two to three 5 ml spoonfuls; in acute cases, three to four 5 ml spoonfuls. Not suitable for children under 12. SETON HEALTHCARE

Femeron Cream

Cream containing miconazole, a highly effective anti-fungal agent which destroys the Candida fungus to soothe and treat external vaginal itching due to vaginal thrush. Apply cream to the external vaginal area twice daily. If symptoms persist, or worsen, see your doctor. CENTRA HEALTHCARE

Femeron Soft Pessary

Effective single-dose treatment for vaginal thrush. The Femeron soft pessary contains miconazole, a highly effective anti-fungal agent which destroys the Candida fungus, giving fast and effective relief from the itching and discharge caused by candidal infections. Read enclosed leaflet carefully before use.

Directions: insert the soft pessary high into the vagina as a single dose, at night. Full instructions for use are provided in the leaflet. Do not let rubber contraceptive products such as condoms and diaphragms come into contact with the pessary. If symptoms do not improve, or if they get worse, tell your doctor.

CENTRA HEALTHCARE

Femigraine

Soluble tablets containing aspirin to relieve migraine and cyclizine hydrochloride, an antihistamine and anti-emetic, to help prevent vomiting and reduce nausea. May cause drowsiness. Do not take if you have a stomach ulcer or other stomach disorder, nor if you are sensitive to aspirin. Consult your doctor if you suffer from asthma, or if you are receiving medical treatment or are pregnant.

Dosage: tablets must be dissolved in half a glass of water. Adults and children over 12 – take two tablets at the first sign of a migraine attack, then if necessary two tablets every four hours. Do not take more than eight tablets in 24 hours. Do not give to children under 12 years unless your doctor tells you to. ROCHE CONSUMER HEALTH

Feminax

Painkillers specially formulated to ease period pain and associated stomach cramps, back ache and headache. Contain paracetamol; codeine phosphate, a mild pain-reliever; caffeine, a stimulant; and hyoscine hydrobromide, used to relieve spasm in abdominal and pelvic muscles. May cause drowsiness. Not recommended for children under 12. Not to be taken by persons suffering from glaucoma.

Dosage: adults and girls over 12 – up to two tablets every four hours. No more than six tablets in 24 hours.

ROCHE CONSUMER HEALTH

Fennings Children's Cooling Powders

Paracetamol powders for the treatment of pain arising from teething, headache, aches, pains and the symptomatic relief of feverish colds, flu and mild feverish conditions.

Dosage, to a maximum of four doses daily: babies 3 months to 1 year – one powder; children 1 year to under 6 years – two powders. The powder may be given in a little milk or jam.

FENNINGS PHARMACEUTICALS

Fennings Little Healers

Tablets containing prepared ipecacuanha for coughs with colds and catarrh. Adults: two tablets three times daily; children over 5: one tablet three times daily. Do not exceed the stated dose. If pregnant seek medical advice.

FENNINGS PHARMACEUTICALS

Fenox Nasal Spray and Drops

To relieve nasal congestion due to head colds, catarrh, blocked sinuses and hay fever. Contains phenylephrine hydrochloride, a decongestant. Use morning and night and every four hours if necessary. Don't use drops for longer than seven days without medical advice.   SETON HEALTHCARE

Fiery Jack Rubbing Ointment

Rub containing capsicum and one of the hottest on the market for back ache, muscular aches and pains, lumbago, and stiff joints. To be applied once or twice daily only, and only to a limited area of skin overlying the painful area. Not to be used by people with delicate or sensitive skin. Never apply to diseased or broken skin. Care should also be taken to avoid sensitive parts of the body and to wash the hands thoroughly after use. Avoid contact with clothing as ointment may stain.   J. PICKLES & SONS

Fynnon Calcium Aspirin

Soluble tablets containing aspirin and calcium carbonate.

Dosage: adults and children over 12: one to two tablets, repeated four-hourly as necessary. Rheumatic sufferers should take one to two tablets at about 9 a.m., 1 p.m., 5 p.m. and 9 p.m. A 5 a.m. dose (with milk) is helpful against morning stiffness but do not exceed eight tablets in 24 hours.

SETON HEALTHCARE

Flurex Cold/Flu Capsules with Cough Suppressant

Capsules containing paracetamol, phenylephrine

hydrochloride and dextromethorphan hydrobromide, for the short-term symptomatic relief of colds and flu. Adults: two capsules every four hours. Maximum 12 capsules in 24 hours. Children 6–12 years: one capsule every four hours. Maximum six capsules in 24 hours. Not recommended for children under 6 years.

SETON HEALTHCARE

Flurex Tablets

Contain paracetamol, the stimulant caffeine and phenylephrine hydrochloride to clear a stuffy nose. Used for the short-term symptomatic relief of colds, flu and catarrh. Not to be taken during pregnancy or when breast-feeding. Not for children under six.

Dosage: adults and children over 12 – one or two tablets to be taken four-hourly as needed. For light infections the dose may be reduced to one tablet every three hours. No more than eight tablets a day. Children 6–12 years – one tablet four-hourly if required. No more than four tablets per day.　SETON HEALTHCARE

Franolyn Chesty Cough

For tight, chesty coughs with congestion. Contains the expectorant guaiphenesin;

theophylline to ease congested airways; and ephedrine, a decongestant.

Dosage: adults – two 5 ml spoonfuls. Children 7–12 years – one 5 ml spoonful. Repeat up to four times a day if necessary. Children under 7 – on medical advice only. Take with or after food. Works without causing drowsiness. People suffering from asthma should consult their doctor before using this product.

JANSSEN PHARMACEUTICAL

Franolyn Dry Cough

Syrup for the relief of dry, irritating coughs, containing dextromethorphan hydrobromide, a cough-suppressant.

Dosage, to be taken up to four times a day: adults – two 5 ml spoonfuls. Children 7–12 years, one 5 ml spoonful. Children under 7 – on medical advice only. Works without causing drowsiness.

JANSSEN PHARMACEUTICAL

Freezone Liquid

A liquid corn-remover containing salicylic acid. Soak the affected foot in warm water for 15 minutes. Dry thoroughly, then rub the corn very gently with a pumice stone to remove any dead skin. Apply Freezone a drop at a time until the corn is covered. Cover with a waterproof plaster. Repeat daily, renewing the plaster each time until the corn can be lifted out. WHITEHALL

Full Marks Lotion

Contains phenothrin for the treatment of head lice infestations. Sprinkle lotion on dry hair and rub gently until the entire scalp is moistened. Allow to dry naturally – use no heat. As all lice and eggs will have been killed, the hair may be shampooed after two hours. While still wet comb the hair with an ordinary comb. Then use a nit comb to remove the dead lice and eggs. Can also be used to treat pubic lice.

Lotion contains isopropyl alcohol which may cause wheezing in patients suffering from asthma or cause stinging or inflammation of the skin in patients with severe eczema. Some people with a normal skin may also experience stinging or inflammation of the skin. NAPP

Fybogel and Fybogel Orange

Sachets of granules containing ispaghula husk, recommended for the treatment of patients needing a high-fibre regimen. Effective in relieving constipation and restoring regular bowel function.

Adults and children over 12 – one sachet morning and evening. Children 6–12 years – half to one level 5 ml spoonful depending on age and size, morning and evening. Children under 6 – on medical advice only.

RECKITT & COLMAN

Gardolex

A traditional herbal remedy containing garlic oil, marshmallow root and parsley for the symptomatic relief of colds and catarrh. MODERN HEALTH

Gaviscon

Liquid for the relief of heartburn and indigestion due to gastric reflux. Contains the antacids sodium alginate, sodium bicarbonate and calcium carbonate. Adults and children over 12: two to four 5 ml spoonfuls after meals and at bedtime, or as directed. This may be followed by a drink of water if desired. If your doctor has advised a low salt diet, please note that each 10 ml contains 141 mg of sodium. Also available in tablet form. RECKITT & COLMAN

Gaviscon 250 Tablets

Mint-flavoured tablets containing alginic acid and the antacids magnesium trisilicate, dried aluminium hydroxide and sodium bicarbonate for the relief of heartburn and indigestion.

Adults and children over 12 – two tablets as needed. Not recommended for children under 12. Tablets should be thoroughly chewed and may be followed by a drink of water.   RECKITT & COLMAN

Gee's Linctus Pastilles

Pastilles to relieve stubborn coughs. Not suitable for children under 12. Contain concentrated camphorated opium tincture (to suppress an unnecessary cough), squill liquid extract (an expectorant), cinnamic acid and benzoic acid (antiseptics), glacial acetic acid (an expectorant) and honey. Suck two pastilles every four hours and at bedtime.

ERNEST JACKSON

Gelcosal

Gel containing salicylic acid, coal tar solution and pine tar for the treatment of psoriasis or dermatitis in the chronic scaling phase. Adults: apply by gentle massage over all the affected area twice daily.

QUINODERM

Gelcotar

Gel containing coal tar solution and pine tar for the treatment of psoriasis and dermatitis in the chronic phase. Adults: apply by gentle massage over all the affected area twice daily.   QUINODERM

Gelcotar Liquid

Liquid containing coal tar and cade oil for the treatment of psoriasis, seborrhoeic dermatitis and dandruff. Adults: wet hair and scalp with warm water, massage in thoroughly. Rinse and repeat. Rinse again. To be used twice weekly.   QUINODERM

Gelusil

Antacid tablets for the relief of hyperacidity, indigestion and heartburn whether occurring alone or in association with a peptic ulcer. Contain magnesium trisilicate and dried aluminium hydroxide.

Dosage: adults – one or two tablets to be chewed or sucked after meals or whenever symptoms arise. Children 6–12 years – half or one tablet. Gelusil tablets contain 561 mg sugar per tablet, so patients suffering from diabetes should seek their doctor's advice first if this is the antacid they prefer to take.   WARNER LAMBERT

Genisol

Lotion containing sodium sulphosuccinated undecyclenic

mono-alkyloamide (an antifungal agent) and purified coal tar fractions to treat dandruff. Wet hair thoroughly and use approximately 10 ml of Genisol as a shampoo. Work well into the scalp with fingers, rinse and repeat. Keep away from eyes.

ROCHE CONSUMER HEALTH

Germolene Cream

Cream containing chlorhexidine gluconate and phenol for minor cuts and grazes, minor burns and scalds, blisters, stings and insect bites, spots and other minor skin conditions, chapped or rough skin. Clean affected area, apply and rub in gently or use white lint or gauze.

SMITHKLINE BEECHAM CONSUMER BRANDS

Germolene Medicated Foot Spray

Aerosol spray containing dichlorophen (a fungicide) and triclosan (to stop bacterial growth) for athlete's foot and foot odour. Adults and children 3 years and over: spray areas of discomfort freely. Maximum six times in 24 hours. Not recommended for children under 3.

SMITHKLINE BEECHAM CONSUMER BRANDS

Germolene Ointment

Ointment containing liquid

paraffin light, methyl salicylate, octaphonium chloride (an antiseptic), petroleum jelly, phenol, starch, lanolin and zinc oxide, for minor cuts and grazes, minor burns and scalds and blisters, sore or rough skin, wash-day hands, sunburn and the symptomatic relief of muscular pain and stiffness.

Adults and children, apply directly or on a dressing and where applicable massage gently.

SMITHKLINE BEECHAM CONSUMER BRANDS

Germoloids Cream

Cream containing lignocaine hydrochloride and zinc oxide for symptomatic relief of pain, swelling, irritation and itching associated with piles and anal itching.

Dosage: adults apply twice a day at minimum of four hourly intervals. Maximum use four times in 24 hours. Not recommended for children under 12 years except on medical advice.

SMITHKLINE BEECHAM CONSUMER BRANDS

Germoloids Ointment

Ointment containing lignocaine hydrochloride and zinc oxide for pain, swelling, irritation and itching associated with piles and anal itching.

Adults apply twice daily and

after bowel movement.
Maximum four applications in
24 hours. Not recommended
for children under 12 years
except with medical advice.

SMITHKLINE BEECHAM CONSUMER BRANDS

Germoloids Suppositories

Suppositories containing
lignocaine hydrochloride and
zinc oxide for the
symptomatic relief of pain,
swelling, irritation and itching
associated with piles and anal
itching.

Adults: one suppository
inserted night and morning,
preferably after a bowel
movement. Maximum four
suppositories in 24 hours. Not
recommended for children
under 12 years except on
medical advice.

SMITHKLINE BEECHAM CONSUMER BRANDS

Gluco-lyte

Oral rehydration treatment
containing essential mineral
salts – sodium chloride,
potassium chloride, sodium
bicarbonate and glucose
monohydrate – for the
treatment of diarrhoea and
fluid loss in infants, children
and adults. Pour contents into
a glass and add 200 ml of
fresh drinking water. For
infants and where drinking
water isn't available, use
freshly boiled and cooled

water. Stir until powder has
completely dissolved.

Dosage: adults and children
over 12 – use one or two
reconstituted sachets after
each loose bowel movement.
Children 1–12 years – use one
reconstituted sachet after each
loose bowel movement.
Infants – substitute equivalent
volumes of reconstituted
solution in place of feeds, or
give the appropriate volume
before breast-feeding.
Artificial or cow's milk feeds
should be re-introduced
gradually when diarrhoea has
lessened.   SETON HEALTHCARE

Glutarol

Wart treatment containing
the disinfectant
glutaraldehyde. Gently rub
the surface of the wart with a
pumice stone or emery board,
or pare down any hard skin.
Apply a few drops of paint to
the wart. Repeat twice daily.
There is no need to use a
sticking plaster.

DERMAL LABORATORIES

Gonne Balm

A warming balm of menthol,
camphor and oils of cajuput,
eucalyptus, turpentine and
methyl salicylate – a counter-
irritant. Particularly useful as
a pre-sports rub. Apply with
gentle massage two or three
times daily and also at night if

necessary. For maximum effect have a hot bath first. This opens the pores and ensures deeper penetration.

LANES

HC45 Hydrocortisone Cream

For treatment of contact dermatitis caused by allergies or irritants and of skin reactions to insect bites. Contains hydrocortisone acetate which reduces inflammation and calms irritated skin. Use sparingly on a small area, once or twice a day for a maximum of seven days. If the condition doesn't improve, consult your doctor. Do not use on the eyes, face, anal or genital areas, or on broken or infected skin such as that caused by impetigo, cold sores, acne or athlete's foot. Do not use during pregnancy or for children under 10 without medical advice.

CROOKES HEALTHCARE

Hedex and Hedex Extra

Easy-to-swallow paracetamol caplets designed for relief from headaches, but effective for treatment of back ache, rheumatic and muscle pains, period pain and toothache. Also relieves fever, aches and pains associated with colds and flu. Hedex Extra contains the stimulant caffeine, so avoid drinking too much tea or coffee while taking these tablets.

Hedex is not suitable for children under six. Dosage: adults – two caplets up to four times daily. No more than eight in 24 hours. Children 6–12 years – half or one caplet up to four times daily. No more than four in 24 hours. Do not repeat more frequently than every four hours. Take with a tumblerful of water.

Hedex Extra: adults only – two caplets up to four times daily. No more frequently than every four hours, and no more than eight caplets in 24 hours.

STERLING HEALTH

Heemex

A soothing, healing ointment containing hamamelis (witch-hazel), compound tinct benzoine and zinc oxide (protective agents). For the symptomatic relief of discomfort, itching and irritation due to internal and external piles. Adults and the elderly should apply Heemex freely night and morning and after every bowel movement.

LANES

Hemocane Suppositories

Suppositories with five ingredients for all-round relief from symptoms of painful internal piles. Contains a local anaesthetic, lignocaine hydrochloride; soothing protective agents zinc oxide and bismuth oxide to help heal raw, tender tissues; benzoic acid, an antiseptic; and cinnamic acid, an antibacterial and antifungal agent. Use one suppository morning and night, and after bowel movements.

Also available as a cream.

INTERCARE

Herbal Laboratories' Herbal Feverfew 125

Tablets containing organically grown feverfew leaf powder which many people have found helpful in the treatment of migraine.   CEDAR HEALTH

Herbelix Specific

A traditional remedy to help relieve catarrh, mucous congestion, rhinitis, head colds and hay fever. The active ingredients are lobelia ethereal tinct, tolu solution and sodium bicarbonate. Suitable for vegans and vegetarians. Gluten free.

Dosage: adults – one 5 ml spoonful taken in a little water at bedtime. Children 7–14 years – half a 5 ml spoonful.

LANES

Hewletts Cream

An antiseptic healing cream containing zinc oxide and lanolin and scented with oil of rose. For use on chapped and broken skin, nappy rash and in nursing hygiene. Apply to the affected areas as and when required.   BIOGLAN

Hill's Balsam Children's Mixture for Chesty Coughs

Syrup containing ipecacuanha liquid extract, citric acid monohydrate, treacle, capsicum tincture, compound benzoin tincture and orange oil for children's chesty coughs. Children 5–12: one 5 ml spoonful three times a day and at bedtime; 1–4: half a 5 ml spoonful three times a day and at bedtime.

WINDSOR HEALTHCARE

Hill's Balsam for Chesty Coughs

Syrup containing guaiphenesin (an expectorant), acetic acid, treacle, capsicum tincture, compound benzoin tincture, aniseed oil and ethanol for chesty coughs. Dosage: adults and children over 12: one to two 5 ml spoonfuls every two to four hours. Not more than twelve 5 ml spoonfuls in 24 hours.

WINDSOR HEALTHCARE

Hill's Balsam for Dry Tickly Coughs

Syrup containing phlocodine, acetic acid, treacle, capsicum

tincture, compound benzoin tincture, aniseed oil and peppermint oil for dry tickly coughs. Adults and children over 12: one 5 ml spoonful three times a day and at bedtime, if preferred in a little warm water. WINDSOR HEALTHCARE

Hill's Balsam Pastilles for Chesty Coughs
Pastilles containing compound benzoin tincture, capsicum oleoresin, peppermint oil, ipecacuanha, tincture lobelia simple and menthol. Suck one when required.

WINDSOR HEALTHCARE

Hioxyl Cream
Cream containing the disinfectant hydrogen peroxide for the treatment of pressure sores, also leg ulcers, minor wounds and infections. Adults: apply freely using a piece of lint or gauze. Repeat application as needed. QUINODERM

Hirudoid
Cream or gel containing the organo-heparinoid 'Luitpold' for the soothing relief of superficial bruising and haematoma. Also for the treatment of superficial thrombophlebitis. Adults and children over 5 – 5–15 cm (2–6 in) to be applied to the affected area up to four times daily and gently massaged into the skin. Not to be used on large areas of skin, broken skin, sensitive areas of skin or mucous membranes. PANPHARMA

Hismanal
Tablets containing the antihistamine astemizole to relieve hay fever without causing drowsiness. Dosage: adults and children over 12 – one tablet once a day on an empty stomach, preferably in the morning. Do not take Hismanal if you are or may be pregnant, or are breast-feeding. Since people vary in their response to medications, it may take two to three days to attain maximum effect. For best results, take Hismanal continuously every day for as long as the hay-fever season lasts. JANSSEN PHARMACEUTICAL

Hofels Cardiomax Garlic Pearles
Highly concentrated essential oil of garlic. One capsule a day to be taken with food and, if preferred, with liquid. SEVEN SEAS

Hofels Odourless Neo-Garlic Pearles and Neo-Garlic Pearles One-A-Day
Fermented garlic extract capsules to avoid taste and odour of garlic.

Dosage: Neo-Garlic Pearles – three capsules daily; One-A-Day – one capsule daily.

SEVEN SEAS

Hofels Original and One-A-Day Garlic Pearles

A traditional herbal remedy for the relief of catarrh, symptoms of rhinitis and other symptoms of common colds and coughs. Dosage – Original: adults three capsules daily, either one before each meal or three before bed. Children 7–12 years – two capsules daily. Dosage: One-A-Day – one capsule a day, preferably with a meal.

Garlic tablets are also available with parsley – take one tablet three times a day before meals.   SEVEN SEAS

Hydromol Cream

Cream containing emollients liquid paraffin, sodium pyrolidone carboxylate, arachis oil, isopropyl myristate and sodium lactate to lubricate and hydrate in dry skin conditions. Adults: apply liberally to the affected area and massage well into the skin as needed.   QUINODERM

Hydromol Emollient

Emollient liquid containing liquid paraffin light and isopropyl myristate, a semi-dispersible bath additive for the treatment of dry skin conditions. Adults and children: one to three capfuls to an 8-inch bath of warm water. Soak for ten to fifteen minutes. Infants: add half to two capfuls to a small bath of warm water.   QUINODERM

Hypercal Cream

A topical herbal remedy traditionally used in the symptomatic treatment of cuts and sores. Combines the healing qualities of calendula (marigold) with the pain-relieving properties of hypericum (St John's Wort). Apply to more than cover the affected area. Cover with plain lint and bandage if necessary.   NELSONS

Ibugel

Clear, fragrance-free gel containing ibuprofen, a proven pain-relieving analgesic. Designed to be absorbed rapidly into the skin for effective relief at the point of pain. Specially formulated for the relief of pain and inflammation associated with conditions such as back ache, rheumatic and muscular pain, sprains, strains and neuralgia.

Lightly apply a thin layer of the gel over the affected area. Massage gently until absorbed. Repeat as required up to three times daily. Keep away from broken skin, the eyes and mucous membranes. Wash hands after use. Not recommended for children under 14. Patients with a history of kidney problems, asthma or aspirin sensitivity should seek medical advice before using this product. Do not use during pregnancy or while breast-feeding.

DERMAL LABORATORIES

Ibuleve

A clear, fragrance-free gel containing the pain-reliever ibuprofen. Designed to be rapidly absorbed into the skin for effective relief at the point of pain and inflammation associated with conditions such as back ache, rheumatic and muscular pain, sprains, strains and neuralgia.

Lightly apply a thin layer of the gel over the affected area. Massage gently until absorbed. Repeat as needed up to three times daily. If symptoms persist for more than a few weeks consult your doctor. Not recommended for children under 14. Patients with a history of kidney problems should seek medical advice before using Ibuleve. Keep away from broken skin, lips and eyes. Not to be used during pregnancy or while breast-feeding.

DDD

Ibuleve Sports Gel

Ibuprofen gel in a rapid action pump-dispenser for the relief of sports injuries. The cool,

clear, fragrance-free gel relieves muscular aches, sprains and strains and reduces inflammation.

Lightly apply a thin layer of the gel over the affected area. Massage gently until absorbed. Wash hands after use. Repeat as required up to three times daily. If symptoms persist for more than a few weeks, consult your doctor. Not recommended for children under 14 years. Patients with a history of kidney problems, asthma or sensitivity to aspirin should seek medical advice before using. Keep away from broken skin, lips and the eyes. Do not use during pregnancy or while breast-feeding.

DDD

Imodium

Capsules containing loperamide hydrochloride, which slows down gut wall muscles to treat diarrhoea. Not recommended for children under 12.

Dosage: two capsules initially, followed by one capsule after each further loose bowel movement up to a maximum of eight a day.

JANSSEN PHARMACEUTICAL

Imuderm Range

A range including body wash, cream, hand and face wash, hair wash, shower gel, which is lanolin-free and free of many chemicals commonly used in other skincare preparations. Suitable for dry skin conditions such as eczema and psoriasis.   GOLDSHIELD

Indian Brandee

Traditional herbal remedy containing cardamom tincture, compound and capsicum tincture to promote warmth and relief for flatulence and digestive discomfort. Adults: up to two 5 ml spoonfuls. Maximum 20 ml in 24 hours. Not for children under 12 years.   ROSMARINE

Infacol

A sugar-free, alcohol-free and colorant-free liquid to help relieve infant colic and griping pain and also effectively assist in bringing up wind. It contains activated dimethicone, which helps trapped gas bubbles join into bigger bubbles which the baby can bring up easily. Suitable for babies of all ages. Infacol has a build-up effect which means it should be given for several days to achieve the best results.

Dosage: 0.5 ml given preferably 20 minutes before each feed. (If necessary this dosage may be increased to 1 ml.) To use – shake the bottle. Fill the dropper by squeezing

the rubber bulb twice. To administer the dose, squeeze the bulb once and release. If symptoms persist, seek medical advice.   PHARMAX

Infaderm Range

A range of baby bath, cream, hair wash and lotion which is lanolin-free, fragrance-free and colouring-free for delicate skin and suitable in the management of eczema.

GOLDSHIELD

Inoven

Ibuprofen caplets to relieve pain, reduce inflammation and lower temperature. Effective in the relief of headaches, symptoms of colds and flu, muscular pain, rheumatic pain, back ache, neuralgia, migraine, period pain and dental pain.

Dosage: adults and children over 12 – initial dose two caplets with water, followed by one or two caplets every four hours if necessary. No more than six caplets in 24 hours. Not suitable for children under 12.

JANSSEN PHARMACEUTICAL

Isogel

A natural-fibre drink containing dried ispaghula husk, a natural source of nonstarch carbohydrate fibre, the fibre type considered to provide the most suitable means of increasing faecal bulk. Ispaghula is obtained from *Plantago ovata*, a plant grown mainly in the southern hemisphere. The outer layers of the dried ripe seeds are milled and made into granules.

Isogel is both effective as a laxative and helpful in the control of diarrhoea associated with disorders such as irritable bowel syndrome, making it an ideal preparation for promoting natural bowel regularity. It's also useful in the management of colostomies.

Dosage: the following dosage is a guide and can be adjusted to suit individual needs. Adults – two 5 ml spoonfuls once or twice daily, preferably at meal-times; children 6 to 12 years – one 5 ml spoonful once or twice daily, preferably at meal-times.   CHARWELL PHARMACEUTICALS

Jaap's Health Salt
Antacid powder containing sodium bicarbonate, tartaric acid and sodium potassium tartrate for the symptomatic relief of indigestion and heartburn, and a mild laxative. Adults take one to two teaspoonfuls in water and repeat two to three hourly as needed. As a laxative, take two teaspoonfuls in water in the morning or at bedtime. Children under 12 years: half the adult dose.

ROCHE CONSUMER HEALTH

Jackson's All Fours
Syrup containing guaiphenesin (an expectorant) for the symptomatic relief of coughs. Adults: two to four 5 ml spoonfuls at bedtime, or at four-hourly intervals. Maximum 120 ml in 24 hours. Not to be given to children under 12.   ROSMARINE

Jackson's Febrifuge
Liquid containing sodium salicylate, for the symptomatic relief of influenza, sore throat and feverish colds, general muscular aches, strains or sprains, rheumatism, lumbago and fibrositis. Adults: one to two 5 ml spoonfuls every six hours or three times a day. Take with equal amount of water. Not for children under 12 years.   ROSMARINE

Junifen
Brand name for the only form of ibuprofen (see page 279) available for children. Suitable for children over 1 year.

Junior Kao-C

Suspension flavoured with cinnamon, nutmeg and clove oils, containing light kaolin – a bulk-forming and absorbent agent, and calcium carbonate, an antacid, to calm the stomach for the treatment of short-term, mild diarrhoea.

Dosage: children over 14 – four 5 ml spoonfuls three times a day; 5–14 years – two 5 ml spoonfuls; 1–5 years – one 5 ml spoonful.

SETON HEALTHCARE

Junior Lemsip

Powder containing paracetamol, phenylephrine hydrochloride – which constricts blood vessels to ease congestion, the expectorant sodium citrate and ascorbic acid for the relief of the symptoms of colds and influenza in children, including the relief of aches and pains, nasal congestion and lowering of temperature. Children 6–12 years: two sachets dissolved in a beakerful of hot (not boiling) water every four hours. Maximum eight sachets in 24 hours. Children 3 years to under 6 years: one sachet dissolved in half a beakerful of hot (not boiling) water every four hours. Maximum four sachets in 24 hours. Not to be given to children under three except on a doctor's advice.

RECKITT & COLMAN

Kalms Tablets

A traditional herbal remedy containing extracts of valerian, hops and gentian to help relieve periods of anxiety, stresses and strains and allow restful sleep. No known evidence of habit-forming effects. Not suitable for children.

Dosage: two tablets three times a day after meals. Do not take during pregnancy or while breast-feeding. Seek medical advice if you're taking other medications or if the condition worsens. LANES

Kamillosan

Ointment containing chamomile in a base containing lanolin – a natural herbal treatment for sore skin conditions that has been used for more than 2000 years – to soothe away soreness from sore nipples and in nappy rash. Apply after breast-feeding. The ointment does not need to be washed off. Breast pads may be used to protect clothing. NORGINE

Karvol Decongestant Capsules

A combination of natural oils, including pine, cinnamon and

menthol, to help clear nasal congestion. Suitable for children and adults. Empty one capsule into hot water and inhale vapour freely. For young children, empty a capsule on to a handkerchief and tie it down securely in the vicinity.   CROOKES HEALTHCARE

Kleer

A traditional herbal remedy for skin disorders and eczema which also helps alleviate inflammations. It contains echinacea, stinging nettle and burdock root.   MODERN HEALTH

KLN Suspension

Liquid suspension containing sodium citrate, kaolin light, peppermint oil and pectin for infantile diarrhoea or abnormally loose bowel action and minor stomach upsets caused by dietary problems. For children, following each bowel movement: 6–12 months one 5 ml spoonful, 1–3 years two 5 ml spoonfuls, 3–10 years four 5 ml spoonfuls.

ROCHE CONSUMER HEALTH

Kwells and Junior Kwells

Melt-in-the-mouth anti-travel sickness tablets containing hyoscine hydrobromide to control motion sickness and nausea caused by disturbances of the inner ear. May cause drowsiness. Can be taken up to 30 minutes before start of journey, or at the onset of nausea. Not to be taken by persons suffering from glaucoma. Children should not be left unattended.

Dosage: Kwells – adults, one tablet every six hours if needed. No more than three in 24 hours. Children over 10 – half to one tablet, not more than one and a half to three in 24 hours.

Junior Kwells: children 8–12 years – one to two tablets, not more than three to six in 24 hours; 3–7 years – half to one tablet, not more than one and a half to three in 24 hours. Children under 3 – only on medical advice.

ROCHE CONSUMER HEALTH

Lacto-Calamine

Soothing calamine lotion with protective zinc oxide, cooling hamamelis water and phenol, for relieving discomfort caused by skin irritations, sunburn, insect bites and stings. Apply as needed.

Also available in cream form.

SCHERING-PLOUGH CONSUMER HEALTH

Lanacane

Soothing cream containing the local anaesthetic benzocaine for the relief of itching and pain of everyday scrapes and cuts, heat rash, nettle rash, itchy, dry skin, sore 'detergent hands', eczema, rectal or vaginal itching. Apply cream to affected area as needed three or four times daily. Not for prolonged use.

COMBE INTERNATIONAL

Lanacort Creme and Ointment

Hydrocortisone cream and ointment to calm the body's reactions to skin disturbances and aid healing. For relief from rashes, redness, itching, skin irritations, inflammation and scaling caused by insect bites, stings and allergic reactions to soaps, jewellery, toiletries and detergents. Use sparingly over a small area once or twice daily for a maximum period of one week. Do not use during pregnancy or for children under 10 without medical advice. Do not use on the eyes, face, ano-genital region, broken or infected skin including that caused by cold sores, acne and athlete's foot.   COMBE INTERNATIONAL

Lasonil

An ointment for bruises, sprains, piles and soft-tissue injuries. Contains heparinoid, an anti-inflammatory agent, and hyaluronidase, an enzyme which makes tissue more

permeable. Unless otherwise directed, apply thickly to the affected area two to three times daily. If symptoms persist, consult your doctor. For external use only.   BAYER

Laxoberal

A laxative containing sodium picosulphate, which is broken down by bacteria in the large intestine to form soft stools usually 10–14 hours after administration.

Dosage: adults – 5–15 ml at night. Children 5–10 years – 2.5–5 ml at night; not recommended for children under 5.   WINDSOR PHARMACEUTICALS

Lemon Eno

Powder containing citric acid, and antacids sodium bicarbonate and sodium carbonate for the symptomatic relief of indigestion, flatulence and nausea.

Dosage: adults 5 g or one sachet dissolved in water every two to three hours if necessary. Maximum 30 g or six sachets in 24 hours. Not recommended for children under 12 years except on medical advice.

SMITHKLINE BEECHAM CONSUMER BRANDS

Lemsip

Powder containing paracetamol, phenylephrine

hydrochloride – to constrict blood vessels and so ease congestion, ascorbic acid and sodium citrate (used as an expectorant) with real lemon for the relief of the symptoms of colds and influenza such as aches and pains and nasal congestion, and for the lowering of temperature. Also available in blackcurrant flavour.

Dosage – adults and children over 12: one sachet dissolved by stirring in hot water. The dose may be repeated after four hours. No more than six doses should be taken in 24 hours. Not for children under 12 except on medical advice.   RECKITT & COLMAN

Lemsip Chesty Cough
Liquid containing the expectorant guaiphenesin for the symptomatic relief of deep chesty coughs and to soothe the throat.

Dosage: adults and children over 12 years – two 10 ml doses. Children 6–12 years – one 10 ml dose; children 2–6 years – one 5 ml dose. Under two years – on medical advice only. Doses up to four times daily.   RECKITT & COLMAN

Lemsip Cold Relief Capsules
Capsules for the treatment of the symptoms of colds and influenza, containing paracetamol, the stimulant caffeine and phenylephrine hydrochloride, which constricts blood vessels to ease congestion. Adults and children over 12: one to two capsules every three to four hours. Do not exceed eight capsules in 24 hours. Not to be given to children under 12 without medical advice.

RECKITT & COLMAN

Lemsip Dry Tickly Cough
Syrupy liquid containing glycerol, honey, citric acid and lemon oil terpeneless for the symptomatic relief of dry, tickly coughs and to soothe the throat.

Dosage: adults and children over 12 – two 5 ml spoonfuls, up to four times daily. Children under 12 – one 5 ml spoonful, up to four times daily.   RECKITT & COLMAN

Lemsip Flu Strength
Sachets containing paracetamol, phenylephrine hydrochloride (to clear a stuffy nose) and ascorbic acid, for the relief of the symptoms of colds and flu.

Dosage: adults and children over 12 – one sachet every four hours. Do not exceed three sachets in 24 hours. Children under 12 years on medical advice only. Junior

Lemsip is available for children from 3–12 years. Do not take any medicine containing paracetamol within four hours of taking this medicine. Lemsip Flu Strength should be dissolved by stirring in hot (not boiling) water and sweetened to taste.

RECKITT & COLMAN

Lemsip Menthol Extra

Sachets containing paracetamol, phenylephrine hydrochloride (a decongestant) and ascorbic acid for the relief of symptoms of colds and influenza. Adults and children over 12 years – one sachet every four hours. Do not exceed four doses in 24 hours.

RECKITT & COLMAN

Lemsip Night Time

A liquid containing paracetamol, dextromethorphan hydrobromide (a cough-suppressant), chlorpheniramine maleate (an antihistamine) and phenylpropanolamine hydrochloride (to ease congestion), for the relief of nasal congestion during colds and influenza, together with the relief of other symptoms frequently associated with these conditions such as fever, aches and cough.

Dosage: adults and children over 12 – one 30 ml dose at bedtime. Children under 12 years on medical advice only. Do not take any medicine containing paracetamol within four hours of taking this medicine. Do not take with any other cold treatment at night. Lemsip Night Time should be taken after mixing with hot (not boiling) water, or without adding hot water, if preferred.   RECKITT & COLMAN

Lenium

Dandruff treatment cream shampoo containing selenium sulphide. Use shampoo twice weekly for two weeks, once a week for a further two weeks and then every three to six weeks as required to maintain control. Use as normal shampoo, but leave second lather on scalp for five minutes. Lenium should not be used within 48 hours of perming or dyeing hair.

CILAG

Librofem

Tablets containing ibuprofen specifically for the relief of period pain. Take two tablets every four hours with a maximum of six tablets in 24 hours.   ZYMA

Liminate

A traditional herbal remedy

for the symptomatic relief of occasional constipation. It contains turkey rhubarb, senna leaf and Irish moss.

MODERN HEALTH

Listerine Antiseptic

A solution for oral hygiene, bad breath and for relief of sore throats. Can also be used as an antiseptic for minor cuts, bites, stings and wounds. Contains the antiseptics benzoic acid, thymol, eucalyptol, with menthol, methyl salicylate and ethanol. For adults and children. Rinse the mouth, teeth and gums vigorously night and morning with half a mouthful of Listerine. Then tilt the head back and gargle for 30 seconds. Don't swallow.

WARNER LAMBERT

Listermint

An oral antiseptic, mouthwash and breath-freshener containing cetylpyridinium chloride, an antiseptic, and zinc chloride, an astringent which 'tightens up' the gum membranes and reduces inflammation. Suitable for adults and children. Rinse the mouth or gargle with half a capful of Listermint every morning. Do not swallow. Do not dilute.

WARNER LAMBERT

Lloyd's Cream

A cool, soothing, odour-free cream containing diethylamine salicylate which provides gentle and effective relief from muscular aches and pains, sprains, rheumatic pain, fibrositis, lumbago and sciatica without reddening the skin.

Gently massage cream into the affected area until it has been fully absorbed. The application may be repeated two or three times a day, or as your doctor directs. Wash hands after use. Not to be used on children aged 6 years and under without medical advice.

SETON HEALTHCARE

Lustys Garlic Perles

Herbal remedy containing essential oil of garlic, available in two potencies and traditionally used to treat the symptoms of the common cold and coughs. Can also be used for temporary relief of the symptoms of rhinitis and catarrh. The higher potency is not recommended for children under 12.

Dosage: adults – one capsule before each meal or up to three at bedtime with a little water. Children 5 to 12 – one capsule of the lower potency twice daily.

LUSTYS NATURAL PRODUCTS

Lustys Herbalene

A powdered blend of dried herbs and seeds including senna leaf, buckthorn, elder leaf and fennel to help relieve temporary or occasional constipation.

Dosage: adults – half to one 5 ml spoonful placed on the tongue and washed down with a little warm water first thing in the morning and last thing at night. Children 7–14 years – half the above dose. Alternatively, Herbalene may be brewed by adding half to one 5 ml spoonful to half a cup of boiling water. Cool and strain before drinking.

LUSTYS NATURAL PRODUCTS

Lyclear Creme Rinse

A creme rinse for the treatment of head lice and their eggs. Contains permethrin, an insecticide. Used as directed, a ten-minute application of the rinse will kill head lice and their eggs. As with all medicines, if you're pregnant or currently taking any other medicine, consult your doctor or pharmacist before using this product.

Lyclear Dermal Cream is a new product for the treatment of scabies infection.

WELLCOME

Lypsyl

Moisturiser for chapped lips available in original flavour, lemon and mint as well as a night-time gel in a tube. Apply as required.   ZYMA

Lypsyl Cold Sore Gel

Contains the local anaesthetic lignocaine hydrochloride, zinc sulphate and cetrimide (an antiseptic) for the symptomatic relief of cold sores.

Adults and children over 12 – apply a small amount to the affected area with your fingertip three to four times daily. Not recommended for children under 12 unless advised by your doctor.   ZYMA

Maalox Suspension

Antacid suspension containing aluminium hydroxide and magnesium hydroxide for the symptomatic relief of heartburn, gastric hyperacidity and gastritis. Adults over 14 years take two to four 5 ml spoonfuls twenty minutes to one hour after meals and at bedtime, or as needed. Not to be given to children under 14 years. Higher strength Maalox TC Suspension also available.

RHONE POULENC RORER

Maalox Plus

Antacid suspension or tablets containing aluminium hydroxide, dimethicone activated, magnesium hydroxide for the symptomatic relief of dyspepsia, heartburn and flatulence. Suspension: adults take one to two 5 ml spoonfuls 20 minutes to one hour after meals and at bedtime, or as needed. Children: dose may be a proportion of the adult dose. Under 5 years a maximum of one 5 ml spoonful three times a day. Tablets: adults one to two tablets well chewed four times daily, 20 minutes to one hour after meals and at bedtime, or as needed.

RHONE POULENC RORER

Maclean Indigestion Tablets

Tablets containing antacids aluminium hydroxide, calcium carbonate and magnesium carbonate light for indigestion, flatulence and nausea.

Adults: one to two tablets sucked or chewed as needed. Maximum 16 tablets in 24 hours. Not for children under 12 years.

SMITHKLINE BEECHAM CONSUMER BRANDS

Massage Balm

A remedy with extracts from arnica flowers, birch leaves, lavender – lavandin oil, and rosemary oil, for the relief of stiffness, fibrositis, muscular and rheumatic pain. Also for the symptomatic relief of bruising, sciatica, lumbago and cramp. Should ideally be used after a warm bath or shower, while the skin is still damp.

WELEDA

Medicaid

Antiseptic cream containing cetrimide for sun- and wind-burned skin, sore, chapped hands, chafing in the intimate areas beneath the breasts and in the crotch, nappy rash, minor burns, cuts and grazes – whenever skin is too sore to touch. Apply liberally to the affected area. Repeat as necessary. For first aid, wash area gently and pat dry before application. For nappy rash, apply after nappy changing, paying particular attention to tiny folds and creases where irritation often begins. Give an extra application at night for protection during the baby's longest sleep period.

NEWTON CHEMICAL

Medicinal Charcoal Biscuits and Tablets by J.L. Bragg

Contain pure vegetable charcoal for the relief of indigestion, wind and heartburn. Also relieve halitosis. Take four or more biscuits during or after meals. Tablets – take two or more after meals.   J.L. BRAGG

Medijel Gel
To relieve mouth ulcers, sore gums and denture rubbing. Contains the local anaesthetic lignocaine hydrochloride and aminacrine hydrochloride, an antiseptic.

Apply gel to the painful area. Repeat the application after 20 minutes if necessary. If symptoms persist, consult your doctor.   DDD

Medijel Soft Pastilles
Pastilles formulated with a soft base to give quick release of the analgesic lignocaine hydrochloride. Also contain the antiseptic aminacrine hydrochloride. Because the pastilles are soft, they avoid the risk of further damage to inflamed or broken gums.

Place pastille against the affected part and let it dissolve slowly. Repeat as necessary. If symptoms persist, consult your doctor.   DDD

Medised
Soothing blackcurrant-flavoured suspension giving pain relief for children from 1–12 years old. Contains paracetamol and a mild antihistamine, promethazine

hydrochloride. Reduces temperature and relieves painful or feverish conditions such as toothache, headache, sore throat, colds and flu. Also dries up a runny nose. May cause drowsiness.

Dosage: children 6–12 years – four 5 ml spoonfuls; 1–6 years – two 5 ml spoonfuls. Under 1 year – on doctor's advice only. The dose should not be repeated more frequently than every four hours, and no more than four doses should be given in any 24-hour period.

MARTINDALE PHARMACEUTICALS

Medised Plain
Sugar-free suspension containing paracetamol. Children 1–6: two 5 ml spoonfuls; 6–12: four 5 ml spoonfuls. Doses four times a day.   MARTINDALE PHARMACEUTICALS

Medised Plain 6+
Sugar-free suspension containing paracetamol for children over six years. Children 6–12: two 5 ml spoonfuls four times a day.

MARTINDALE PHARMACEUTICALS

Meggozones
Pastilles containing menthol, benzoin and liquorice to soothe soreness in the throat, relieve coughs and reduce catarrh. Adults – allow one

pastille to dissolve slowly in the mouth as needed. Maximum daily dosage – 15 pastilles. If the mouth becomes sensitive, irritated or sore, discontinue use.

SCHERING-PLOUGH CONSUMER HEALTH

Meltus Adult Dry Cough Elixir

Sugar- and colour-free elixir containing dextromethorphan hydrobromide, a cough-suppressant and pseudo-ephedrine hydrochloride, a decongestant. May cause drowsiness. Asthmatics should consult their doctor before using this product.

Dosage: adults and children over 12 only – one 5 ml spoonful to be taken four times a day.   SETON HEALTHCARE

Meltus Adult Expectorant and Junior

Linctus containing the expectorant guaiphenesin and cetylpyridinium chloride, an antiseptic, as well as sucrose and honey, for the symptomatic relief of coughs and catarrh in influenza, colds and mild throat infections. Not suitable for children under 12.

Dosage: one or two 5 ml spoonfuls swallowed slowly every three or four hours. Junior version – for children over two years of age.

Dosage, to be taken three or four times daily: children over 6 – two 5 ml spoonfuls; 2–6 years – one 5 ml spoonful.

SETON HEALTHCARE

Meltus Baby Cough Linctus

Sugar- and colour-free blackcurrant-flavoured linctus containing dilute acetic acid, an expectorant, for the symptomatic relief of irritating and distressing coughs often accompanying colds, especially for babies over three months old and young children.

Dosage, to be given slowly: children over 2½ years – two 5 ml spoonfuls; 1–2½ years – one 5 ml spoonful. Babies 3 months to 1 year – half a 5 ml spoonful. Repeat as needed every two or three hours.

SETON HEALTHCARE

Menthol and Wintergreen Heat Rub

Counter-irritant heat rub containing methyl salicylate, eucalyptus oil, camphor, menthol and mustard oil, to ease muscular pain and stiffness caused by rheumatic conditions including fibrositis and lumbago. Also effective for sprains and bruises. Apply two or three times daily over the affected muscles and joints. Massage gently but firmly.   SETON HEALTHCARE

Mentholair Steam Bath

A blend of natural essential oils including menthol, eucalyptus, peppermint, rosemary and lavender which have been traditionally used to help relieve cold symptoms.

MENTHOLATUM

Mentholatum Vapour Rub

Blended from natural menthol and eucalyptus with extracts of pine. Also contains methyl salicylate. The vapour from these ingredients clears congestion, eases breathing and relieves soreness. Can also be used to relieve itching, insect bites and stings, nettle rash or dry skin. A nasal inhaler and antiseptic lozenges are also available.   MENTHOLATUM

Merocaine

Lozenges containing an antiseptic – cetylpyridinium chloride, and a local anaesthetic – benzocaine, to relieve pain and discomfort from severe sore throat due to tonsillitis and pharyngitis. Also helpful in easing pain from gum infections. Suitable for adults and children over 12. Allow to dissolve slowly in the mouth. Take one every two hours as needed. Do not exceed eight lozenges in 24 hours. If symptoms persist or are severe, or are accompanied by fever, headache, nausea and vomiting, consult your doctor.   MARION MERRELL DOW

Merocets

Sore throat lozenges to soothe irritated and inflamed tissues. Contain cetylpyridinium chloride, an antibacterial agent. Suitable for adults and children over six. Dissolve slowly in the mouth. One lozenge every three hours.

MARION MERRELL DOW

Merothol

Lozenges to relieve sore throats due to colds and to relieve nasal congestion. Contain the antibacterial agent cetylpyridinium chloride and soothing menthol and eucalyptus oil. Suitable for children over 6. Dissolve slowly in the mouth. One every three hours or as often as needed.   MARION MERRELL DOW

Merovit

Lozenges containing the antibacterial agent cetylpyridinium chloride and Vitamin C for the relief of sore throats caused by colds. Suitable for adults and children over 6 years of age and should be allowed to dissolve slowly in the mouth. One lozenge every three hours.   MARION MERRELL DOW

Metamucil

A natural laxative containing ispaghula husk. Adults and children over 12 should take one rounded 5 ml spoonful. Children 6–12, a quarter to one level 5 ml spoonful. Usually taken one to three times a day depending on need and response. Continued use for two to three days may be needed for most benefit. Add dosage to 150 ml cool water, milk, fruit juice or other liquid. Adequate fluid intake should be maintained. Not to be taken in cases of intestinal obstruction, faecal impaction or a previously discovered hypersensitivity to ispaghula – when it causes unpleasant diarrhoea, for example.   PROCTER AND GAMBLE

Metanium

Ointment containing titanium dioxide, titanium peroxide, titanium salicylate and titanium tannate in a silicone paraffin base for the treatment and prevention of nappy rash.   CHANCELLOR

Migraleve

Tablets to relieve migraine headache, nausea and vomiting. Not suitable for children under 10. May cause drowsiness. Pack contains eight pink and four yellow tablets. Pink tablets contain the pain-relievers paracetamol and codeine phosphate and the antihistamine buclizine hydrochloride. Yellow tablets do not contain buclizine hydrochloride.

Adults should take two pink tablets at the first sign of a migraine attack. If further treatment is needed, take two yellow tablets every four hours. Maximum dose – two pink and not more than six yellow tablets in 24 hours.

Children 10–14 years – take one pink tablet initially. If necessary, follow with one yellow tablet every four hours. Maximum dose – one pink and not more than three yellow tablets in 24 hours.

Packs of pink only or yellow only tablets are also available.

CHARWELL HEALTH CARE

Milk of Magnesia

A stomach-upset remedy for all the family. Contains magnesium hydroxide for the relief of indigestion, over-acidity, heartburn and flatulence. Can also be used as a laxative.

Dosage: adults one to two 5 ml spoonfuls. Children 3–12 years, one 5 ml spoonful. As a laxative – adults, two to three 15 ml spoonfuls at bedtime. Repeat nightly, reducing dose each night until constipation is relieved. Children 1–12 years, one to two 5 ml spoonfuls at bedtime. Under 1 year – only as recommended by your doctor. Can be taken in milk or water if desired.

Also available in tablet form.   STERLING HEALTH

Mil-Par

A laxative emulsion containing magnesium hydroxide and liquid paraffin. Not recommended for children under 3.

Dosage: adults one to two 15 ml spoonfuls before breakfast or at bedtime. Children over 7 – half to one 15 ml spoonful at bedtime; 3–7 years – one to two 5 ml spoonfuls at bedtime. Can be mixed with half a glass of milk or water if desired.

STERLING HEALTH

Moorland

Tablets for the relief of indigestion, heartburn and flatulence. Contain the antacids bismuth aluminate, magnesium trisilicate, dried aluminium hydroxide gel, heavy magnesium carbonate, light kaolin and calcium carbonate.

Dosage: two tablets dissolved slowly in the mouth after each meal and last thing at night, or when required.

SETON HEALTHCARE

Morhulin

Contains cod-liver oil and zinc oxide to provide a barrier to protect baby's skin from contact exposure to moisture. Use at every nappy change. Can also be used to treat eczema, pressure sores, varicose ulcers and minor wounds.   SETON HEALTHCARE

Morsep

An antiseptic cream containing cetrimide – an active antiseptic which helps fight infection – and Vitamin A, which is known to have healing properties. Ideal for the treatment of sore nipples, nappy rash, minor burns and scalds. Also suitable as an emollient for patients suffering from incontinence.

For sore nipples – simply apply to the affected area. For nappy and urinary incontinence rash – carefully wash and dry skin before applying to affected areas. Ensure that nappies or underclothes are rinsed thoroughly to remove all traces of soap and detergent. For minor burns and scalds – do not wash, but apply cream on a piece of gauze.   NAPP

Movelat

Rubefacient cream and gel containing mucopoly-saccharide polysulphate and salicylic acid for the relief of symptoms associated with painful inflammatory conditions of the musculoskeletal system, including traumatic conditions such as sprains and strains.

Dosage: adults and children over 12 – massage 5–15 cm (2–6 in) of cream or gel into the affected area up to four times daily. Should not be used on large areas of skin, broken or sensitive areas of skin, or on mucous membranes. Not suitable for children under 12.   PANPHARMA

Mrs Cullen's Powders
Contain aspirin and caffeine for the relief of headaches, colds, flu, neuralgia, rheumatic and period pains. Not suitable for children under 12. Take a powder immediately when colds and flu symptoms are experienced. Repeat every four hours. For other pain, take one powder and repeat every three or four hours as necessary. Mix powder in a little water or fruit drink.

CULLEN AND DAVISON

Mucron
Tablets for the relief of nasal congestion, containing phenylpropanolamine hydrochloride, which constricts blood vessels to ease congestion, and paracetamol.

Take one tablet two to four times a day with a maximum of four tablets in 24 hours.

ZYMA

Mucron Junior Syrup
Syrup for the relief of nasal congestion in children. Contains phenylpropanolamine hydrochloride, a decongestant, and vinegar of ipecacuanha, an expectorant.

Dosage: children 6–12 years – one to two 5 ml spoonfuls; 2–6 years – one 5 ml spoonful up to four times daily. Allow four hours between doses.

ZYMA

Mycil
Double-action ointment for treating athlete's foot. Contains tolnaftate, an antifungal agent, and benzalkonium chloride, an antiseptic. Rub into infected parts morning and night. Continue treatment for at least a week after the infection has cleared. Also available as powder and foot spray. Powder contains tolnaftate and chlorhexidine hydrochloride. Spray contains tolnaftate.   CROOKES HEALTHCARE

Mycota Cream
To treat athlete's foot. Cream contains the fungicides undecenoic acid and zinc undecenoate. Apply night and

morning. Also available as powder. Continue treatment for one week after all signs of infection have disappeared. Spray containing undecenoic acid and the fungicide dichlorophen available from Seton Healthcare.

CROOKES HEALTHCARE

Natracalm

Herbal remedy for the stress and strain of everyday life and to help disturbed nights. Tablets contain an aqueous alcoholic extract from a species of passiflora, a plant that has been used for medicinal purposes since the early nineteenth century. Take one tablet three times a day with meals. If necessary, a further tablet may be taken at bedtime.   ENGLISH GRAINS HEALTHCARE

Natrasleep

Combines two traditional herbal ingredients – hops and valerian – which together have been recognised for hundreds of years as having excellent sleep-inducing and relaxing properties with no known side-effects. If you are taking a prescribed medicine, consult your doctor before using this product.

ENGLISH GRAINS HEALTHCARE

Naturest

A non-habit-forming traditional remedy for the treatment of temporary or occasional sleeplessness. Tablets contain passiflora aqu ext. – extract of passiflora, a herbal tranquilliser. Not recommended for children under 12.

Dosage: adults – two tablets three times a day after meals and up to three tablets at bedtime. If, after five days, you're still experiencing disturbed sleep, consult your medical adviser.   LANES

Nelsons Arnica Cream

A topical herbal remedy traditionally used in the symptomatic treatment of bruises. Prepared from the Alpine plant *Arnica montana*. It's a healing and soothing agent when applied to bruising resulting from injuries, falls, blows and contusions. Apply gently to bruised surfaces.   NELSONS

Nelsons Calendula Cream

A topical herbal remedy prepared from marigolds, traditionally used in the symptomatic treatment of sore and rough skin. Apply a little cream and rub away lightly.   NELSONS

Nelsons Evening Primrose Cream

A skin cream made from the seeds of the evening primrose flower – particularly soothing when applied to dry or 'tired' skin. NELSONS

Nelsons Graphites Cream

A homoeopathic remedy for dermatitis containing sixth potency graphites – a soothing application which helps protect sensitive skin against further irritation. Apply gently to the affected area as required. NELSONS

Nelsons Haemorrhoid Cream

A topical herbal remedy traditionally used in the symptomatic treatment of piles. Prepared from fresh plant tinctures including calendula and hamamelis (witch-hazel). Wash affected area with warm water and apply cream as needed. NELSONS

Nelsons Hay Fever Tablets

A homoeopathic remedy for the relief of hay fever with sixth homoeopathic potency of *Allium cepa, Euphrasia officinalis* and *Sabadilla officinarum*. Suck or chew two tablets at two-hourly intervals for six doses, then three times daily until symptoms subside.

Children should take half the adult dose. NELSONS

Nelsons Rhus Tox. Cream

A topical herbal remedy traditionally used in the symptomatic treatment of rheumatic conditions. Also for strains and the effects of over-lifting. Prepared from the fresh leaves of *Rhus toxicodendron*. Massage gently into the affected area as required. NELSONS

Nelsons Teething Granules

A homoeopathically prepared remedy to help bring relief from the distressing symptoms of teething. The sixth homoeopathic potency of chamomilla helps the body overcome the symptoms and may be safely taken by small infants. Tip on to a clean, dry spoon the equivalent of a pinch of granules (do not touch with the fingers). Put the granules directly into the child's mouth every two hours for up to six doses. NELSONS

Nelsons Travel Sickness Tablets

A homoeopathic remedy for the relief of travel sickness with sixth homoeopathic potency of Apomorph, Staphisagria, Cocculus, Theridion, Petroleum, Tabacum and Nux Vomica.

Suck or chew two tablets hourly for two hours before the journey. Take two more tablets hourly during the journey if necessary. Children should take half the adult dose.   NELSONS

Nicabate
Nicotine patches in three different strengths to help stop smoking. Apply one patch to the skin daily for 10 weeks.   MARION MERRELL DOW

Nicobrevin
Capsules containing menthyl valerate, quinine, camphor and eucalyptus oil to help give up smoking.   INTERCARE PRODUCTS

Niconil Patches
Patches in two different strengths to help give up smoking.   ELAN PHARMA

Nicorette
Chewing gum containing nicotine to help give up smoking. Adults: chew one piece when urge to smoke is felt. Maximum 15 pieces in 24 hours. Nicorette Plus also now available.   KABI PHARMACIA

Nicorette Patch
Patches in three different strengths containing nicotine to help give up smoking. Use for 12 weeks.   KABI PHARMACIA

Nicotinell
Nicotine-replacement patches in three different strengths designed as an aid to giving up smoking. You must not smoke while using the patches. As your body adjusts to not smoking you should gradually reduce the size of the patch over a period of up to 12 weeks until you no longer need to use them.

Adults only: apply one patch at the same time each day (preferably first thing in the morning) to a clean, dry and hairless area of the skin. The front or side of the chest, back or the upper arm are recommended. Leave the patch on for 24 hours, then remove and dispose of before applying the next patch.

Not to be used by non-smokers. Not recommended for people under 18 years of age. Do not use if you have serious heart disease, are pregnant or breast feeding. If you are under the care of a doctor or taking prescribed medication, consult your GP or pharmacist before using this product.   ZYMA

Night Cough Pastilles
Contain extract of wild cherry bark and codeine phosphate, a cough-suppressant, to relieve tickly coughs. Not suitable for children under 12. Dosage –

adults may take up to four pastilles in any two-hour period, but no more than 15 in any 24-hour period.

ERNEST JACKSON

Night Nurse Capsules

Capsules containing dextromethorphan hydrobromide (a cough suppressant), paracetamol, and promethazine hydrochloride (an antihistamine) for the symptomatic relief of colds, chills and influenza, at night.

Adults: two capsules just before bedtime. Children 6–12 years one capsule just before bedtime. Not recommended for children under 6 years except on medical advice.

SMITHKLINE BEECHAM CONSUMER BRANDS

Night Nurse Liquid

Liquid containing the same active ingredients as Night Nurse Capsules, for colds, chills and influenza (night use).

Adults: 20 ml just before going to bed. Children 6–12 years 10 ml just before going to bed. Not recommended for children under 6 except on medical advice.

SMITHKLINE BEECHAM CONSUMER BRANDS

Nirolex

A pleasantly flavoured, soothing linctus containing guaiphenesin (an expectorant), ephedrine hydrochloride (a decongestant), menthol, sucrose and glycerol, to relieve the symptoms of chesty coughs without causing drowsiness.

Dosage: adults and children over 12 (unless your doctor gives you different instructions) – two 5 ml spoonfuls; children 5–12 years – one 5 ml spoonful. Repeat the dose every four hours up to four times in 24 hours if needed. For children under 5, use Nirolex for children. Do not exceed the stated dose. If symptoms do not go away after three days, consult your doctor. Patients suffering from asthma should consult their doctor before using this product. BOOTS

Nirolex for children

Specially formulated sugar-free linctus for children from 1–12 years. Contains the expectorant guaiphenesin to relieve tight, chesty coughs.

Dosage: children 5–12 years – two 5 ml spoonfuls; 1–5 years – one 5 ml spoonful. Repeat the dose every four hours up to four times in 24 hours if necessary. Contains no artificial colours. BOOTS

Nirolex Lozenges

Contain dextromethorphan hydrobromide (a cough-suppressant) to relieve the symptoms of dry, tickly coughs.

Adults and children over 6 – suck one lozenge when the cough is troublesome. Adults and children over 12 – take up to 10 lozenges in 24 hours if needed; children 6–12 years – not more than two lozenges within any four hours and not more than seven in any 24-hour period. Children under 6 should not be given these lozenges. Do not exceed the stated dose.   BOOTS

Noctura

A homoeopathic remedy for the relief of insomnia. Contains the sixth homoeopathic potency of Kali Brom, Coffea, Passiflora, Avena Sativa, Alfalfa and Valeriana. Take two tablets four hours before retiring and two tablets at bedtime. A further two tablets may be taken during the night if required.   NELSONS

Normacol and Normacol Plus

Granules containing sterculia, a natural fibre product, for the treatment of constipation. Dosage: adults one or two sachets or one to two heaped

5 ml spoonfuls, once or twice daily after meals. Children 6–12 years: one half of the above amount. Children under 6 on the discretion of the doctor.

Normacol Plus also contains the natural laxative frangula. Adults: one or two sachets once or twice daily after meals or as directed by physician. Reduced dosage may be given to children from 6–12 years as directed by physician. The granules should be placed dry on the tongue and, without chewing or crushing, swallowed immediately with plenty of liquid (water or a cool drink).   NORGINE

Nulacin

Antacid tablets containing calcium carbonate, whole milk with dextrins and maltose, magnesium trisilicate, magnesium heavy oxide for relief from heartburn and acid indigestion, hiatus hernia, symptoms of peptic ulcer and pain from hyperacidity. Adults only: one tablet as needed between meals and at bedtime, with a maximum of eight tablets a day.   GOLDSHIELD

Nupercainal

Cream containing a local anaesthetic, cinchocaine, for the relief of piles. Apply as required, not more than three times a day. ZYMA

Nurofen

Ibuprofen tablets effective in the relief of headaches, cold and flu symptoms, rheumatic pain, muscular pain, back ache, feverishness, migraine, period pain, dental pain and neuralgia. Also available in soluble form. Not suitable for children under 12.

Dosage: initial dose two tablets with water. Then, if necessary, one or two tablets every four hours. No more than six tablets daily.

CROOKES HEALTHCARE

Nurse Harvey's Gripe Mixture

Gripe water with dill oil, caraway oil, weak ginger tincture and the antacid sodium bicarbonate to relieve the pain of wind, tummy upsets and colic.

Dosage: children over 1 year – three to four 5 ml spoonfuls; 6–12 months – two to three 5 ml spoonfuls; 2–6 months – two 5 ml spoonfuls; 1–2 months – one 5 ml spoonful; birth to 1 month – half a 5 ml spoonful. Give one dose during or after a feed. No more than eight doses in 24 hours. HARVEY SCRUTON

Nurse Sykes' Powders

Powder containing caffeine, paracetamol and aspirin for mild to moderate pain and the symptomatic relief of rheumatic aches and pains, fibrositis. Also symptomatic relief of influenza, feverishness and feverish colds. Adults: one powder with a little water every four hours. Maximum six powders in 24 hours. Not recommended for children under 12 years except on medical advice. ROSMARINE

Nylax

Laxative tablets containing phenolpthalein, powdered senna leaf and bisacodyl (a laxative). For short-term use only. Not suitable for children. One or two tablets to be taken at bedtime. A bowel movement is generally produced in 6–12 hours. Do not use during pregnancy or while breast-feeding. Do not take if any gastro-intestinal blockage is present.

CROOKES HEALTHCARE

Nytol

Tablets containing diphenhydramine hydrochloride (an antihistamine) for use as an aid to the relief of temporary sleep disturbance. Two tablets to be taken 20 minutes before going to bed, or as directed by a doctor. Not recommended for children under 16.

STAFFORD MILLER

Odourless Garlic One-A-Day

Odourless garlic powder capsules. Take one capsule every day with water. For the beneficial effects of garlic, see 'Herbal remedies' under COLD, THE COMMON p.34.

EVANS

Oilatum Cream

Cream containing arachis oil to reduce moisture loss in dry skin conditions. Use as often as needed. Apply to the affected area and rub in well. Especially effective immediately after washing.

STIEFEL

Oilatum Emollient

A bath oil producing an emulsion of dispersed oil in the bath water and an even film on the surface to aid the treatment of dry skin conditions. Contains liquid paraffin, which replaces oil and water and hydrates the keratin – a protein in the outer layer of the skin, and the emulsifier wool alcohol. Suitable for infants.

Adult's or child's bath – add one to three capfuls to a 20-cm deep bath of water. Soak for 10–20 minutes. Pat dry.

Infant's bath – add half to two capfuls to a basin of water. Apply gently over entire body with a sponge. Pat dry. The oil should always be used with water, either added to a bath or rubbed into wet skin. STIEFEL

Oilatum Gel

An emollient shower gel containing light liquid paraffin for the treatment of dry skin conditions. Daily application is recommended. Gel should always be applied to wet skin, normally as a shower gel.

STIEFEL

Oilatum Soap

A gentle soap with vegetable oil to help reduce dryness. Use as ordinary soap. Using very little warm water, massage rich creamy lather into the skin with fingers or face cloth. Rinse off, again using very little water. Pat dry. Suitable for infants. STIEFEL

Olbas Oil Inhalant Decongestant

A blend of six pure plant oils combining the essential oils of peppermint, eucalyptus, cajuput, clove, juniper berry and wintergreen with menthol. Can be used as an inhalant or to relieve muscular discomfort and rheumatic pain such as lumbago and fibrositis, sprains or pulled muscles –

essential oils applied to the skin produce a feeling of warmth and a local anaesthetic action. If using as a rub, sponge painful areas with warm water if possible and dry thoroughly. Then gently and thoroughly massage Olbas Oil into the affected part. Treatment may cause perspiration.   LANES

Olbas Pastilles

Plant remedy for the symptomatic relief of colds, coughs, catarrh, sore throats, flu, catarrhal headache and nasal congestion. Contain olbas oil, which soothes the throat and as pastilles dissolve they release vapours to help clear the head. Contain no gelatine, so are ideal for vegetarians and vegans.   LANES

Opazimes

Tablets for the relief of diarrhoea, upset stomach, 'holiday tummy' and mild forms of gastro-enteritis. Contain the antacid dried aluminium hydroxide gel, as well as light kaolin, belladonna dry extract and morphine hydrochloride.

Dosage: adults – two tablets every four hours to a maximum of eight tablets in one 24-hour period. Children over 6 years – one tablet

every four hours to a maximum of four tablets in one 24-hour period. Not to be given to infants.   RYBAR

Opticrom Allergy Eye Drops

Drops containing sodium cromoglycate for the relief and treatment of seasonal allergic conjunctivitis. Adults and children: one or two drops in each eye four times daily.   FISONS

Optrex Clearine Eye Drops

For temporary relief of redness of the eye due to minor eye irritations such as dust, smoke and chlorine from swimming pools. Contain distilled witch-hazel to cool and naphazoline hydrochloride to relieve inflammation. For use by adults and children over 12 only. Gently squeeze one or two drops into each eye, no more than four times daily.

Not to be used by contact-lens wearers except under medical supervision. Do not use this product if you suffer from glaucoma or any serious eye disease or if you have had previous eye surgery. If you're being treated for high blood pressure, depression, heart disease, diabetes or increased thyroid activity, consult your doctor before using these drops. If you experience severe eye pain, changes of vision or discharge from the eye, or if the condition worsens or persists for more than one day, consult your doctor.   CROOKES HEALTHCARE

Optrex Eye Drops

Soothing eye drops with cooling witch-hazel preserved with a small amount of the antiseptic benzalkonium chloride. For the relief of minor eye irritations caused by dusty or smoky atmospheres, driving or close work. Safe to carry in handbag or pocket. Not suitable for use with hydrophilic (soft) contact lenses. Gently squeeze one or two drops into each eye to obtain soothing relief. Discard any eye drops remaining three months after first opening the container.   CROOKES HEALTHCARE

Optrex Eye Lotion

Gentle eye lotion with cooling witch-hazel and a small amount of the antiseptic benzalkonium chloride, to soothe tired and sore eyes. For the relief of minor eye irritations caused by dusty or smoky atmospheres, driving or close work. Also available in drop form. Not suitable for use with soft contact lenses. Always clean eye bath by boiling in water before use. Fill a third full. Do not dilute lotion. Bend head slightly forward, apply the eye bath and rock the head from side to side for at least half a minute, keeping the eyelid open so that the lotion bathes the eye's surface thoroughly. Repeat with fresh lotion to the other eye.   CROOKES HEALTHCARE

Optrex Hayfever Allergy Eye Drops

Fast, soothing treatment for itchy, allergy eyes. Drops contain sodium cromoglycate, benzalkonium chloride (an antiseptic), disodium edetate and purified water. Adults and children over 5: one or two drops into each eye, four times daily. Do not use while wearing soft contact lenses.

CROOKES HEALTHCARE

Oraldene

A solution containing hexetidine, a bactericide and fungicide, for the treatment of mouth infections such as gingivitis, chronic periodontitis, stomatitis, ulcers, bad breath and oral thrush. Also useful before and after dental surgery, in geriatric nursing and in treating tonsillitis and pharyngitis.   WARNER LAMBERT

Oruvail Gel 2.5%

Gel containing ketoprofen for the relief of acute painful musculoskeletal conditions, caused by trauma, such as sports injuries, sprains, strains and contusions. Adults: apply a thin layer of gel to the affected area three times a day for up to seven days. Not recommended for children.

RHONE POULENC RORER

Otex Ear Drops

Glycerol solution drops containing urea hydrogen peroxide to soften hardened ear wax. Adults and children: five drops into the ear two or three times a day for three to four days.   DDD

Otrivine

Nasal decongestant containing xylometazoline hydrochloride, available in drop or spray form for adults and children. Dosage: one application in each nostril two to three times daily.

Also available as Otrivine Children's Formula Nasal Drops. Children under 12 – one or two drops in each nostril once or twice daily. Not to be used for infants of less than three months.   ZYMA

Otrivine-Antistin

Eye drops containing xylometazoline and antazoline sulphate for allergic conjunctivitis including hay fever. Adults and children over 12: one or two drops three times daily. Children 5–12: one drop two or three times daily.   CIBA VISION OPTHALMICS

Ovex

Contains mebendazole to treat threadworms. The tablets are orange-flavoured and may be chewed or swallowed whole. Adults and children over 2 years – take one tablet. Not suitable for children under 2.

A single tablet of Ovex will kill threadworms. However, it may not destroy the eggs, which can cause re-infection. It's therefore highly recommended that a second tablet is taken after two weeks. If you are pregnant or think you may be, do not take this product.

Larger packs of mebendazole are now available to treat the whole family.   JANSSEN PHARMACEUTICAL

Oxy 5 and 10 Lotion

Lotions containing different strengths of benzoyl peroxide for stubborn spots and acne. Wash area and dry. Apply lotion to area once daily for first week, thereafter twice daily if no irritation or discomfort occurs.

SMITHKLINE BEECHAM CONSUMER BRANDS

Panadeine

Paracetamol and codeine phosphate tablets for the relief of headache, migraine, toothache, colds and flu, period pains and rheumatic pains. Not recommended for children under 7. Take with a tumblerful of water.

Dosage: adults – two tablets every four hours as needed. No more than four doses in 24 hours. Children 7–12 years – half to one tablet every four hours as needed. No more than four doses in 24 hours.

STERLING HEALTH

Panadol and Panadol Extra

Paracetamol available in tablet, capsule or soluble form. Panadol Extra contains an additional ingredient, the stimulant caffeine. Suitable for the relief of headache, migraine, back ache, rheumatic and muscle pains, neuralgia, toothache and period pains. Also relieves discomfort in colds, flu, sore throats and helps reduce temperature. Panadol Baby and Infant Elixir and Panadol Junior (see below) can be given to children under 12. Panadol capsules and Panadol Extra should only be given to children under 12 on medical advice.

Dosage: adults – two tablets four times daily, but no more frequently than every four hours. No more than four doses in 24 hours.

STERLING HEALTH

Panadol Baby and Infant

Strawberry-flavoured paracetamol suspension to relieve the pain of teething, toothache and sore throats and to reduce the feverishness often associated with colds and flu and with childhood infections such as chicken pox, whooping cough, measles and mumps. Contains no aspirin, sugar or alcohol. Suitable for babies and children from two months to 12 years old.

Dosage: children 6–12 years – two to four 5 ml spoonfuls; 1–6 years – one to two 5 ml spoonfuls; 3–12 months – half to one 5 ml spoonful; 2–3 months – half a 5 ml spoonful. Repeat the dose every four hours if necessary, but do not exceed four doses within 24 hours. If symptoms persist, consult your doctor. Do not give this product to children for more than three days without consulting your doctor. Do not give to babies less than two months old except on medical advice. If your baby was born prematurely and is less than

three months old, consult
your doctor prior to use.

STERLING HEALTH

Panadol Junior

Paracetamol for children to
relieve aches and pains such as
headache, toothache, sore
throat and discomfort due to
colds and flu. Will also help
lower raised temperature.
Suitable for children aged
3–12 years. Dissolve sachet in
cold water.

Dosage: children 6–12 years
– one to two sachets; 3–6
years – one sachet, but for
both age ranges no more than
four doses in 24 hours. Do
not take more frequently than
at four-hourly intervals, up to
the maximum daily dose.

STERLING HEALTH

Panadol Ultra

Tablets containing
paracetamol and codeine
phosphate for rheumatic pain,
sciatica, lumbago, strains and
sprains, neuralgia and
migraine. Also for headache,
backache, muscle pain, period
pain and for relieving
discomfort in colds, influenza
and sore throat.

Adults: two tablets every
four hours as needed. Do not
take more than eight tablets
in 24 hours. Not to be given
to children under 12.

STERLING HEALTH

Panda Baby Cream

Zinc and castor oil cream with
lanolin for the relief of
symptoms of nappy rash and
as a protective water-resistant
cream for dry chapped skin.
Apply directly to the skin.

THORNTON & ROSS

Panoxyl Aquagel 2.5, 5, 10 and Panoxyl Wash

Wash and gels for the
treatment of acne. Apply once
daily after washing the
affected area. Contain benzoyl
peroxide. STIEFEL

Paraclear and Junior Paraclear

Soluble paracetamol tablets
for the relief of mild and bad
headache, migraine pain,
neuralgia, rheumatic and
muscle pains, period pains and
toothache. Also reduces
temperature and relieves
feverishness and the major
symptoms of colds and flu.
Paraclear must be taken in
half a glass, or less, of water.
Not suitable for children
under six.

Dosage: adults – one to two
tablets. No more than eight
tablets in 24 hours. Children
6–12 years – half to one tablet
up to four times a day. Do not

repeat dose more frequently than every four hours.

Junior Paraclear – for children's painful and feverish complaints. Soluble paracetamol tablets forming a strawberry-flavoured solution. Children 6–12 years – two to four tablets; 1-5 years – one to two tablets; 3 months to 1 year – one tablet. If necessary dose can be repeated every four hours, but do not give more than four doses in 24 hours. Do not give to children under 3 months except on a doctor's advice.

ROCHE CONSUMER HEALTH

Paraclear Extra Strength

Tablets containing caffeine and paracetamol for headache, neuralgia, backache, rheumatic and muscular pain, period pain, teething pain, and the relief of the symptoms of colds and sore throats, and reduction of fever in influenza.

Adults: one to two tablets with water every four to six hours as needed. Maximum eight tablets in 24 hours. Not recommended for children except under medical supervision.   ROCHE CONSUMER HEALTH

Paracodol

Capsules and soluble tablets containing paracetamol and codeine phosphate for strong pain relief in headaches, migraine, cold and flu symptoms including raised temperature and sore throats, muscular and rheumatic pains, neuralgia, period pain and toothache. Capsules not recommended for children under 12.

Dosage: adults – one to two capsules, repeat every four to six hours if necessary, with a maximum of eight capsules in 24 hours. Soluble tablets: adults – as capsules. Children 6–12 years – half to one tablet. Repeat every six hours if necessary, with a maximum of four tablets in 24 hours.

ROCHE CONSUMER HEALTH

Paramol

A powerful new pain reliever, containing the highly effective compound dihydrocodeine and paracetamol. Dihydrocodeine is one of the strongest pain-relieving compounds and until recently it has only been available on prescription. Paramol combines dihydrocodeine with the tried and trusted pain relief of paracetamol. As it is one of the strongest pain relievers you can buy, it must only be used as directed. For the treatment of headache, migraine, feverish conditions, period pains, toothache and other dental pain, back ache and other muscular aches and pains.

Dosage: adults and children over 12 – one or two tablets may be taken every four to six hours. Do not take more than eight tablets in any 24-hour period. If you suffer from asthma or have breathing difficulties, consult your doctor or pharmacist before taking Paramol. Not suitable for children under 12. NAPP

Pavacol-D

Sugar-free cough mixture containing pholcodine, a cough-suppressant, for the symptomatic treatment of coughs due to upper respiratory tract infection.

Dosage: adults – one or two 5 ml spoonfuls as needed. Children 6–12 years – one 5 ml spoonful four or five times daily; 3–5 years – one 5 ml spoonful three times daily; 1–2 years – half a 5 ml spoonful three or four times daily.

BOEHRINGER INGELHEIM

Penetrol Catarrh Lozenges

Relieve the symptoms of catarrh, hay fever and nasal congestion. Contain menthol; ammonium chloride, an expectorant; phenylephrine hydrochloride, to clear a stuffy nose; and creosote, a disinfectant. Not suitable for children under 10. Suck two, one after the other and then one every two to three hours as required. SETON HEALTHCARE

Penetrol Inhalant

Menthol and peppermint oil inhalant to relieve the symptoms of catarrh, hay fever and nasal congestion.

SETON HEALTHCARE

Pepcid AC

Tablets containing famotidine for relief from the symptoms of heartburn, dyspepsia and excess acid. Adults and children over 16 years – take one tablet. When symptoms are associated with food or drink take one tablet one hour before eating. Repeat the dose if symptoms return, up to a maximum of two tablets in a 24-hour period. CENTRA HEALTHCARE

Phenergan Elixir

Sugar-free elixir containing promethazine hydrochloride (an antihistamine) for urticaria and travel sickness. Children over 10 years: 25 ml; 5–10 years: 10–25 ml; 1–2 years: 5–15 ml. Not recommended for children under 1 year. Give at bedtime unless two doses needed during the day. In this case give the lowest dose. Travel sickness: low dose the night before repeated in six to eight hours.

RHONE POULENC RORER

Phenergan Tablets

Tablets containing promethazine hydrochloride (an antihistamine) for the symptomatic treatment of allergic conditions of upper respiratory tract and skin including allergic rhinitis, urticaria and allergic reactions. Adults and children over 10 years: one tablet at night increased to two or three if necessary. For allergies one tablet two to three times daily.

RHONE POULENC RORER

Phensedyl Plus

Liquid containing promethazine hydrochloride (an antihistamine), pseudoephedrine hydrochloride (a decongestant) and pholcodine (a cough suppressant) to relieve dry coughs, clear congestion and soothe a sore throat. Adults one to two 5 ml spoonfuls three to four times a day.

RHONE POULENC RORER

Phensic

Tablets containing aspirin and caffeine for mild to moderate pain. For symptomatic relief of minor upper respiratory tract infections such as colds and flu.

Adults take two tablets every three to four hours as needed. Maximum 12 tablets in 24 hours. Not recommended for children under 12 except on medical advice.

SMITHKLINE BEECHAM CONSUMER BRANDS

Pepto-Bismol

Liquid suspension containing bismuth subsalicylate (an antacid) for upset stomach, indigestion and nausea. Controls common diarrhoea. Adults 30 ml repeated every half to one hour if needed. Maximum of 240 ml in 24 hours. Children 10–14 years: 20 ml every half to one hour if needed. Maximum 160 ml in 24 hours. 6–10 years: 10 ml every half to one hour if needed. Maximum 80 ml in 24 hours. 3–6 years: 5 ml every half to one hour if needed. Maximum 40 ml in 24 hours.

PROCTER AND GAMBLE

Pholcodine Cough Pastilles

Contain pholcodine, a cough-suppressant, to relieve a persistent cough. Not suitable for children under 12. Adults should take one or two pastilles every four hours.

ERNEST JACKSON

Phor Pain and Phor Pain Double Strength

Ibuprofen tablets for the treatment of rheumatic and muscular pain, backache and neuralgia, headache, toothache, migraine, neuralgia, period pains and symptoms of colds and flu.

GOLDSHIELD

Phytocil Powder

Powder to treat athlete's foot. Contains phenoxy-propan-2-ol, chlorophenoxy-ethanol (an antifungal agent) and zinc undecanoate. Apply twice daily and dust into socks and shoes.   ROCHE CONSUMER HEALTH

Pileabs Tablets

Herbal tablets containing powdered slippery elm bark and cascara sagrada, a herb with a long tradition of use in the relief of constipation. To help ease constipation and the itching, irritation and discomfort due to piles. Gluten free. Suitable for vegetarians.

Dosage: adults should take two tablets with a little water three times a day before meals.   LANES

Piriton Syrup

Syrup containing chlorpheniramine maleate (an antihistamine) for the symptomatic control of allergic conditions including hay fever, vasomotor rhinitis, urticaria and insect bites. Adults: 10 ml four to six hourly. Children 6–12 years: 5 ml four to six hourly; 2–5 years: 2.5 ml four to six hourly; 1–2 years: 2.5 ml twice daily. Not recommended for children under 1 year.

ALLEN & HANBURYS

Piriton Tablets

Tablets containing chlorpheniramine maleate (an antihistamine) for the symptomatic control of allergic conditions including hay fever, vasomotor rhinitis, urticaria and insect bites. Adults: one tablet four-to-six hourly. Maximum six tablets in 24 hours. Children 6–12 years: half a tablet four-to-six hourly. Maximum three tablets in 24 hours.

ALLEN & HANBURYS

Pollon-Eze

Tablets containing astemizole, an antihistamine, sold over the counter since 1988, for relief from hay fever without causing drowsiness. Adults and children over 12 – one tablet once a day on an empty stomach, preferably in the morning. If you are pregnant or think you may be, do not take this product. Available in a calendar pack. Since people vary in their response to medications, it may take two to three days to attain maximum effect. For best results, take Pollon-Eze continuously every day for as long as the hay-fever season lasts.   CENTRA HEALTHCARE

Polytar Liquid

Concentrated antiseptic tar-medicated scalp cleanser for the treatment of seborrhoea, psoriasis, itching scalp and dandruff. Contains tar, cade oil, coal-tar solution, arachis oil, extract of crude coal tar and oleyl alcohol – a blend of coal and wood tars to relieve scaling, itching and oiliness. It's thought that tar compounds are able to penetrate the stratum corneum – the tough, waterproof, top layer of the skin – and slow down the division of cells.

Use as shampoo once or twice weekly, or as recommended by your doctor.
    STIEFEL

Polytar Plus

A concentrated antiseptic, medicated scalp cleanser containing Polytar (as in Polytar Liquid) for the treatment of scalp disorders such as dandruff, psoriasis, seborrhoea, eczema and pruritis. Use as shampoo but massage vigorously. Use once or twice weekly.   STIEFEL

Potter's Acidosis

Herbal tablets containing meadowsweet, charcoal medicinal vegetable and rhubarb, traditionally used for the symptomatic relief of indigestion, stomach ache, heartburn and acid stomach. Adults two tablets three times a day after meals. At least one full course (10 days) may be necessary for full effect. POTTER'S

Potter's Ana-Sed Pain Relief Tablets

Herbal remedy containing hops, dogwood jamaica, passiflora dry extract, wild lettuce and pulsatilla dry extract, used for relief of minor aches, tenseness and irritability. A traditional remedy to promote calmness and natural sleep. Adults: one or two tablets three times daily and two at bedtime. Not recommended for children.
    POTTER'S

Potter's Antibron

A traditional herbal remedy containing wild lettuce, lobelia, coltsfoot, euphorbia, pleurisy root and senega for the symptomatic relief of coughs. Adults: two tablets three times a day. Children over 7 years: one tablet three times a day.   POTTER'S

Potter's Catarrh Pastilles

Contain menthol, pumilio pine oil, creosote and eucalyptus to soothe the symptoms of catarrh. One pastille to be sucked as often as required. Breathe through the nose while sucking the pastille to allow the decongestant properties to work directly on the respiratory system. Not recommended for children.

ERNEST JACKSON

Potter's Chest Mixture
Liquid containing horehound, pleurisy root, senega, lobelia and acetum scillae, a traditional herbal remedy for the symptomatic relief of coughs and catarrh of the upper respiratory tract. Adults one 5 ml spoonful every three hours.

POTTER'S

Potter's Cleansing Herb Tablets
Tablets containing senna leaves tinnevelly, aloes, cascara bark, dandelion root and fennel seed, traditionally used for the symptomatic relief of occasional constipation and feelings of bloatedness. Adults one or two tablets at bedtime or when necessary.

POTTER'S

Potter's Comfrey Ointment
Ointment containing comfrey root liquid extract, a traditional herbal remedy used for the symptomatic relief of

bruises and sprains. Adults and children: bathe the affected area in warm water and apply the ointment morning and night.

POTTER'S

Potter's Cough Pastilles
Sugar-free pastilles with liquorice extract, menthol, benzoin tincture, aniseed oil, clove oil, peppermint oil and capsicum for the relief of bronchial catarrh, coughs and colds. Dissolve one pastille slowly in the mouth when required.

ERNEST JACKSON

Potter's Nodoff Passiflora
Tablets containing passiflora dry extract, a herbal remedy traditionally used as an aid to promote natural sleep. Adults two tablets at teatime and two at bedtime.

POTTER'S

Potter's Piletabs
Tablets containing pilewort, agrimony dry extract, cascara dry extract and collinsonia, a traditional herbal remedy for the relief of piles aggravated by constipation. Adults: two tablets three times a day. Elderly: two tablets morning and night.

POTTER'S

Potter's Psorasolv
Ointment containing sulphur, zinc oxide, starch, poke root liquid extract and clivers soft extract, a traditional herbal

remedy for the symptomatic relief of mild psoriasis. Adults: apply up to four times a day.

POTTER'S

Potter's Raspberry Leaf Tablets

A herbal remedy containing raspberry leaf dried aqueous extract traditionally used for the symptomatic relief of painful menstrual cramps. Adults: one to two tablets after each meal.   POTTER'S

Potter's Sciargo

Herbal tablets containing juniper berry oil, clivers dry extract, shepherds purse, uva ursi dry extract and wild carrot traditionally used for the symptomatic relief of sciatica and lumbago. Adults: two tablets three times a day.

POTTER'S

Potter's Skin Clear Tablets

Tablets containing echinacea root and echinacea dry extract, a herbal remedy traditionally used for symptomatic relief of minor skin conditions and blemishes. Adults: two tablets three times a day.   POTTER'S

Potter's Slippery Elm Stomach Tablets

Tablets containing peppermint oil, clove oil, slippery elm bark and cinnamon traditionally

used for indigestion, dyspepsia, heartburn and flatulence. Adults one or two tablets to be chewed after each meal, up to five a day.

POTTER'S

Potter's Sore Throat Pastilles

Contain glycerin and thymol to soothe a sore throat. One or more pastilles to be dissolved slowly in the mouth whenever required.

ERNEST JACKSON

Potter's Tabritis

A herbal remedy containing clivers dry extract, uva ursi dry extract, burdock root dry extract, elderflowers, prickly ash bark, yarrow and poplar bark dry extract traditionally used for the symptomatic relief of rheumatic pain and stiffness. Adults: two tablets three times a day.   POTTER'S

Powerin

Strong pain-relieving tablets containing aspirin, paracetamol and caffeine, for the treatment of headache, migraine, neuralgia, rheumatic, period and dental pains and the symptoms of colds and flu. Not suitable for children under 12.

Dosage: one or two tablets every four hours. No more than six in any 24 hours.

WHITEHALL

PR Freeze Spray

Spray relief for muscular pain and stiffness, lumbago, sciatica, fibrositis, sprains and bruises. Contains trichlorofluoromethane, which has a cooling effect on the skin, and dichlorodifluoromethane, to relieve pain. Hold the can approximately 45 cm away from painful area and spray for three to five seconds. Repeat once or, if necessary, twice, at 30-second intervals. Do not repeat this treatment more than three times a day. Do not spray on head, neck, fingers or toes. Not to be used on children under 6.

CROOKES HEALTHCARE

PR Heat Spray

Spray relief for muscular and rheumatic pain, sprains and bruises. Works by warming the skin over the painful area. Contains the counter-irritants methyl salicylate and ethyl nicotinate, and camphor. Hold can about 15 cm away from painful area and spray two or three short bursts. Repeat up to twice daily. Spray may have a stronger effect on some people than on others, so use on a small area first. Use sparingly, as over-application can cause discomfort.

CROOKES HEALTHCARE

Premiums

Antacid tablets containing magnesium trisilicate, dried aluminium hydroxide gel, light magnesium carbonate, creta and peppermint oil, to neutralise excess acid and give relief from heartburn, acid indigestion and sour stomach.

NEWTON CHEMICAL

Preparation H Suppositories

Suppositories or ointment to ease the pain and irritation of piles. Use morning and night and after each bowel movement. Contains shark-liver oil and alcohol-soluble extract of live yeast cells. These work 'empirically' – that is to say, they have been found to be beneficial in some people – doctors don't really know why.

Preparation H Ointment is also available.   WHITEHALL

Prioderm Cream Shampoo

Contains malathion to treat head-lice infestation. Use as ordinary shampoo but leave second lather on for at least five minutes. While the hair is wet comb with an ordinary comb, then use a nit comb. This treatment should be carried out a total of three times at three-day intervals. Also effective for the treatment of pubic lice.   NAPP

Prioderm Lotion

Contains malathion for the treatment of head lice. Sprinkle lotion on the hair and rub in until entire scalp is moistened. Allow the hair to dry naturally – use no heat. Hair may be shampooed after two hours. While still wet, comb the hair with an ordinary comb. Then use a nit comb to remove the dead lice and eggs. Can also be used to treat pubic lice and scabies.

Lotion contains isopropyl alcohol, which may cause wheezing in patients suffering from asthma, or stinging or inflammation of the skin in patients with severe eczema. Some patients with a normal skin may also experience stinging or inflammation of the skin. In these cases it may be more appropriate to use Prioderm Shampoo.   NAPP

Pripsen

Powder containing piperazine phosphate and sennosides, the main active ingredient of the laxative senna fruit, to treat threadworm and roundworm. Pripsen acts by paralysing the adult worms which are then expelled by the gentle laxative action of standardised senna.

All members of the household should be treated with Pripsen on the same day, with a follow-up dose 14 days later. This helps to ensure complete treatment of threadworm infection by eliminating those worms which were in the egg or larval stage when the first dose was given. One pack contains two sachets. The dose from one sachet should be taken at bedtime by adults and in the morning by children. Stir the contents into a small glass of milk (or water) and drink at once, any unused powder being discarded. Adults and children over 6: one sachet. Children 1–6: two-thirds of a sachet (one level 5 ml spoonful). Infants three months to one year: consult your doctor. If you believe you may be pregnant, consult your doctor before using this product. Do not take if you have kidney disease or have ever suffered from epilepsy.

                SETON HEALTHCARE

Probase 3

Dermatological cream and lotion to moisturise dry skin conditions. Apply as often as required. Suitable for all the family.

        SCHERING-PLOUGH CONSUMER HEALTH

Proflex

Tablets containing ibuprofen for the relief of back and muscular pain. Also available in capsules designed to release slowly: these are called Proflex Sustained Relief Capsules. Dosage, adults only: two tablets every four hours with a maximum of six in 24 hours, or one to two capsules twice a day with a maximum of four in 24 hours.   ZYMA

Proflex Cream

Contains ibuprofen, a topical analgesic and anti-inflammatory treatment for the fast relief of the symptoms of rheumatic and muscular pain, back ache, sprains, strains, lumbago and fibrositis.

Dosage: adults – apply 4–10 cm (1½–4 in) of cream three or four times daily and massage it into the skin over a large area of the affected site. Not recommended for children under 14. Do not use during pregnancy or while breast-feeding. Patients with a history of kidney problems, asthma or aspirin sensitivity should seek medical advice before using this product.

ZYMA

Propain

Analgesic tablets containing paracetamol, codeine phosphate, diphenhydramine hydrochloride (an antihistamine) and caffeine. For the treatment of migraine, headache, toothache, muscular pain and period pain, and the symptomatic relief of flu, feverishness and colds. May cause drowsiness. Do not take during pregnancy or while breast-feeding.

Dosage: adults and children over 12 – one or two tablets every four hours, with not more than ten tablets in 24 hours. Avoid excessive intake of coffee or tea when taking these tablets.   PANPHARMA

Psoriderm Bath Emulsion

Contains coal tar, which has long been advocated as a therapeutic agent in the management and treatment of psoriasis.

Add 30 ml of the emulsion to a standard bath of warm water. Soak for five minutes, then pat dry.   DERMAL LABORATORIES

Pulmo Bailly

Liquid containing guaiacol and codeine for the symptomatic relief of coughs associated with colds, flu, bronchial catarrh, laryngitis and pharyngitis.

Dosage: adults – up to two 5 ml spoonfuls; children 5–15 years – one 5 ml spoonful. The dose to be taken in half a small glass of water three times daily before meals, and repeated at bedtime. Not recommended for children under 5.   SYNTEX PHARMACEUTICALS

Pyralvex

Analgesic anti-inflammatory with an antiseptic base to treat the pain of mouth ulcers and denture irritation quickly and effectively. Contains salicylic acid and rhubarb extract. Each bottle has its own applicator brush, allowing the solution to be applied exactly where it is needed.

Adults and children over 12 – apply three to four times daily using the brush provided. Not to be used by children under 12. Each pack must only be used by one person.   NORGINE

Quiet Life Tablets

Herbal remedy with no known evidence of habit-forming effects to help relieve periods of worry, irritability, stresses and strains, and to promote sleep. A blend of valerian, hops and passiflora with motherwort, wild lettuce and three B vitamins, thiamine, riboflavin and nicotinamide.   LANES

Quinoderm Cream

Cream containing benzoyl peroxide and potassium hydroxyquinoline sulphate for the treatment of acne. Adults: apply thinly two or three times daily by gentle massage over all the affected area.

Quinoderm Cream 5 and Lotio-Gel 5% also available.

QUINODERM

Quinoped Cream

Cream containing benzoyl peroxide and potassium hydroxyquinoline sulphate for the treatment of athlete's foot. Adults: apply twice daily by gentle massage over all the affected area.   QUINODERM

Radian-B

A topical analgesic range containing counter-irritants to provide fast and lasting relief from muscular aches and pains. Suitable for adults and children over six. Best applied after a hot bath. The range consists of:

Radian-B Liniment containing menthol, camphor, ammonium salicylate and salicylic acid for relief over large surface areas. Massage in and repeat 10–15 minutes later. Apply up to three times a day, reducing to morning and evening when acute symptoms subside.

Radian-B Rub with menthol, camphor, methyl salicylate and capsicin (made from peppers). Massage in to ease pain.

Radian-B Spray, with the same ingredients as the liniment, but with the advantage of reaching awkward areas. Spray lightly for two to three seconds, and repeat if necessary after 10–15 minutes.

There are also Radian-B mineral bath and mineral bath salts to soothe away aches and pains. ROCHE CONSUMER HEALTH

Ralgex Cream
Cream containing capsicum oleoresin, glycol monosalicylate and methyl nicotinate for muscular pain and stiffness, including backache, sciatica, lumbago, fibrositis and rheumatic pain.

Adults apply as needed up to four times a day. Not recommended for children under 12 years except on medical advice.

SMITHKLINE BEECHAM CONSUMER BRANDS

Ralgex Freeze Spray
Spray containing glycol monosalicylate, isopentane, and methoxymethane, for the symptomatic relief of muscular pain and stiffness, including backache, sciatica, lumbago, fibrositis and rheumatic pains, and strains and bruises associated with sports injuries and stiffness following sporting exercise.

Adults and children over 5: apply two to three short bursts on to site of pain up to four times a day. Not to be used for children under 5.

Also available in low-odour formula.

SMITHKLINE BEECHAM CONSUMER BRANDS

Ralgex Stick
Embrocation stick containing capsicum oleoresin, ethyl salicylate, glycol monosalicylate, menthol, and methyl salicylate for the symptomatic relief of muscular pain and stiffness including backache, sciatica, lumbago, fibrositis and rheumatic pain.

Adults: clean painful area and, after trial use, apply gently and liberally. Do not rub or massage. Not recommended for children under 12 years except on medical advice.

SMITHKLINE BEECHAM CONSUMER BRANDS

Rap-Eze
Fast-acting orange-flavour indigestion tablets containing calcium carbonate for relief from indigestion, heartburn, acid indigestion, nervous indigestion, flatulence, upset stomach, dyspepsia, biliousness and indigestion during pregnancy. Also available in a mixed fruit flavour pack.

Dosage: two tablets to be sucked or chewed as needed, up to a maximum of 16 tablets a day. Not recommended for children under 12.   ROCHE CONSUMER HEALTH

Rapolyte

Oral rehydration therapy containing the essential salts and minerals sodium chloride, sodium citrate and potassium chloride. Also contains glucose. Add contents of a sachet to 200 ml fresh drinking water. For infants and if drinking water is unavailable, boil water for one minute and allow to cool. Stir well until the contents are dissolved.   JANSSEN PHARMACEUTICAL

Rappell

An ozone-friendly pump spray containing piperonal, produced from a natural source, to keep hair free of lice during periods when lice infections are likely. Can also be used after treatment for head lice to prevent reinfection or if other family members have had treatment for head lice. During head-lice epidemics, it's best for all the family to use Rappell.

Adults and children aged two years and above: style hair as normal each morning and then spray on Rappell. The number of sprays needed will vary according to hair length. As a guide, apply between five and 25 sprays at a time. Allow hair to dry naturally – use no heat. Head-lice infections should be treated immediately they are detected, then use Rappell to prevent reinfection.

Avoid spraying Rappell on to the face and eyes. If a child has sensitive skin or suffers from asthma, use with caution to ensure these conditions are not aggravated. If so, discontinue use immediately. Children under two years with head lice should be referred to their doctor. For external use only. Flammable. Do not expose to heat or flame.

CHARWELL HEALTH CARE

RBC

Rybar Bite 'n' Burn soothing cream for immediate relief of insect bites, stings, nettle rash, sunburn and itching. Contains antazoline hydrochloride, an antihistamine; cetrimide, an antiseptic; and cooling calamine and camphor. Apply to affected area every three hours as necessary. If symptoms persist after two to three days, consult your doctor.   RYBAR

Regulan

Sachets containing Ispaghula husk, a miscible fibre – that means it disperses in water. Used for regulating bowel movements and softening the stools.

Dosage: adults – one or three sachets daily; children 6–12 years – half to one level 5 ml spoonful one to three times daily. PROCTER AND GAMBLE

Reguletts

Chocolate-flavoured laxative tablets containing phenolphthalein for relieving occasional constipation. Take at bedtime for overnight action. Not suitable for children under 12. Adults and children over 12 chew one to two tablets carefully before swallowing. Do not take during pregnancy except on medical advice, nor while breast-feeding. SETON HEALTHCARE

Rehidrat

Oral electrolyte mixture containing sodium chloride, potassium chloride, sodium bicarbonate, citric acid, glucose, sucrose, fructose plus flavourings for the prevention and correction of mild and moderate dehydration and the management of diarrhoea. Dissolve one sachet in 250 ml of drinking water – for infants the water should be freshly boiled and cooled. SEARLE

Remegel

A chewable tablet containing calcium carbonate for the relief of acid indigestion, heartburn and upset stomach associated with these conditions.

Dosage: adults – chew one or two pieces of Remegel as symptoms occur. Repeat hourly if symptoms return, up to a maximum of 12 pieces in a 24-hour period. Not recommended for children.

WARNER LAMBERT

Rennie and Rennie Gold

Antacid tablets to relieve acid indigestion, heartburn, nervous indigestion, acidity, flatulence, upset stomach, dyspepsia or biliousness. Also available in spearmint flavour. Rennie contains calcium carbonate and light magnesium carbonate, Rennie Gold calcium carbonate. Suck or chew two tablets as needed. Repeat whenever discomfort is felt, to a maximum of 16 tablets a day for Rennie, 14 for Rennie Gold. ROCHE CONSUMER HEALTH

Resiston ONE

Nasal spray containing sodium cromoglycate and xylometazoline for allergic rhinitis with nasal congestion. Adults and children over 8: one squeeze to both nostrils four times a day. Should be used continually throughout the hay fever season to give effective defence, even when free from symptoms.   FISONS

Resolution

Lozenges containing nicotine, Vitamin A, ascorbic acid and Vitamin E. Dissolve one or more slowly in the mouth to ease desire to smoke.

PHOENIX HEALTH

Resolve

Sachets of effervescent granules containing citric acid, paracetamol, potassium bicarbonate, sodium bicarbonate, sodium carbonate and Vitamin C for headache with gastric upset. For headache and nausea which occur with migraine.

Adults: one sachet every four hours as needed. Maximum four sachets in 24 hours. Not for children under 12 years.

SMITHKLINE BEECHAM CONSUMER BRANDS

Ress Q

Pastilles containing soothing tincture of benzoin and benzalkonium chloride solution, an antiseptic, to relieve pain caused by mouth ulcers and sore gums. Adults (including the elderly) and children over 3 should dissolve one pastille in the mouth every two hours, up to a maximum of eight pastilles in any 24-hour period.

ERNEST JACKSON

Rheumasol

A herbal medicine used for the relief of muscular pain and stiffness associated with back ache, sciatica, lumbago, fibrositis, rheumatism and painful joints. Tablets contain two plants known through the centuries for their specific action in rheumatic conditions and said to have anti-rheumatic and anti-inflammatory properties – guaiacum resin, extracted from the ornamental evergreen tree, and prickly ash bark. One tablet to be taken three times a day with meals.   ENGLISH GRAINS HEALTHCARE

Rhuaka Herbal Syrup

Syrup containing senna-concentrated infusion, cascara liquid extract and rhubarb concentrated infusion for occasional constipation.
Adults: 20 ml at bedtime. Children 7 years and above: 5 ml at bedtime. Not to be given to children under 7 years.

ROSMARINE

Rinstead Adult Gel

For immediate relief of mouth ulcers. Contains benzocaine, a local anaesthetic, and chloroxylenol to cover the sore area with a protective coat of soothing antiseptic. Also relieves pain from denture chafing, sore gums, cheek bites and soreness after extraction of teeth. For adults and children over 12. Apply to the sore area with a clean finger or swab up to six times a day.

SCHERING-PLOUGH CONSUMER HEALTH

Rinstead Pastilles

Contain soothing menthol and the antiseptic chloroxylenol, to relieve pain and aid the healing of mouth ulcers. Allow one pastille to dissolve slowly in the mouth about every two hours.

SCHERING-PLOUGH CONSUMER HEALTH

Rinstead Teething Gel

Sugar-free teething gel containing lignocaine for pain relief and cetylpyridinium chloride (an antiseptic). Gently massage gel into affected part of the gums. The anaesthetic will start to work immediately and the cooling effect of the gel will help take some of the 'fire' out of the inflamed gums. If needed, the application may be repeated every three hours. Do not exceed more than eight applications in 24 hours.

SCHERING-PLOUGH CONSUMER HEALTH

Robitussin Chesty Cough Medicine

Sugar-free expectorant containing guaiphenesin to relieve chesty coughs without causing drowsiness. Not recommended for children under 2.

Dosage to be taken four times a day. Adults – one 10 ml measure. Children 6–12 years – one 5 ml measure; 2–6 years – one 2.5 ml measure. Contains a sugar substitute (carbohydrate content approximately 1 gm per 5 ml) which should be safe for people with diabetes.

WHITEHALL LABORATORIES

Robitussin Chesty Cough with Congestion Medicine

A sugar-free expectorant linctus containing guaiphenesin and pseudoephedrine hydrochloride, a decongestant, to clear up blocked noses without causing drowsiness. Not suitable for children under 2.

Dosage to be taken three times a day. Adults – one 10 ml measure. Children 6–12 years – one 5 ml measure; 2–6 years – one 2.5 ml measure. Contains the same sugar substitute as Robitussin Expectorant, above, so should be safe for people with diabetes. WHITEHALL LABORATORIES

Robitussin Dry Cough Medicine

Sugar-free linctus containing dextromethorphan

hydrobromide, a cough-suppressant, to relieve dry, irritating coughs without causing drowsiness.

Dosage: adults one 10 ml measure three or four times daily. Children 6–12 years, one 5 ml measure three or four times daily. Contains a sugar substitute (carbohydrate content approximately 1 gm per 5 ml) which should be safe for people with diabetes.

WHITEHALL LABORATORIES

Robitussin Junior Persistent Cough Medicine

Junior version of the above, to relieve children's dry, irritating coughs without causing drowsiness. Children 6–12 years – one 10 ml measure three or four times daily; 1–6 years – one 5 ml measure three or four times daily. Not recommended for children under one year.

WHITEHALL LABORATORIES

Salatac Gel

Contains salicylic acid and lactic acid for the treatment of warts, corns and callouses. Soak the affected area in warm water for two to three minutes every night. Dry thoroughly. Apply one or two drops of gel and allow to dry. No plaster necessary. The following evening, carefully remove and discard the elastic film formed from the previous application and re-apply gel. An emery board is included in every pack to abrade stubborn warts.

DERMAL

Samaritan Menthol and Wintergreen Cream

Cream containing menthol, methyl salicylate for the symptomatic relief of muscular pain and stiffness including backache, sciatica, lumbago, fibrositis and rheumatic pain. Adults and children: apply a small quantity to the affected area once or twice a day and at night.

THORNTON & ROSS

Sanatogen One-A-Day Garlic Perles

Pure essential oil of garlic capsules to help support the body's natural defences. Take one capsule daily.

ROCHE CONSUMER HEALTH

Savlon

Liquid antiseptic disinfectant and cream containing cetrimide, an antiseptic, and chlorhexidine gluconate, an antiseptic and disinfectant. Use as required.

ZYMA

Savlon Bath Oil

An oily liquid containing liquid paraffin and acetylated wool alcohols for the symptomatic relief of dry skin conditions.

Adults – add 15–20 ml to a standard bath of water. Immerse the affected areas in the bath water for 10–20 minutes. Pat dry with a towel. Alternatively, use a similar amount smoothed on to wet skin following a shower. Rinse off thoroughly and pat dry.

Infants and children – add 5–10 ml to a small bath or washbasin of water. Immerse the affected areas for several minutes. Alternatively, sponge gently and repeatedly over the affected areas. Pat dry with a towel.   ZYMA

Savlon Dry
Antiseptic first-aid aerosol spray for minor skin abrasions. Contains povidone iodine, an antiseptic. Use as required.   ZYMA

Savlon Junior
Liquid containing chlorhexidine gluconate, an antiseptic and disinfectant, for the cleansing and disinfection of minor wounds, including insect bites and stings. Use undiluted and apply as needed to the affected area.   ZYMA

Savlon Nappy Rash Cream
For the treatment and prevention of nappy rash. Contains dimethicone, a water-repellent, and cetrimide, an antiseptic. Use as required.   ZYMA

Scholl Athlete's Foot Range
Cream, powder, solution and spray liquid all containing tolnaftate for the prevention and treatment of athlete's foot. Use products twice daily.   SCHOLL CONSUMER PRODUCTS

Scholl Corn and Soft Corn Removers and Callous Removers
Pads and discs containing salicylic acid for corn and callous removal. Apply daily until corn or callous can be removed.

Caution: if the seal on any of the packs are broken do not use. Do not apply if the area around the corn is inflamed or if the skin is broken. Keep out of reach of children. Not to be used by diabetics or in cases of severe circulatory problems, except after a doctor's permission and recommendation. Children under the age of 16 should seek medical advice before use.   SCHOLL CONSUMER PRODUCTS

S.C.R. Cream
A treatment for cradle cap containing salicylic acid in an easily washed off cream base. It was originally formulated at Great Ormond Street Hospital for Children.   J. PICKLES

Sea-Legs

Travel sickness tablets containing meclozine hydrochloride, an antihistamine. May cause drowsiness.

Dosage: adults and children over 12 – two tablets. Children 6–12 years – one tablet; 2–6 years – half a tablet. As Sea-Legs remain active for 24 hours, take the previous night or about one hour before the journey starts. Can also be taken for relief when you feel sickness coming on. As with all medicines, do not take during pregnancy except on medical advice.   SETON HEALTHCARE

Search Dental Rinse

Contains cetylpyridinium chloride (an antiseptic) to remove the bacteria which form plaque. Also stops plaque coming back for several hours after use.

Directions: adults and children over 6 – use as part of a good oral hygiene routine. Brush teeth as advised by your dentist or hygienist and then rinse for at least 30 seconds with 10 ml of this product. May be used full strength or diluted with an equal volume of water, warm if desired. Use every three hours or as often as required.

STAFFORD-MILLER

Seldane

Tablets containing the antihistamine terfenadine to relieve symptoms of hay fever while avoiding drowsiness. One tablet lasts 24 hours. Seldane will not normally affect your ability to drive or perform tasks requiring concentration. However, as with all drugs, care should be taken initially because there may be rare exceptions. Adults and children over 12: one tablet daily when symptoms require. Not to be used during pregnancy unless medically directed.

MARION MERRELL DOW

Senlax

Chocolate laxative tablets with natural senna. Adults and children over 12 should take one tablet at bedtime. Children 6–12 years – half a tablet.   INTERCARE

Senokot

Tablets, granules or syrup containing standardised senna for the management of constipation. The correct dose of Senokot is the smallest required to produce a comfortable, soft-formed motion. It varies between individuals, but is generally found within the following ranges:

Adults – two tablets (up to four on medical advice) or one 5 ml spoonful of granules (up to 10 ml on medical advice) or 10 ml of syrup (up to 20 ml on medical advice) at bedtime.

Children over 6 – half the adult dosage, taken in the morning; children 2–6 years – Senokot syrup only, half to one 5 ml spoonful.

The tablets can be taken with a drink; the granules can be stirred into hot milk, sprinkled on food, or eaten as they are.   RECKITT & COLMAN

Setlers

Peppermint- or spearmint-flavoured tablets containing calcium carbonate for heartburn, including heartburn of pregnancy, indigestion, dyspepsia, nausea and flatulence. Dosage: adults one to two tablets sucked slowly as needed. Maximum 16 tablets in 24 hours. Not recommended for children under 12 years.

SMITHKLINE BEECHAM CONSUMER BRANDS

Setlers Tums

Assorted fruit-flavoured tablets containing calcium carbonate for the symptomatic relief of acid indigestion, heartburn, flatulence and nausea. Adults one to two tablets sucked or

chewed as needed. Maximum 16 tablets in 24 hours. Children 6–12 years: one tablet sucked or chewed. Maximum four tablets in 24 hours. Not to be given to children under six years.

SMITHKLINE BEECHAM CONSUMER BRANDS

Shen Garlic Tablets

Concentrated, organically grown Chinese garlic. Take one or two tablets three times a day before meals. A daily intake of six tablets provides the equivalent of an average-sized garlic clove.   LANES

Sinotar

A traditional herbal remedy for symptomatic relief of blocked up sinuses and catarrh. Contains elderflower, marshmallow root and echinacea.   MODERN HEALTH

Sinutab

Tablets containing paracetamol and phenylpropanolamine hydrochloride, a drug that constricts blood vessels to ease congestion. For the relief of sinus congestion and associated headache. Also helpful in the relief of sinus pain, fever and congestion associated with the common cold, flu and hay fever. Not

suitable for children under six.
Do not take during
pregnancy.

Dosage: adults – two tablets
three times daily. No more
than six tablets in any 24-
hour period. Children 6–12
years – one tablet three times
daily. No more than three
tablets in any 24-hour period.

WARNER LAMBERT

Sinutab Nightime

Tablets containing
paracetamol,
phenylpropanolamine
hydrochloride (a
decongestant) and
phenyltoloxamine citrate (an
antihistamine) for the
symptomatic relief of sinus
and facial pain, nasal and sinus
congestion and headache
when associated with acute
and chronic sinusitis, allergic
and vasomotor rhinitis,
influenza and the common
cold.

Adults: one tablet at night.
Not recommended for
children.　　　　WARNER LAMBERT

Snowfire

A tablet for the treatment of
chapped hands and chilblains.
Contains yellow soft paraffin
to moisturise and protect, and
15 natural herbal extracts
including benzoin,
marshmallow and thyme oil,
which are all healing

ingredients, and nutmeg and
clove oil which bring warmth
to chilblains. Wash the hands
or feet in warm water, then
gently rub in some of the
tablet. Alternatively some of
the tablet may be spread on a
bandage or lint and applied to
the affected area.　　J. PICKLES & SONS

Snuffle Babe

A mild vapour rub containing
eucalyptus oil, menthol and
thyme oil for young babies
and children. The formula
contains no camphor which is
said to irritate the skin of
young babies. Lightly rub a
small amount of Snuffle Babe
on to chest, throat and back.
Leave bed coverings loose so
that beneficial vapours
emitted may be inhaled during
the night. Keep away from
eyes. Do not use on infants'
nostrils. For external use only.

J. PICKLES & SONS

Solarcaine

Lotion containing the local
anaesthetic benzocaine and
antiseptic triclosan for relief
from the pain of sunburn and
for general first aid – cuts,
bites, scratches and minor
burns. Apply freely to the
skin. Limit use to three to
four times daily. Not suitable
for children under 3. Not for
deep or puncture wounds or
serious burns nor for

prolonged or extensive use.

Also available in cream form and as an ozone-friendly spray.

SCHERING-PLOUGH CONSUMER HEALTH

Solpadeine

Strong pain relief in soluble tablets or capsules containing paracetamol, codeine phosphate and caffeine. For treatment of migraine, headache, rheumatic pain, period pains, toothache, neuralgia, colds, flu, sore throat and feverishness. Capsules not suitable for children under 12. Tablets not for children under 7. Tablets should be dissolved in a tumblerful of water.

Dosage: adults – two tablets or capsules up to four times daily. No more than eight in 24 hours. Children 7–12 years – half to one tablet up to four times daily, not more often than every four hours. No more than four tablets in 24 hours.

Do not give Solpadeine to children for more than three days without consulting a doctor.   STERLING HEALTH

Solpadeine Tablets

Tablets containing caffeine, paracetamol, and codeine phosphate for pain relief in migraine, headache, rheumatic pain, period pain, toothache, neuralgia, colds, influenza, sore throat and feverishness. Adults: two tablets every four hours as needed. Maximum eight tablets in 24 hours. Not to be given to children under 12 years.   STERLING HEALTH

Sominex

Tablets containing the antihistamine promethazine, to relieve temporary sleep disturbances. Prolonged sleep disturbance should always be dealt with by your doctor. For bedtime use only.

Adults – one tablet at bedtime. May be taken up to one hour after going to bed when sleep is difficult to achieve. Not to be given to children under 16 except on medical advice. Do not exceed the stated dose. Causes drowsiness.   BEECHAM

Soothene Ointment

An antiseptic ointment containing methyl salicylate, camphor and zinc oxide, with a blend of witch-hazel, eucalyptus oil and ti-tree oil. For the treatment of scratches, stings, chilblains, spots, pimples and other common skin problems.   LANES

Sootheye Eye Drops

Eye drops containing zinc sulphate (an astringent) for the symptomatic treatment of minor eye irritations. Adults and children: one or two drops up to three or four times daily.   RHONE POULENC RORER

Stoppers

Nicotine-replacement lozenges available in three flavours – original, peppermint and chocolate orange – for use as an aid to giving up smoking.

CHARWELL HEALTH CARE

Strepsils

Throat lozenges for adults and children, available in original flavour, honey and lemon, Vitamin C and menthol and eucalyptus. Contain two antiseptics, dichlorobenzyl alcohol and amylmetacresol. Dissolve one lozenge slowly in the mouth every two to three hours.

CROOKES HEALTHCARE

Stubit

Lozenges containing purified nicotine. Dissolve a lozenge in the mouth in place of smoking a cigarette.   PICKLES

Stugeron

Travel-sickness tablets containing cinnarizine, an antihistamine. May cause drowsiness. Tablets may be sucked, chewed or swallowed.

Dosage: adults and children over 12 – two tablets two hours before travelling. One further tablet every eight hours as needed. Children 5–12 years – one tablet two hours before travelling. A further half-tablet every eight hours as needed.

JANSSEN PHARMACEUTICAL

Sudafed.Co

Tablets containing paracetamol and the decongestant pseudoephedrine hydrochloride to relieve cold and flu symptoms such as aches and pains, feverishness, blocked-up nose and sinuses, without causing drowsiness.

Dosage: adults and children over 12 – one tablet three times a day. Children 6–12 years – half a tablet three times a day. Safety advice as for Sudafed Expectorant, below.   WELLCOME

Sudafed Expectorant

Contains guaiphenesin and pseudoephedrine hydrochloride to fight congestion. To loosen stubborn mucus, clear chesty coughs and help relieve the symptoms of nasal congestion such as blocked sinuses, stuffed-up nose or catarrh. Does not cause drowsiness.

Dosage, to be taken three times a day. Adults and children over 12 – two 5 ml spoonfuls. Children 6–12 years – one 5 ml spoonful; 2–5 years – half a 5 ml spoonful. As with all medicines, if you're pregnant or currently taking any other medicine, consult your doctor or pharmacist before taking this product.

WELLCOME

Sudafed Elixir

A mixture containing the decongestant pseudoephedrine hydrochloride to relieve colds and flu symptoms such as blocked sinuses, stuffed-up nose and catarrh without causing drowsiness. Dosage and safety advice as for Sudafed Expectorant, above.

WELLCOME

Sudafed Linctus

Contains dextromethorphan hydrobromide, a cough-suppressant, and the decongestant pseudoephedrine hydrochloride, to soothe and control dry coughs and help relieve the symptoms of nasal congestion such as blocked sinuses, stuffed-up nose and catarrh. Dosage and safety advice as for Sudafed Expectorant, above, but also avoid alcoholic drink.   WELLCOME

Sudafed Nasal Spray

Contains a topical decongestant (oxymetazoline hydrochloride) which reduces inflammation of the nose; also reduces mucus secretions and

so acts to relieve nasal congestion in colds, hay fever, allergy or sinusitis.

The spray works in minutes and lasts for up to 12 hours. The special metered dose spray gives a precise dosage of decongestant to the nasal passage to help you breathe freely both during the day and while you sleep.

Adults and children 6 years and over – one or two sprays should be given into each nostril two or three times a day. Use for more than seven days is not recommended. Do not swallow.   WELLCOME

Sudafed Tablets

Contain the decongestant pseudoephedrine hydrochloride to relieve cold and flu symptoms such as blocked sinuses, stuffed-up nose and catarrh without causing drowsiness. Adults and children over 12 only – one tablet three times a day.

WELLCOME

Sudocrem

An antiseptic healing cream for the treatment of cuts and grazes, nappy rash, sunburn, acne, eczema, bed sores, chilblains and minor burns. Contains the antiseptics benzyl alcohol and benzyl benzoate, skin protectors zinc oxide and lanolin, and preservative benzyl cinnamate.

Sudocrem Baby Lotion is also available.   PHARMAX HEALTHCARE

Suleo-C Carbaryl Lotion

A lotion containing carbaryl to kill head lice. Keeping head upright, rub the lotion well in until scalp and all hair are thoroughly moistened. This could take up to one bottle per head. If applying to a child, hold a towel to the forehead to protect the eyes. Allow hair to dry naturally in a well-ventilated room. Don't use a hairdryer. Shampoo in normal manner with an ordinary shampoo. A hairdryer may now be used.

Not to be used on infants less than six months old except under medical supervision.   NAPP

Suleo-C Carbaryl Shampoo

Contains carbaryl to eradicate head lice infection. Treatment should consist of three shampoo applications at intervals of three days. Use as normal shampoo, but leave second lather on head for five minutes. Rinse off with clean water. Comb out hair with a fine-toothed comb and then dry.   NAPP

Suleo-M Malathion Lotion

A lotion to kill head lice. Use as directed for Suleo-C Carbaryl Lotion, above.   NAPP

Sun E45

From the makers of Cream E45 (see p.179), a perfume-free range containing titanium dioxide, a non-irritant sunscreen, that gives protection against UVA and UVB rays, while allowing a gradual tan. For children and adults with sun-sensitive skin.

The range includes UVA/UVB sun block cream SPF25 – for fair skin types, children and adults who always burn and never tan. Ultra UVA/UVB Protection Lotion for children and adults who always burn and sometimes tan. High UVA/UVB Protection Lotion for people who sometimes burn, but will tan and want to take care of their skin.

Sun E45 is long-lasting and water-resistant, so it doesn't require frequent re-application – every three hours is usually enough, unless you rub it off while towelling yourself dry.

CROOKES HEALTHCARE

Sunerven

A traditional herbal remedy which helps to calm the stresses of modern living and so aid restful sleep. It contains

valerian, passiflora,
motherwort and vervain.

MODERN HEALTH

Syndol

Tablets specially formulated to
relieve tension headache.
Syndol contains paracetamol,
codeine phosphate and
doxylamine succinate (an
antihistamine) and the
stimulant caffeine. Adults and
children 12 years and older:
take one or two tablets every
four or six hours as needed
for relief. Do not exceed eight
tablets per day. Syndol tablets
should not be taken
continuously over prolonged
periods in the maximum dose.
Do not exceed the stated dose.
May cause drowsiness.

MARION MERRELL DOW

Tabmint

Chewing gum containing
silver acetate for giving up
smoking. Chew one to two
pieces at least 15 minutes
before smoking, up to a
maximum of six pieces in 24
hours. Works by spoiling the
taste of cigarettes.

ROCHE CONSUMER HEALTH

Tagamet 100

Tablets containing cimetidine
for the short-term relief of
dyspepsia, hyperacidity and
heartburn. Adults and
children over 16: two tablets
when symptoms appear. If,
after this dose, symptoms
persist for more than one
hour, a second dose may be
taken, but no more than four
tablets in any period of four
hours. Maximum eight tablets
in 24 hours. To prevent night-
time heartburn – one tablet
one hour before bedtime. Not
suitable for children under 16.

SMITHKLINE BEECHAM CONSUMER BRANDS

Tancolin

Children's linctus containing
dextromethorphan
hydrobromide (a cough
suppressant) and Vitamin C
for coughs, particularly those
associated with inflamed and
infected conditions of the
upper respiratory tract.
Children, up to three times
daily: 6–12 months half a 5 ml
spoonful; 1–3 years one 5 ml
spoonful; 3–6 years two 5 ml
spoonfuls; 6–12 years three
5 ml spoonfuls.

ROCHE CONSUMER HEALTH

TCP Antiseptic Liquid

Aqueous glycerol solution of
phenol and halogenated
phenols which gives the
combined benefits of local
anaesthetic to soothe pain and
an antiseptic to fight infection.
For cuts, grazes, bites and
stings, boils, spots, pimples,
minor burns and stings, dilute

with an equal quantity of water and apply freely. For boils, spots and pimples use undiluted every four hours.

CHEMIST BROKERS

TCP First Aid Antiseptic Cream

Cream containing TCP antiseptic, chloroxylenol and triclosan. Cleanse affected area and apply freely.

CHEMIST BROKERS

TCP Ointment

Ointment containing TCP antiseptic, iodine, methyl salicylate, precipitated sulphur, tannic acid, camphor, and salicylic acid for piles and itching. Apply night and morning. Can cause a slight staining of underwear.

CHEMIST BROKERS

TCP Throat Pastilles

Blackcurrant, lemon, orange or honey and menthol flavoured pastilles containing TCP antiseptic for a sore throat. Suck one occasionally. You can also gargle twice a day with TCP liquid diluted with five parts of water.

CHEMIST BROKERS

Teejel Gel

A sugar-free gel for the relief of pain in teething. Can also be used to treat mouth ulcers, denture irritation and cold sores. Contains an antiseptic, cetalkonium chloride, and an analgesic, choline salicylate, which is closely related to aspirin but is more soluble, enabling it to be absorbed through the mucosa of the mouth and other parts of the body. The gel shouldn't be used if a baby is being prescribed, or is allergic to, aspirin.

SETON HEALTHCARE

Throaties

Range of pastilles. Throaties Originals contain soothing benzoin tincture and menthol for chest and throat relief for the symptoms of coughs and colds. Throaties Blackcurrant Flavour Pastilles and Throaties Lemon, Honey and Menthol Flavour soothe minor throat irritations and ease dry tickling coughs. Blackcurrant Flavour contains honey, ascorbic acid and menthol. Lemon contains honey, lemon oil and menthol. May be taken with reasonable freedom.

Throaties Extra are pastilles for the relief of sore throats and the symptoms of bronchial catarrh, coughs and colds. Contain soothing benzoin tincture, menthol and aniseed oil. Dissolve one pastille slowly in the mouth when required.

Other soothing pastilles

from the same manufacturer include Liquorice and Aniseed Lozenges, Honey and Rosehip Lozenges, Menthol and Eucalyptus Lozenges, Proctor's Pinelyptus Pastilles (for loss of voice, relief of husky voice, minor throat irritations and coughs), Glycerine Thymol Pastilles (for sore throats), Lemon, Glycerine and Honey Pastilles, Blackcurrant and Glycerine Pastilles, clear Blackcurrant and Glycerine Pastilles, Orange and Glycerine Pastilles, Glycerine and Natural Oil of Lemon Pastilles, Lemon and Lime Pastilles, Pine and Eucalyptus Pastilles (to relieve a husky voice), Cough Pastilles with Eucalyptus and Menthol, and Gale Force Ferociously Strong Lozenges. There is also a range of sugar-free fruit pastilles.   ERNEST JACKSON

Tinaderm Cream

Contains tolnaftate to treat athlete's foot. Twice daily wash and dry the feet before massaging cream into affected area.

SCHERING-PLOUGH CONSUMER HEALTH

Tinaderm Plus Powder and Powder Aerosol

Contain tolnaftate. Recommended for use in conjunction with Tinaderm Cream to treat athlete's foot. Both products kill and prevent athlete's foot, control wetness and fight odour. Twice daily, dust or spray affected areas above, below and between the toes after using Tinaderm Cream. To prevent re-infection, use inside socks, stockings or shoes.

SCHERING-PLOUGH CONSUMER HEALTH

Tixylix Cough and Cold

Fruit-flavoured medicine containing pseudoephedrine hydrochloride (a decongestant), chlorpheniramine maleate (an antihistamine) and pholcodine (a cough-suppressant), to soothe children's coughs, dry up runny noses and help clear congestion.

Dosage, to be administered by an adult: using the measuring cup provided, give the following doses six-hourly as required. Do not exceed three doses in 24 hours. Children 6–10 years – one to two 5 ml spoonfuls; 3–5 years – one 5 ml spoonful; 1–2 years – half a 5 ml spoonful. May cause drowsiness. If your child is taking other medicines, consult your doctor or pharmacist before giving Tixylix Cough and Cold.

INTERCARE

Tixylix Daytime

Medicine with pholcodine (a cough-suppressant) to relieve children's dry, tickly coughs without causing drowsiness.

Dosage, to be administered by an adult: using the measuring cup provided, give the following doses six-hourly as required. Children 6–10 years – one to two 5 ml spoonfuls; 3–5 years – one 5 ml spoonful; 1–2 years – half a 5 ml spoonful. Do not exceed the stated dose. If your child is taking other medicines, consult your doctor or pharmacist before giving Tixylix Daytime.   INTERCARE

Tixylix Decongestant Inhalant

Contains menthol, eucalyptus oil, camphor and turpentine oil. The natural, aromatic vapours relieve congestion and clear blocked noses. Whether your child has a cold, catarrh, flu or hay fever, the inhalant will ease their breathing and so let them sleep more comfortably.

For children aged one year or more, snip the top of a capsule and sprinkle contents on to bed linen, pillow or nightwear. For babies aged 3–12 months, sprinkle on to a handkerchief. The contents of one capsule may also be tipped into 500 ml (1 pt) of hot water. Ensure the bowl of water is out of reach of the child and allow them to inhale the vapours. Do not leave the child alone with the bowl.

Not to be taken internally. Avoid contact with the skin and direct contact with the eyes and nostrils.   INTERCARE

Tixylix Night Time

Blackcurrant-flavoured children's cough linctus to relieve troublesome, tickly coughs. Contains promethazine hydrochloride, an antihistamine, and pholcodine, a cough-suppressant. Also eases sore throats, runny and blocked-up noses. May cause drowsiness. Aids restful sleep. Use the measuring cup provided to give doses two to three times a day. Children 6–10 years – 5–10 ml; 3–5 years – 5 ml; 1–2 years – 2.5ml.   INTERCARE

Tramil 500

Paracetamol capsules offering fast pain relief in easy to swallow form for the treatment of headache, migraine, neuralgia, rheumatic, period and dental pains and the symptoms of colds and flu. Not suitable for children under six.

Dosage: adults – two capsules every four hours. Not suitable for children under 12. Maximum eight capsules in any 24-hour period. WHITEHALL

Transvasin

Heat rub containing ethyl nicotinate, hexyl nicotinate and tetrahydrofurfuryl salicylate to relieve muscular aches and pains.

Gently massage Transvasin into the affected area until it has been fully absorbed. The application may be repeated two or three times a day, or as your doctor directs. Wash hands after use. Not to be used on broken or sensitive skin, or if you are sensitive to the product or any of its ingredients. Transvasin Heat Spray also available.

SETON HEALTHCARE

Travel Calm Tablets

Fast-acting tablets with hyoscine hydrobromide to prevent the unpleasant and distressing effects of travel sickness. Within 20 minutes most travellers will be protected from sickness caused by car, plane or boat journeys. Travel Calm Tablets are best taken 20 minutes before the start of your journey.

Dosage: adults and children over 12 – one tablet; children 7–12 years – half to one tablet; 3–7 years – quarter of a tablet.

Doses may be repeated in six to eight hours if necessary. Babies and children under 3 should not be given this medicine. Do not take more than three doses in 24 hours.

Not to be used during pregnancy or if you suffer from the eye condition glaucoma. May cause drowsiness. If affected, do not drive or operate machinery. Avoid alcoholic drink. BOOTS

Tri-Ac

Face-wash lotion treatment and preventative for acne. Contains ethyl lactate, a mild antiseptic, and zinc sulphate, an astringent. Use as required.

ZYMA

Triludan and Triludan Forte

Tablets containing the antihistamine terfenadine for the effective treatment of hay fever, rhinitis, insect bites and nettle rashes while avoiding drowsiness. Triludan will not normally affect your ability to drive or perform tasks requiring concentration. However, as with all drugs, care should be taken initially because there may be rare exceptions.

Dosage – adults and children over 12: one tablet twice daily (or two tablets together in the morning if preferred). Children 6–12: half a tablet twice daily.

Triludan Forte contains a higher dose of terfenadine. Adults and children over 12 should take one tablet in the morning. Neither form of Triludan should be taken during pregnancy unless medically directed.

MARION MERRELL DOW

Triogesic

Decongestant (phenylpropanolamine hydrochloride) and analgesic (paracetamol) tablets to clear nasal and sinus congestion and the headache and pain that accompany colds and sinusitis. Not recommended for children under 6. Not to be taken during pregnancy or while breast-feeding.

Dosage, to be taken up to four times daily, leaving at least four hours between doses: adults and children over 12 – one to two tablets. Children 6-12 – one tablet.

INTERCARE

Triominic

Decongestant cold and allergy relief tablets containing pheniramine maleate, an antihistamine, and phenylpropanolamine hydrochloride, a decongestant. Not recommended for children under 6. Not to be

taken during pregnancy or while breast-feeding.

Dosage, to be taken up to four times a day, leaving at least four hours between doses: adults and children over 12 – one tablet. Children 6–12 years – half a tablet. INTERCARE

Tyrocane

Colour-free, sugar-free throat lozenges containing the antiseptic cetylpyridinium and the antibiotic tyrothricin with the local anaesthetic benzocaine, for the relief of pain and minor infections in the mouth and throat. Not suitable for children under 12. Adults (including the elderly) and children over 12 may suck one lozenge every three or four hours as needed. Do not take more than seven lozenges a day or 15 lozenges in three days. SETON HEALTHCARE

Tyrocane Junior Antiseptic Lozenges

Sugar-free, orange-flavoured lozenges containing the antiseptic cetylpyridinium chloride to help fight against infections in the throat and nose. Not suitable for children under 6. One lozenge to be sucked slowly as needed. Do not take more than eight lozenges in one day.

SETON HEALTHCARE

Tyrozets

Aniseed-flavoured lozenges for minor mouth and throat irritations, secondary irritation following a tonsillectomy and other mouth and throat surgery. Contains an antibiotic, tyrothricin, and a local anaesthetic, benzocaine. Not recommended for children under 3. Adults should dissolve one lozenge slowly in the mouth every three hours, with a maximum of eight lozenges in 24 hours. Reduce dosage for children. Do not use for longer than five consecutive days.

MERCK, SHARP AND DOHME

Ulc-Aid

Sugar-free soothing throat lozenges for mouth ulcers and sore throat. Contain tyrothricin, an antibacterial agent; benzocaine, a local anaesthetic; and cetylpyridinium chloride, an antiseptic. Not suitable for children under 12. Adults (including the elderly) and children over 12 – suck one lozenge slowly every three or four hours as required. Do not take more than seven lozenges a day or 15 lozenges in three days.   SETON HEALTHCARE

Ulc-Aid Gel

Contains an antiseptic, cetylpyridinium chloride, and a local anaesthetic, lignocaine hydrochloride, for the treatment of mouth ulcers. Suitable for adults and children. Apply a little gel to the ulcer with a clean fingertip or swab. May be repeated after 20 minutes and then every three hours if necessary. Not suitable for treating teething problems in babies.   SETON HEALTHCARE

Uvistat

Sun-protection range that protects against both UVA and UVB rays. Products contain the sunscreens mexenone, ethyl hexyl p-methoxycinnamate and butyl methoxydibenzoylmethane. Some also contain micronised titanium dioxide, a reflectant sunscreen.

Uvistat Babysun Factor 12 and 22 protect young skin. Both are water-resistant. Factor 22 should be used on fair-skinned and very young children, while Factor 12 is ideal for older children to build a tan gradually while helping to protect the skin from sun damage.

The adult Uvistat range provides protection from Factor 20 (high-protection sunblock) to Factor 4 (low-protection sun cream). Uvistat Lipscreen Factor 15 is also available.   WINDSOR PHARMACEUTICALS

Vagisil

A cream containing lignocaine base (lidocaine) to relieve feminine itching, burning and irritation. Helps prevent further irritation by reducing the urge to scratch. Adults and children over three years: apply to the affected area three or four times a day. Not suitable for children under 3 years. COMBE INTERNATIONAL

Valderma range

Valderma Active Gel contains benzoyl peroxide to treat more stubborn spots and acne. Apply once or twice daily to the whole of the affected areas. Very fair-skinned people should apply gel cautiously for the first few days. Continue daily treatment while spots persist, then apply two or three times a week to help keep skin clear.

Valderma Antibacterial Cream contains potassium hydroxyquinoline sulphate, an antibacterial agent, and chlorocresol, an antiseptic, for the treatment of everyday spots. Use two or three times a day, especially at night and in the morning.

Valderma Antibacterial Soap contains trichlorocarbanilide, an antibacterial agent, to help keep skin clear, clean and free from spots. Also contains

lanolin to soften and smooth the surface of the skin. Use at least twice daily, as oil and dirt soon build up again, even while you are asleep.

ROCHE CONSUMER HEALTH

Vapex

Inhalant containing menthol for relief from colds and nasal catarrh. Sprinkle a few drops on your handkerchief, then inhale vapour deeply and often during the day. A drop on your pillow acts while you sleep. ROCHE CONSUMER HEALTH

Vasogen

Cream with a triple-action formula; contains calamine to alleviate soreness immediately, zinc oxide to soothe and heal and silicone which forms a protective layer on your baby's skin. The silicone (dimethicone) acts by isolating the area from further irritation while other ingredients take effect. Vasogen's silicone barrier helps prevent nappy rash, too. Use regularly, especially with the last nappy change in the evening. This ensures that your baby's skin is protected throughout the night, when exposure to a wet nappy is prolonged. Vasogen is also ideal for cracked or sore hands, and bed sores. PHARMAX

Veganin

Tablets containing paracetamol, aspirin and codeine phosphate for the relief of the symptoms of flu and all kinds of mild to moderate pain especially headache, period pain, rheumatism and toothache. Not suitable for children under 12.

Dosage: adults – one or two tablets to be swallowed every three or four hours up to a maximum of eight tablets in 24 hours.   WARNER LAMBERT

Vegetex

A traditional herbal remedy for symptomatic relief from muscular rheumatic pain, lumbago and fibrositis. Contains celery, buckwheat, black cohosh and horseradish.

MODERN HEALTH

Veno's Cough Mixture

Syrup containing liquid glucose and treacle for dry, persistent, irritating, unproductive cough. Adults take one to two 5 ml spoonfuls every two to three hours. Children 3–12 years take one 5 ml spoonful every two to three hours as needed. Not to be given to children under 3 years except on medical advice.

SMITHKLINE BEECHAM CONSUMER BRANDS

Veno's Expectorant

Mixture containing liquid glucose, guaiphenesin (an expectorant) and treacle for coughs (including bronchial cough) and chesty catarrh, particularly following colds and flu.

Adults take two 5 ml spoonfuls every two to three hours. Children 3–under 12: one 5 ml spoonful every two to three hours. Not to be given to children under 3 years except on medical advice.

SMITHKLINE BEECHAM CONSUMER BRANDS

Veno's Honey and Lemon

Syrup containing liquid glucose, lemon juice and purified honey for tickly coughs and non-inflamed sore throats. Adults take three 5 ml spoonfuls every two to three hours. Maximum 120 ml in 24 hours. Children 6–12 years take two 5 ml spoonfuls every two to three hours. Maximum 80 ml in 24 hours. Children 1–6: one 5 ml spoonful every two to three hours. Maximum 40 ml in 24 hours. Not to be given to children under 1 year.

SMITHKLINE BEECHAM CONSUMER BRANDS

Vicks Children's VapoSyrup

Formulated to relieve children's dry coughs quickly

and without causing drowsiness, so it's suitable for use both day and night by children from 3–11 years. Contains dextromethorphan hydrobromide (a cough-suppressant) and no artificial colorants.

Shatterproof bottle has a new Accutip dispenser to give accurate, easy dosing and to prevent drips, spills and messiness.

Dosage: children 6–11 years – fill to the 15 ml mark in dosing cup provided; 3–5 years – fill to the 7.5 ml mark. Repeat every six hours as needed, but no more than four doses per day. Do not administer to children under 3 except on medical advice. Not to be used by patients suffering from asthma except on medical advice.

PROCTER AND GAMBLE

Vicks ColdCare

Cold-treatment capsules containing paracetamol to relieve aches and pains and bring down temperature; dextromethorphan hydrobromide, a cough-suppressant; and phenylpropanolamine hydrochloride, to ease congestion without causing drowsiness.

Dosage: adults and children over 12 – two capsules every

four hours, maximum of eight in 24 hours. Children 6–12 years – one capsule every four hours, maximum of four in 24 hours. If you're under the care of your doctor or receiving continual prescribed medication or if you are pregnant, consult your doctor before using this product.

PROCTER AND GAMBLE

Vicks Cough Syrup Expectorant

Syrup to help loosen and ease chesty coughs. Contains guaiphenesin, an expectorant; cetylpyridinium chloride, an antiseptic; and sodium citrate.

Dosage: adults and children over 12 – two 5 ml spoonfuls. Children 6–12 years – one 5ml spoonful. Every three hours as needed.   PROCTER AND GAMBLE

Vicks Inhaler

Plastic holder containing camphor, menthol and pine needle oil for the relief of nasal congestion associated with allergic and infectious upper respiratory tract disorders. Adults and children: insert into each nostril in turn and inhale as frequently as needed.   PROCTER AND GAMBLE

Vicks Medinite

Syrup containing paracetamol, dextromethorphan hydrobromide (a cough suppressant), pseudoephedrine hydrochloride (a decongestant) and doxylamine succinate (an antihistamine) for the treatment of symptoms of the common cold. Adults: 30 ml in measuring cup at bedtime. Children 10–12 years: 15 ml in measuring cup at bedtime.

PROCTER AND GAMBLE

Vicks Sinex Decongestant Nasal Spray

Spray containing menthol, cineole, and oxymetazoline hydrochloride (relieves nasal congestion) for the symptomatic relief of congestion of the upper respiratory tract due to the common cold, hay fever and sinusitis. Adults and children over 6 years: one to two sprays per nostril every six to eight hours. Not to be used in children under 6 years.

PROCTER AND GAMBLE

Vicks Ultra Chloraseptic

Throat spray containing benzocaine for the symptomatic relief of sore throat pain. Adults and children over 13 years: three sprays to the back of the throat. Repeat every two to three hours to a maximum of eight doses in 24 hours. Children 6–12 years: one spray to the back of the throat. Repeat every two to three hours to a maximum of eight doses in 24 hours. Not to be used for children under 6 years.

PROCTER AND GAMBLE

Vicks Vapo Rub

Vapour rub decongestant for colds. Contains menthol, camphor, turpentine oil, eucalyptus, nutmeg, cedar wood oils and thymol. Use at first sign of a cold to get maximum benefit.

Children and adults – rub liberally on to chest, throat and back – cover whole area for maximum effect. Apply especially at bedtime. Leave nightclothes loose to allow vapours to be inhaled easily. For babies (over six months) apply lightly to chest and back. Rub in gently.

Can also be used as an inhalant.

PROCTER AND GAMBLE

Vicks Vaposyrup for Chesty Coughs

Syrup containing guaiphenesin (an expectorant) to loosen mucus, soothe and coat the throat and make the cough more productive. Adults: three 5 ml spoonfuls every four hours as needed. Maximum 90 ml in 24 hours. Children 6–11 years: two 5 ml spoonfuls every four hours as needed. 2–5 years: one 5 ml spoonful every four hours as needed. Maximum 30 ml in 24 hours. Not to be given to children under 2 years.

PROCTER AND GAMBLE

Vicks Vaposyrup for Chesty Coughs with a Blocked Nose

Vicks Vaposyrup for Chesty Coughs with a decongestant phenylpropanolamine hydrochloride to relieve coughs and a blocked nose. Adults: three 5 ml spoonfuls every six hours as needed. Maximum 60 ml in 24 hours. Children 6–11 years: one 5 ml spoonful every six hours as needed. Maximum 20 ml in 24 hours. Not to be given to children under six years.

PROCTER AND GAMBLE

Vicks Vaposyrup for Dry Coughs and a Blocked Nose

Decongestant syrup containing phenylpropanolamine hydrobromide and dextromethorphan hydrobromide (a cough suppressant) for dry cough and a blocked nose. Adults: three 5 ml spoonfuls every six hours as needed. Maximum 60 ml in 24 hours. Children 6–11 years: one 5 ml spoonful every six hours as needed. Maximum 20 ml in 24 hours.

Not for children under 6 years.   PROCTER AND GAMBLE

Vicks Vaposyrup for Dry Coughs

Contains dextromethorphan hydrobromide, a cough-suppressant, for dry coughs and a cough-irritated throat. Not suitable for children under six.

Dosage: adults and children over 12 – three 5 ml spoonfuls. Children 6–12 years – one 5 ml spoonful. Repeat every six hours as needed. No more than four doses a day.   PROCTER AND GAMBLE

Vita-E Range

Gel, ointment and cream containing a naturally occurring form of Vitamin E. Vitamin E ointment and cream have traditionally been used as an adjuvant for healing skin, for example, in burns and ulcerating conditions.   BIOGLAN

Vitathone Chilblain Ointment

Ointment containing methyl nicotinate for relief of itching chilblains. Adults apply to the affected area, rubbing in gently, every two to three hours.   SETON HEALTHCARE

Wash E45

A washing cream for cleansing dry, sensitive and

irritated skin. Free from perfume, soap and detergents. Contains a blend of mineral oils and zinc oxide to help the skin retain natural moisture. Use on face or body, wherever skin feels dry. Apply direct on to dry skin, even before a bath or shower. Massage lightly and rinse off. Take care not to slip. And, as with soap, avoid contact with the eyes.

CROOKES HEALTHCARE

Wasp-Eze

Spray relief from stings – wasp stings, mosquito bites, nettle stings, bee stings, jellyfish stings, ant bites. Contains the antihistamine mepyramine maleate and the local anaesthetic benzocaine. Stings should be removed if possible.

Hold spray very close to skin (about 5 mm away). Spray affected area until all pain has gone – this may take up to five seconds. Repeat once after 15 minutes if necessary. Do not apply to broken skin or use near eyes.

Mosquito bites sometimes produce reactions several hours later. If symptoms persist or worsen, consult your doctor. SETON HEALTHCARE

Wax-Aid Ear Drops

Medicated drops containing turpentine and arachis oil to soften the wax; local pain-reliever and antibacterial agent chlorbutol; and paradichlorobenzene to relieve the symptoms associated with hardened wax in the ears and to aid its removal. Put three or four drops into the affected ear morning and night until the wax softens and can easily be removed with cotton wool.

SETON HEALTHCARE

Waxsol

Odourless, non-staining drops containing docusate sodium which disintegrates ear wax fast. Not to be used in the presence of perforation of the ear drum or inflammation of the ear. If pain or inflammation is experienced, treatment should be discontinued. NORGINE

Wax Wane Ear Drops

Ear drops containing turpentine oil, chloroxylenol and terpineol to soften hard wax in the ear before removal by syringing. Adults and children: 4–5 drops in ear and plug with cotton wool, repeat two to three times daily for a few days. THORNTON & ROSS

Windcheaters

Capsules containing activated dimethicone to break down the tiny bubbles of gas so that trapped wind can be passed easily, bringing welcome relief from the discomfort that wind so often causes. As dimethicone is not absorbed by the body, it does not alter the delicate acid balance of the stomach or disrupt the normal process of digestion.

Dosage: one to two capsules three to four times daily or as required.   NAPP

Witch Doctor

Antiseptic and astringent natural witch-hazel gel formulation to soothe skin irritation, bruises, itching, insect bites, stings, sunburn and minor burns. Squeeze gel directly on to affected area. Leave to dry. Do not use in eyes. Also available in solid form – Witch Stik.   ETHICHEM

Woodward's Gripe Water

Sugar- and alcohol-free liquid containing sodium bicarbonate and dill seed oil, terpeneless for the symptomatic relief of the distress associated with wind in infants up to one year old. Children 1 month–6 months: 5 ml; 6 months–1 year: 10 ml may be given during or after each feed or up to six times in 24 hours. Not to be given to babies under 1 month.   LRC PRODUCTS

Woodward's Teething Gel

Gel containing lignocaine hydrochloride, alcohol and cetylpyridinium chloride for relief of pain associated with teething problems. Place a small quantity of gel on to a pad of cotton wool or a clean finger and rub gently into baby's gum. Repeat after 20 minutes and then every three hours if necessary. Not recommended for babies under three months.

LRC PRODUCTS

Zam-Buk Medicated Ointment

Contains eucalyptus oil, camphor, thyme oil and colophony (made from pine oils) to aid gentle healing of minor cuts and grazes, chapped hands, chilblains, sore aching feet. To treat minor cuts and grazes – bathe gently, apply ointment lightly, use a dressing. For chapped hands and chilblains – rub gently into the affected area. For aching feet – bathe feet in warm water, then rub in ointment. Discontinue use and consult your doctor if excessive irritation or inflammation develops. People with delicate skin may react to the ingredients in this product.   ROCHE CONSUMER HEALTH

Zensyls

Lime-flavoured antiseptic throat therapy in a lozenge. Contains benzalkonium chloride solution. Suitable for adults and children over 5. Dissolve one lozenge slowly in the mouth as required.

ERNEST JACKSON

Zirtek

Antihistamine tablets containing cetirizine dihydrochloride for the treatment of hay fever, allergic rhinitis and allergic skin conditions while avoiding drowsiness. One tablet for 24 hour control. Adults: one tablet daily. Not recommended for children except on medical advice.

UCB PHARMA

Zovirax

Cold sore cream containing acyclovir for cold sores of the lip and face caused by the herpes simplex virus. Early use can stop a cold sore developing. Adults and children: apply five times each day for five days, starting during the tingle phase. If healing is incomplete continue for a further five days. WELLCOME

Zubes

Medicated lozenges with citric acid, menthol and aniseed oil for gentle, effective relief from sore throat, cough and cold symptoms. The warming vapours help soothe and clear your tubes.

Dosage: adults suck one lozenge every half an hour; children 6–12 years – one lozenge every hour; under 6 years – one lozenge every two hours. Available in original, blackcurrant, cherry and honey and lemon. ERNEST JACKSON

Unbranded Products

All these medicines can be bought from your pharmacist, and a limited range will be available in supermarkets under own brand labels. In many cases unbranded or own brand products will be cheaper than well-known brands. Ask your pharmacist for advice.

I have given examples of unbranded products commonly used to treat minor ailments – but your pharmacist will be able to give you further information on products you can buy. As with all medicines, do always follow the instructions on the particular product you have bought and if symptoms persist consult your doctor.

Aspirin

Used for the symptomatic relief of mild to moderate pain. Generally the dose is every four hours as needed, with a maximum of four doses a day. Not suitable for children under 12, asthmatics, anyone suffering from stomach ulcers and those allergic to aspirin.

Calamine Lotion B.P.

This lotion is applied to the skin for the relief of the symptoms of mild sunburn and other minor skin conditions.

Cetrimide Cream B.P.

An antiseptic cream for chapped hands, minor skin abrasions, minor cuts and nappy rash.

Oil of Cloves (own brand)

An oil made from dried flower buds which helps relieve toothache by numbing the sore area. To use, soak a small piece of cotton wool and apply to tooth. If toothache persists, consult your dentist or doctor.

Co-codamol Tablets B.P.

Painkilling tablets containing

codeine phosphate and paracetamol. Adults: one or two tablets generally repeated in four hours if necessary. Children 6–12 years: half to one tablet repeated in four hours if necessary. Maximum adult dose: eight tablets in 24 hours. May cause constipation.

Co-codaprin Tablets B.P.

Painkilling tablets containing codeine phosphate and aspirin. Adults: one or two tablets generally taken every three or four hours with a maximum of 8 tablets in 24 hours. Do not take if you have a stomach ulcer, are asthmatic or allergic to aspirin. Not for children under 12 years unless directed by your doctor. May cause constipation.

Embrocation White B.P.

The embrocation is rubbed in to the skin for the relief of symptoms of rheumatism, lumbago, sciatica and sprains.

Epsom Salts B.P.

The salts are added to water and drunk for occasional constipation or mixed to a lotion as a dressing for the relief of pain from sprains. Beware: very powerful and quick-acting remedy.

Friar's Balsam B.P.

Added to hot water this can be inhaled to relieve congestion and symptoms of the common cold. Can stain plastic basins.

Gee's Linctus B.P.

A linctus used to treat chesty coughs, which may cause drowsiness.

Glycerin B.P.

Glycerin is mixed with some water and can be taken for the relief of sore throat symptoms or to moisturise rough and chapped skin.

Glycerin Suppositories B.P.

Stimulant suppositories containing glycerin for the relief of occasional constipation.

Hydrogen Peroxide Solution 3%, 6%, 9%

A solution to dilute for use as a mild disinfectant, mouthwash or gargle. Follow dilution instructions carefully.

Ibuprofen

Ibuprofen can be bought from your pharmacist under own brand names. They are painkilling tablets used for the relief of headaches, the symptoms of colds and flu, muscular pain, back pain, feverishness, migraine, period pain, dental pain and neuralgia. Do not use if you are asthmatic or have a stomach ulcer as it contains aspirin. Ibuprofen is not suitable for children under 12 except for the branded product Junifen (page 209). Usual dosage is two tablets initially, followed by one or two tablets every four hours. Don't take more than 1200 mg a day.

Iodine Tincture B.P.

This tincture is used as an antiseptic on minor wounds, cuts and abrasions.

Kaolin and Morphine Mixture B.P.

For the relief of diarrhoea in adults.

Kaolin Mixture B.P. and Kaolin Mixture Paediatric B.P. 1980

Mixtures used for the relief of diarrhoea and upset stomachs in adults and children.

Lanolin B.P.

Lanolin can be rubbed into the skin to treat and relieve dryness. Some people are allergic to lanolin.

Magnesium Sulphate Paste B.P.

A drawing ointment for boils which is applied to the skin as a poultice.

Magnesium Trisilicate Mixture B.P.

An antacid mixture for the relief of the symptoms of indigestion, heartburn and dyspepsia.

Menthol and Eucalyptus Inhalation B.P. 1980

Added to hot water and inhaled for the relief of coughs, colds and blocked noses.

Paracetamol

A mild to moderate pain-reliever for the treatment of headache, migraine, neuralgia, toothache, sore throat, period pains, aches and pains, including muscle pain and backache. Also for the symptomatic relief of influenza, feverishness and feverish colds.

Dosage – generally adults and children over 12: one to two tablets every four hours. Maximum eight tablets in 24 hours. Follow instructions on label.

Pholcodine Linctus B.P.

A linctus used as a cough suppressant to soothe dry or irritating coughs. Not recommended for children under five years.

Senna Laxative Tablets

Tablets containing the
stimulant laxative senna used
to treat occasional
constipation.

Simple Linctus B.P. and Paediatric Simple Linctus B.P.

A linctus used for the relief of
the symptoms of coughs in
adults and children.

Sodium Bicarbonate B.P.

Mixed with water can be used
as an occasional remedy for
the symptoms of heartburn,
indigestion and dyspepsia.
May also be used externally as
a lotion for the relief of the
symptoms of insect bites and
sunburn. Not suitable for
people with high blood
pressure, renal problems or
those on a salt-restricted diet.

Surgical Spirit B.P.

Spirit applied to the skin to
prevent bedsores and for
hardening the skin of the feet.

Thymol Glycerin Compound B.P.

Diluted with water this can be
used as a mouthwash or a
gargle in throat infections.

Witch Hazel Distilled B.P.C. 1973

A mild astringent for
cleansing the skin and for the
removal of make up. A herbal
remedy traditionally used for
the relief of cuts, sprains,
bruises and minor scalds.

Vitamins, Minerals and Supplements

VITAMINS

Vitamins are an essential part of your diet – and as long as you eat a well-balanced diet, remembering that the fresher the food, the higher the vitamin content, you should get all the vitamins you need. The exception to this rule is Vitamin D, which is created in our skin when we are exposed to sunshine. But the simple fact that vitamins are readily available in fresh food doesn't seem to prevent us spending more and more money each year on vitamins – the figure reached £81 million in 1990!

One of the reasons for this could be that today's busy lifestyles mean we don't always eat the sort of food we ought to, and bad habits can make things worse – smoking, for instance, depletes the body of Vitamins B6, B12, C and E. On the other hand, with our generally raised consciousness about healthy eating, we

know that we need vitamins and, to make sure we get them, many of us like to take supplements. Children, growing rapidly, have a greater demand for some vitamins than adults and many parents choose to give supplements in order to guarantee that their children have enough, especially if they are fussy eaters.

Vitamin A

Essential for growth, strong bones and teeth in children, Vitamin A raises resistance to infections, aids healing, promotes tooth and skin health and is needed for night vision. It's now thought that an excessive intake of Vitamin A in pregnancy may lead to birth defects.

Vitamin A comes in two forms – retinol and carotene. Carotene is found in green vegetables and in red/orange-coloured foods like peaches, apricots and carrots, but has to be converted into retinol in the body. Other good sources of Vitamin A include liver, kidney, milk (although semi-skimmed and skimmed contain much less), egg yolk, butter and margarine.

Supplements available: Seven Seas Natural Vitamins A and D Capsules.

The B Vitamins

The three main B vitamins – thiamin (B1), niacin, and riboflavin (B2) – work together to release energy from food. They also help maintain the health of our digestion, skin and nervous system.

Good sources of thiamin include cereals, egg yolk, fresh pineapple, peanuts, wheatgerm, kidney and liver; sources of riboflavin are liver, milk, brewers' yeast powder, cottage cheese, poultry and mushrooms; and of niacin, meat and green leafy vegetables.

Vitamin B5, pantothenic acid, helps cortisone release and increases energy. Good sources include beans, chick peas, nuts, egg yolks, avocado pears and royal jelly.

Vitamin B6 – pyridoxine – is essential to help the body convert protein so that it can use it; it also promotes health of skin, nerves and muscle. Good sources are meat, fish, wholemeal foods, milk, cabbage, yeast and wheatgerm. Some women find B6 helpful in overcoming pre-menstrual syndrome, of which common physical symptoms are headaches, a general feeling of bloatedness and tenderness in the breasts. Emotional symptoms include weepiness, forgetfulness, anxiety or depression and bad temper. It's suggested that you take Vitamin B6 three days before problems are expected and continue throughout your period. Some women also claim that B6 supplements have helped reduce nausea in pregnancy.

Vitamin B12 is vital for cell formation and is important in the production of red blood cells. Good sources include dairy produce, fish, wheatgerm, beef and pork.

Folic acid, another of the Vitamin B complex, is essential for growth and blood formation. There's evidence to suggest that it might help prevent spina bifida if taken by women before conception. At the end of 1992 the Chief Medical Officer asked doctors to advise all women who were planning a pregnancy in the near future to take 0.4 mg of folic acid daily before trying to conceive and until the twelfth week of pregnancy. Studies in the UK and the USA have shown that it prevents neural tube defects during pregnancy. Examples of supplements available are Lanes Preconceive Folic Acid Tablets. Good sources are offal, green vegetables, oranges, eggs, yeast and cereals.

Supplements available: Benerva Compound Vitamin B, Benerva Tablets 50 mg, Becosym Forte Vitamin B Complex and Berocca Effervescent Vitamin B Group (Roche); Cytacon Liquid or Tablets, a vitamin B supplement for vegetarians, vegans and the elderly; Golden Health Vitamin B Complex (English Grains); Sanatogen Vitamin B Complex; Vitamin B Complex (Evans); Benadon Vitamin B6 50 mg (Roche); Comploment B6 Continus Tablets (Napp); Golden Health Vitamin B6 (English Grains); Sanatogen Vitamin B6 50 mg; Vitamin B6 50 mg capsules (Evans).

Vitamin C

Essential for the health of cells, blood vessels, gums and teeth, for the healing of wounds and to help absorb iron from food. Also needed for connective tissue in skin,

ligaments and bone.

It's argued that Vitamin C supplements can help replace the Vitamin C used up rapidly as the body fights colds and flu, and therefore help maintain good health. There is no convincing evidence that large doses of Vitamin C will prevent colds, but many people take it in the belief that it will. Fortunately, Vitamin C is one of the vitamins that can safely be taken in larger doses than are required for the body's everyday needs.

It is water-soluble and can be lost during cooking. Oxidation also causes loss of Vitamin C in food that is kept hot – in canteens, for instance.

Good sources include blackcurrants, oranges, new potatoes, strawberries and green leafy vegetables.

Supplements available: Centurion Vitamin C Pastilles (Ernest Jackson); Golden Health Vitamin C (English Grains); Redoxon Vitamin C 50 mg and 500 mg tablets (Roche); Redoxon Chewable Vitamin C 250 mg and 500 mg (orange- or blackcurrant-flavoured tablets from Roche); Redoxon Effervescent Vitamin C 1000 mg (lemon- or lime-flavoured tablets from Roche); Sanatogen Chewable Vitamin C 30 mg (Roche), and Vitamin High C 500 mg.

Vitamin D

Needed to absorb the calcium from food necessary for healthy teeth and bones. Lack of Vitamin D causes rickets – poor bone formation – in children, and adults may suffer from loss of calcium in the bones – osteomalacia.

Good sources include cod-liver oil, oily fish, butter, milk, egg yolk, chicken and beef liver.

Supplements available: Cod-Liver Oil Capsules (for Vitamins A and D – Evans); Crookes Halibut-Liver Oil Capsules (Vitamins A and D); Golden Health Cod-Liver Oil (English Grains); Sanatogen Natural Cod-Liver Oil Liquid or Capsules; Seven Seas Pure Cod-Liver Oil (lemon flavour).

Vitamin E

Also known as tocopherol and 'the vitality vitamin', Vitamin E protects the fats that are part of the structure of all cells and is vital for healthy cell structure. It protects the lungs and other tissues from damage by pollutants. It's been suggested that it may be necessary for development and maintenance of healthy red blood cells, smooth muscle, skin and other tissues. Good sources include vegetable oils, wholemeal bread, wholegrain cereals, egg yolks, nuts and green vegetables.

Supplements available: Crookes Wheatgerm Oil Capsules; Ephynal Vitamin E 50 mg (Roche); Golden Health Vitamin E (English Grains); Sanatogen Vitamin E 400 iu; Vitamin E 200 iu (Evans).

Multivitamin supplements available: Crookes Multivitamins without Iron and Multivitamins with Iron; Golden Health Children's Multivitamins A, C and D and Multivitamins and Iron (English Grains); Haliborange Orange, Mixed Flavour, Multivits with Calcium and Iron and Haliborange Liquid (Reckitt & Colman); Sanatogen Multivitamins, Multivitamins and Iron, Children's Vitamin Syrup, Children's Vitamins, Children's Vitamins and Minerals; Supradyn Ten Multivitamins for Children (Roche); Vitabites Children's Chewable Vitamins A, C and D (English Grains), Vita-E Succinate Tablets 50 and 200 iu (Bioglan).

Anti-oxidant Vitamins

New combinations of vitamins and minerals are appearing on pharmacy shelves regularly.

One of the latest additions you've probably noticed is the anti-oxidant vitamins – Vitamins E, C and beta carotene. Beta carotene is converted to Vitamin A in the body.

These supplements are said to work together to protect the body against the damaging effects of free radicals and reduce the harmful oxidation of fats in the blood. Free radicals are reactive chemicals produced in the body as part of its natural processes which can damage tissues and the delicate balance of the cell structure. Increased levels of free radicals have been associated with, among other things, pollution in the environment and excess ultraviolet light. Or, in simple terms, medical research can now support what some nutritional experts have been saying for years – that certain food components play a vital role in protecting us from disease.

The nutrients concerned are trace minerals, such as selenium, see also page 287, and certain vitamins, particularly A, C and E. Selenium is found in bread and cereals, mushrooms, garlic and Brazil nuts; Vitamin A in carrots; Vitamin E in green, leafy vegetables, as is Vitamin C which is also found in citrus fruits. Past research has suggested that patients taking pills containing selenium and Vitamins A and E regularly over a five-year period lived longer and had fewer episodes of cancer than those not taking the pills.

Supplements available include Arocin Beta Carotene (Modern Health), Redoxon Protector Beta Carotene with Vitamins C and E, Sanatogen Anti Oxidant Vitamins E, C and Beta Carotene (Roche Consumer Health), Selenium ACE, Seven Seas Pulse Anti-Oxidant Fruit and Vegetable Extracts with Vitamins C, E and Beta Carotene.

MINERALS

As with vitamins, whether or not mineral supplements are required to maintain the health of an adult eating a regular, average diet is still open to doubt. However, doctors will prescribe supplements of iron, for example, to those groups at special risk of developing a deficiency at certain times in their lives – pregnant women and the elderly, for instance. Vitamins and minerals are also recommended medically for some children and nursing mothers. For an iron deficiency anaemia, the prescription of iron will usually be essential, as will Vitamin B12 for macrocytic anaemia.

Vitamins receive a lot of publicity and most people now know something about their benefits. However, comparatively few people know much about minerals. Some of their names will be familiar, though. Calcium, sodium (salt), iron and iodine, for instance, are commonly known to be a necessary part of a healthy diet.

The idea of eating minerals may not sound very appetising, but of course we actually absorb them without realising it from a wide range of everyday foods. Some foods are richer in minerals than others, but much depends on the mineral content of the soil in which grains, fruit, nuts and vegetables are grown and, in the case of meat and fish, the mineral content of the foods which the animals themselves have eaten.

Modern farming methods, the widespread use of fertilisers and pollution of the environment have depleted the mineral content of the soil. Food-processing and refining also remove valuable minerals and we may only absorb a small proportion of the minerals we do eat. Add the fact that many people are eating less in order to control their weight and it is easy to see why lack of minerals may be fairly common.

Calcium

Helps build and maintain healthy bones and teeth. Because our bones are continually building and remodelling themselves, we all need calcium throughout our lives, even when our bodies stop growing. Up until our mid twenties we can increase the amount of calcium in our bones, but after this age women especially start to lose more than can be replaced. Recent medical evidence suggests that an adequate intake of calcium early in life can help to limit this loss.

Often in our attempts to eat less fat these days we may also be cutting down on calcium, which is found in certain foods with a higher fat content. Calcium is absorbed more effectively in the presence of Vitamin D.

Iron

Important for physical strength, stamina and mental alertness. Available: Fersaday Iron Supplement (Goldshield).

Trace Elements

Other less well known but equally essential minerals include phosphorus, magnesium, manganese, zinc, chromium, copper and selenium.

The good news is that only a tiny regular amount of each of the minerals is needed to keep us healthy; in fact some (iodine, iron, zinc and selenium, for example) are known as trace elements because the amount required is so minute – though nonetheless essential.

Not all deficiency symptoms are as dramatic as those of lack of iodine – the development of a goitre and underfunctioning of the thyroid gland – but more and more evidence is emerging that many common ailments may be caused or aggravated by prolonged deficiency of one or more of the essential minerals and that correct daily intake can have a protective and preventive effect upon our health.

Some research has shown that two minerals in particular – zinc and selenium – have a beneficial effect upon our immune (disease-fighting) system. Zinc-containing lozenges, sucked every two hours during the day while symptoms last, are suggested to shorten the usual duration of a cold. Studies indicate that adequate daily amounts of selenium can protect against heart disease, relieve arthritis and possibly slow down the ageing process.

Another study shows that a deficiency of selenium in the diet increases the risk of developing cancer. So how much do we need? The British soil (except in parts of Norfolk) is particularly lacking in selenium. It is estimated that the average diet in this country provides about 60 micrograms a day and that our daily requirement is around 200 micrograms. So it would seem a wise precaution to take a daily supplement. Selenium, to be effective, must be taken with Vitamin E. Vitamins A and C are also thought to increase its benefits. For example, Seven Seas Selenium with Vitamin E in Cod Liver Oil.

Minerals interact with each other in our body and too much of one can inhibit the action of another. Taking supplements should therefore be approached cautiously so that the right balance is achieved – seek your pharmacist's advice if in doubt.

Multivitamin and Mineral Supplements available:

Larkhall Natural Health produce a vast range of vitamins, minerals and food supplements under the brand names Cantassium, Octovit One-a-Day Multivitamin with Mineral Tablets (Goldshield), Trufree and Aquamaid.

Wassen International produce Selenium ACE – formulated for the middle-aged and elderly; Magnesium OK – for women from 16 upwards; Confiance – for women at the menopause and onwards; Genesis for men and women from 16 upwards; Pollen B; Sitosterol-B for all ages.

Other supplements available include: Biovital Multivitamins Plus Iron, Calcia, a calcium, iron and vitamin supplement especially formulated for women (English Grains); Golden Health Calcium with Vitamins A and D (English Grains); Haliborange Multivitamin Plus Calcium and Iron; Sanatogen Multivitamins and Calcium, Multivitamins and Minerals and Multivitamins and Evening Primrose Oil; Supradyn Multivitamins with Minerals (capsules or effervescent tablets containing 12 vitamins and eight minerals, from Roche);

Totavit Multivitamins and Minerals Capsules (Seton Healthcare; Pharmaton Capsules; Vitabiotics. Seven Seas, Boots and Lanes also produce a wide range of vitamins and minerals.

There are also tonics available over the counter such as Effico Tonic, which contains two B vitamins, B1 and nicotinamide, as well as caffeine, or Seven Seas Vitamin and Mineral Tonic containing Vitamins A and D, iron, glycerophosphate (an appetite restorative) and some trace minerals. And also Z Span Spansule Capsules (Goldshield).

Many adults take tonics to help build up vitality after illness, when they suffer a loss of appetite or when they feel tired, listless or run down. But when taking a preparation containing Vitamins A and D, as well as iron, make sure you aren't actually taking more of these supplements than you should. There is a Recommended Daily Allowance (RDA) and it is wise to stick to that. If you are in any doubt about the RDA, and you are taking more than one preparation, do seek the advice of your professional pharmacist.

OTHER SUPPLEMENTS

There is now a whole range of other supplements appearing more frequently on the pharmacy and health-shop shelves. These include oil of evening primrose, fish oils, ginseng and royal jelly supplements.

Oil of Evening Primrose

The very words have a soothing ring to them and indeed the old herbal name for the evening primrose was 'king's cure all'. Although we should not take this too literally, scientific studies are beginning to show that the oil does have healing and protective properties and may relieve conditions as diverse as arthritis, eczema, premenstrual syndrome, circulatory disorders and even multiple sclerosis.

It seems that the magic ingredient of the oil is an essential fatty acid, gamma linolenic acid – GLA for short. This is not normally available in our diet (except in human breast milk), but is produced in the body and in turn is needed for the body to form prostaglandins, substances which have a wide range of beneficial effects – they can reduce inflammation, lower blood pressure, help prevent thrombosis (blood-clotting) and aid the immune (disease-fighting) system. As we age, our body's natural production of GLA may diminish because of illness, stress and other factors. To guard against a deficiency, a supplement of evening primrose oil will provide a direct supply of GLA. You can now also buy supplements containing a rich source of GLA, known as Starflower Oil.

Supplements available: Efamol range; Epoc Pure Oil of Evening Primrose with Vitamin E; Evening Primrose Oil 500 mg (Evans); Golden Health Evening Primrose Oil (English Grains); Roche Starflower Oil 250 mg or 500 mg; Sanatogen Pure Evening Primrose Oil enriched with Oil of Borage 250 mg

Fish Oils

Every three minutes someone dies of heart disease in the UK – that amounts to 200,000 people every year. We would all like to avoid a heart attack, if possible, and it seems that the Japanese and the Eskimos – who eat a lot of fish and rarely suffer from heart attacks – may have the answer.

This unique protection from fish oils comes from essential fatty acids called EPA (eicosapentaenoic acid) and DHA (docosahexaenoic acid), part of a group called Omega-3. Studies of EPA and DHA have shown that they decrease production of substances involved in causing inflammation and thrombosis as well as lowering the level of blood fats. The reduction of blood fat levels also reduces the risk of arteriosclerosis (the narrowing and hardening of the arteries that supply the heart muscle with blood).

Supplements available: Haliborange Fish Oil Tablets; Sanatogen Pure Fish Oil Capsules, Cod Liver Oil Capsules, One-A-Day Cod Liver Oil Capsules, Cod Liver Oil and Multivitamin Capsules and Cod Liver Oil Liquid; Pulse Pure Fish Oils

Ginseng
Otherwise known as the 'Root of Life', this is the root of a plant which has been used in the Far East for more than 5,000 years. It is said to contain beneficial organic acids, vitamins, minerals, enzymes and amino acids

which are thought to build up general vitality and increase energy. It is also thought to increase blood pressure – so caution is necessary in those known to be hypertensive.

Supplements available: Red Kooga Ginseng (English Grains); Sanatogen Korean Ginseng Capsules

Royal Jelly
In nature royal jelly is fed exclusively to the queen bee, enabling her alone to become fertile and lead a long and productive life. It provides a rich source of vitamins, minerals and amino acids. It is likely that while it is vital for the queen bee, it has few, if any, benefits for people when studied scientifically. But the queen bee's reliance on it provides some people with a 'fairytale' reason for taking it. They just think it 'does you good', but can't rationalise it to my satisfaction.

Supplements available: Fresh Royal Jelly Capsules (Evans); Golden Health Royal Jelly with Honey; Sanatogen Royal Jelly

Glossary

Analgesic   Painkiller – aspirin, paracetamol, ibuprofen.

Antibiotic   A 'naturally' produced substance which destroys or inhibits the growth of germs within the body.

Anticholinergic   A chemical that prevents the passage of impulses down 'reflex' nerve pathways in the body and so can relieve symptoms or produce a beneficial effect. The substance hyoscine can do this. It is used in medicines which prevent the bowel cramps associated with irritable bowel syndrome.

Antihistamine   A medicine which relieves the symptoms caused by a histaminic response in the tissues. Histamine belongs to a group of chemicals known as the amines. These are released by tissues when they are inflamed and the histamine causes many of the unpleasant symptoms that arise.

Anti-inflammatory   A medicine which reduces the swelling, redness, pain and overheating in inflamed tissues of the body. These can be caused by the damage of an accident, an infection or an allergy. A common example is aspirin, which can be given to remove such inflammation – and the associated pain – in an arthritic joint, for example.

Antipyretic   A medicine which helps to bring down the body's temperature, which rises when an infection is present. Such a rise in temperature can, in itself, cause feelings of illness. Paracetamol and aspirin are antipyretics.

Antiseptic   A chemical substance which prevents sepsis – another name for a harmful infection. In everyday use, the word describes those substances which can be used on or in the body.

Antispasmodic   A medicine taken to relieve spasm in muscles (also see anticholinergic).

Antitussive   A medicine taken to relieve a cough.

Astringent   A substance which dries up excessive secretion – usually by being applied to the surface of the skin or a lining membrane in the throat.

Decongestant   A medicine which removes congestion – often water – from inflamed tissues. Nasal drops for a bunged-up nose are an example.

Emollient   A substance which softens and soothes.

Expectorant   A medicine which 'loosens the phlegm' and allows lung secretions to be coughed up more readily.

Keratolytic   An application which dissolves the top, hard, non-living layers of the skin, which are made of keratin. This can make it easier for effective medicines to penetrate into the deeper, living layers of the skin.

Linctus   Syrupy liquid containing a variety of ingredients, all of which are given to soothe or loosen the cough.

Pessary   A medicated, usually bullet-shaped object, designed to dissolve in and deposit medicines within the vagina.

Prostaglandin   A naturally occurring chemical, widely spread throughout the body and in many different forms. The prostaglandins play a part in regulating blood pressure or body temperature; the way in which the blood clots; the acid secretion within the stomach; and in the control of inflammation – to mention only a few.

Seborrhoeic   Associated with excessive secretion of sebum produced by sebaceous glands at the bottom of hair follicles.

Suppository   A bullet-shaped object designed to dissolve and deliver medicines in the lower bowel.

Vasoconstrictor   A substance which constricts the tiny arteries – the arterioles – and can prevent or treat congestion as a result.

Useful Addresses

Ainsworth Homoeopathic Pharmacy, 38 New Cavendish Street, London, W1M 7LH. Telephone: 071-935 5330.

British Homoeopathic Association, 27a Devonshire Street, London, W1N 1RJ. Telephone: 071 935 2163

National Institute of Medical Herbalists, 9 Palace Gate, Exeter EX1 1JA. Telephone: 0392 426022 (Mrs Chacksfield)

Proprietary Association of Great Britain, Vernon House, Sicilian Avenue, London WC1. Telephone: 071 242 8331 (Can be contacted for information on the non-prescription medicine industry as well as self-medication.)

Raynaud's and Scleroderma Association Trust, 112 Crewe Road, Alsager, Cheshire, ST7 2JA. Telephone: 0270 872 776